MW01283907

Sasquatch Rising 2013
Dead Giants Tell No Tales

How DNA Breakthroughs and
Backyard Visits Reveal
The Greatest Story of Our Time

Christopher Noël

Cover illustration: Jeffrey Caramagna
Cover design: N. Schumaker/northernlightsindustries.com
Author photo: Malcolm Campbell
Published by CreateSpace. In rare cases, their printing is
    substandard. If images in this book are not clear, please
    request an immediate replacement copy from Amazon.com;
    they are quite responsive.

Also by the Author

Doctor White's Monkey (stories)
In the Unlikely Event of a Water Landing:
A Geography of Grief (memoir)
Hazard and the Five Delights (novel)
The Sea Monkey Tombs (novel)

Acknowledgements

I'd like to thank those veteran researchers who first welcomed me into the field in 2005 and early 2006; the appreciative readers of the first edition, *Impossible Visits*; my faithful, eagle-eyed supporter J., whose Delta SkyMiles regularly send me south; and my mother, whom I've dragged long enough up the dizzying mountain trail.

I particularly wish to honor the habituators who have willingly contributed to this book, in their desire to reveal nuances of this inter-species dance and to help teach the world how to meet members from the huskier side of our family without fear or malice. That is, I praise the ongoing work of all who—with profound fascination and humility—allow *themselves* to be habituated every day.

Table of Contents

Chapter Six
A Scientific Revolution Gains Ground—
Main Milestones Pre-Specimen

Chapter Seven
Mystery Solved!
(on the back of a further mystery)
DNA Results Reveal Half-Human Genesis

{*The Yeahoh, An Old Kentucky Folktale*}

They inhabit these forests so comfortably and inconspicuously, are enough like us to have shrewdly escaped our notice, but have not our territorial competitiveness or would long since have come out of hiding and waged war for diminishing woods. Perhaps they are not lower animals after all, but an evolutionary advance—have grown beyond poor *Homo sapiens* and understand the world well enough that they have no need to construct a civilization upon it.

—from *Wild Life*, by Molly Gloss

The term "Sasquatch" was coined in 1926 by J.W. Burns, a school teacher and newspaper reporter at a British Columbian Chehalis reservation. He collected Native American accounts of massive, hairy men said to live in the forest, which they called by various names, including *sokqueatl* and *soss-q'tal*. He noted the similar-sounding terms for the creatures and decided to consolidate them into one, which also resembles the word for the figure in the Chehalis dialect where Burns lived: *sesqac*. As a proper name in English, Sasquatch is capitalized.

Preface

One thing is clear: 2013 will go down as The Year of the Sasquatch.

What is less clear is exactly how it will all play out. Turf battles and infighting among researchers and groups with vested interests will continue obscuring the picture, but hard evidence is finally in position to win the day.

Here is what I know so far, on the first day of this pivotal year.

1. The Melba Ketchum DNA study includes three complete Sasquatch genomes and demonstrates that the creature originally resulted from hybridization between *Homo sapiens* and another primate species. She has been hounded by detractors since her November 2012 announcement of genetic findings soon to be published, but her raw data is solid and extensive. What may require refinement is Ketchum's *interpretation* of this data, in that we might need to push the era of interbreeding further back than 15,000 years ago. Upon release, this proof will mark the first scientific validation of our zoological next of kin and will vindicate thousands of eyewitnesses who have endured harsh ridicule for sharing their stories.

2. The long-awaited Erickson Project footage is due to be released along with the Ketchum study data. At least one of the clips—clear video of a female in Kentucky—is tied directly to Sasquatch tissue and blood samples gathered at the same site and contributing to the DNA data.

3. What happened just outside of San Antonio, Texas, on September 6th, 2012, has yielded several minutes of perfect, close-range film of a male Sasquatch—nearly nine feet tall—going about his business before being brutally gunned down. This footage, which matters to me far more than the frozen carcass, will soon be seen by millions as part of a Minnow Films documentary. The event occurred in a forest "tent city" where the towering visitor had been spotted for years, nabbing food from campsites,

and where he had learned to lose his fear of humans and the natural stealth of an apex predator, surviving instead as a docile scavenger.

This book devotes 250 of its 425 pages to similar situations unfolding at habituation sites across North America, places where our two species interact. But instead of ending in slaughter, these relationships flow forward as a subtle, ongoing dance, featuring mutual respect and fascination.

I hope that the detailed accounts presented here will help to establish legal protection by assembling a vivid, highly textured infrastructure of knowledge and compassion—the best barrier standing between Sasquatch and its would-be trophy hunters.

Christopher Noël
Northeast Kingdom, Vermont
January 1, 2013

Prologue

Trickster is a boundary-crosser. Every group has its edge, its sense of in and out, and trickster is always there, at the gates of the city and the gates of life. His mischievous actions continue to keep our world lively and give it the flexibility to endure [so that] human beings have a way to enter into the play of fate and uncertainty, and from that play this world constantly arises.

—from *Trickster Makes This World*,
by Lewis Hyde

The first time I see a Sasquatch, I don't even know it.

It's November 8ᵗʰ, 2008, at 9:15 PM. I'm visiting the habituation site I've called Texas #2, and the woman of the house has made an impressive bonfire in her backyard. She and I, her twenty-year-old daughter, and her daughter's friend, are roasting hot dogs and marshmallows, laughing and joking around.

From time to time, I move away from the firelight and scan along the nearby tree line with my thermal camera, which reads "heat signatures." Yes, I do notice that vague bar of light (heat) projecting horizontally, low to the ground, from a pile of old lumber and debris, but I don't judge it worthy of a closer look; after all, I've geared myself for upright giants, swaying and peeking out from behind trees.

It's not until nine days later, back home in Vermont, that I review the footage and realize that this bar of light is actually *moving*, and in a peculiar way, tough to interpret. The front end keeps thrusting forward and down, to the right. I assume this object on my computer monitor must be a hog or a sheep, or *something* ordinary in the woods, perhaps choking or bellowing, making some call that we can't hear, thanks to the loudly crackling bonfire.

I send this curious video clip around to the habituators' group—people who are experiencing repeat Sasquatch visits to their properties. They are puzzled, until the Oklahoma habituator says the magic word. She's noticed that as the "head" moves, it *splays,* like the fingers of a hand, flexing. I look again, and again, and then in an abrupt gestalt shift, the true nature of the image jumps out at me unmistakably. This long, bright object is, in fact, a huge left forearm and hand, slung over a dark, pointed board, the hand actually seen *cupping* the tip of the board at times, the rest of the figure presumably crouched and hidden behind the woodpile.

Three times, the Sasquatch stretches its hand like this, out and down, flicking, like someone with a cramp or filled with nervous energy. If it hadn't moved, no identification would have been possible.

I grew up in a village of 750, in Vermont. When I'd explore the woods behind our house, I'd peer into hollow trees and rabbit holes, scan along ridgelines to catch sight of a Hobbit, a gnome, a hulking figure from *Where The Wild Things Are,* or some such utterly *other* kind of creature, non-human yet also *like* us, and strangely sympathetic. The forest as a whole seemed like a house much larger on the inside than on the outside, rewarding belief, unfolding room by room, pocket by secret pocket.

The idea of Sasquatch first reared up before me when I was twelve, thanks to the Patterson/Gimlin Film. Of course, I wanted to travel right away to the Pacific Northwest, where this creature actually *lived,* and over the years, this vision persisted, imprinted and always astir, serving me in the way of an elusive deity at the horizon, lush because unattainable.

If I didn't have Sasquatch, though, I did have the ravine, just a mile from our house—steep, five hundred feet deep, a mile long, a quarter mile across, thick with pines. As a teenager, I felt drawn to it, as to some otherworldly, timeless spot on Earth.

And now, thirty-five years later, having learned a thing or two about this primate species, I've returned to the ravine at middle age, spent hundreds of hours exploring and camping here, and never encountered another human being.   But I have encountered Sasquatch and their handiwork. If you're down inside the ravine in the middle of the night, unable to see two feet in front of you, and something thirty feet away in the blackness is circling you for six hours straight, snapping branches and thumping the ground, human civilization itself can seem a distant, pale fiction.

One snowy morning in 1992, my twenty-six-year-old fiancée was killed in a car accident. Later, seeking some dramatic right angle back into life, I made a solo expedition to British Columbia, to the little town of Bella Coola, which has logged hundreds of Sasquatch sightings over the years. I flew to Vancouver, rented a mini-van, and drove the hundred and forty-five miles due north, eager to trek the forests. Unfortunately, I found I was so afraid of grizzly bears that I didn't dare venture more than fifty feet from my vehicle. Instead, I interviewed locals who claimed to have seen this "hairy man of the forest." They were credible and understated, these townsfolk. Indeed, one young man claimed to have seen just the leg—white, furry, thick—of something walking upright in his backyard, the rest of the body obscured by darkness. He told me several times, "I'm not saying I know what it was. I saw *something*." In the post office, I quizzed an ancient, five-foot fellow, who lived way back up in the mountains.

"Yup, I did see a Sasquatch once. About thirty years ago now. He was totally covered in brown fur like a bear, but he walked on two legs, across the field, and then climbed over my split-rail fence." He tugged on his white beard while I braced for the mind-bending proportions. "Oh, I'd say he was about my size."

Ten years after I lost my fiancée, my father died suddenly of a heart attack. A scholar and writer, he'd been a life-long champion of the human imagination, including *my* imagination, in the most robust sense of the word—not reduced to the merely fanciful but, in the sense of poetic imagination, endowed with the potency of true insight. This death, too, sent me back to the long dream. On-line, I found the Bigfoot Field Researchers Organization, a group that had been actively studying the

Sasquatch phenomenon for years.   I joined up, and attended ten expeditions in far-flung regions of North America, traveling more than nineteen thousand miles. I met like-minded men and women, and my childhood prayer of a forest hosting upright *others* finally stopped feeling so childish. The very ground itself now seemed renewed, re-enchanted, courtesy of great five-toed footprints.

Still: If only I could actually *live* in one of these Sasquatch "hot spots."

At home in Vermont, though, life was blooming. I had finally fallen in love again, and together, she and I brought a girl child into the world. At forty-five, I'd become a first-time father.

But before our daughter was even a year old, her mother and I parted ways; the split felt like another death.

And just then, I met a man who lives just six miles down the road, an Ojibwa Native American who became my brief mentor, sharing years of experiences and opening my eyes to stick structures and other signs in the woods, all suggesting the inconceivable: *local* Sasquatch. Indeed, I soon came to recognize that members of their species spend time in the very ravine I'd discovered as a boy.

I'm not suggesting any mystical, causal relationship between these three deaths and my approach to this creature, but I do think that they have thrown me open to what lies beyond the human, yet offers kinship.

But back to the night of the bonfire, at Texas #2, because this story takes another twist. Nineteen months after I first shot the thermal footage, a fellow researcher re-appraises it for me, boosting the contrast in a bit of due videographic diligence I should have performed long before. (Had I slyly veiled my own vision, reluctant to see more?) Now, in addition to the subject's left forearm and hand, one can plainly make out a large pair of eyes—just, incidentally, where one would *expect* to see them—glowing white and warm, very near the ground, peering out at us through a gap in the boards of the woodpile, as our small group plays by the fire. Above them, the cooler dome of the head. And on the opposite side, our visitor's *right* forearm, too, even the fingers, thumb angled off.

In light of this breaking news, the habituator takes a tape measure to the main tree seen in the footage. It is 6.5 inches thick. Using this valuable scale, one can derive the distance between the two large eyes (from midpoint to midpoint): 4.75 inches. I immediately check the distance between my own eyes: 2.25 inches. This, I learn, is the average span between human eyes generally.

See video on YouTube: "Woodpile Sasquatch"

More than anything, Sasquatch reminds me of the gods of Mount Olympus. Embedded in nature yet seeming to stand beyond it, both transcendent and more emphatically terrestrial than ourselves, they cannot be circumscribed or contained. They seem to travel wherever they will, like quicksilver, otherwise known as Mercury, otherwise known as Hermes, fleet of foot, messenger between realms, shape-shifter, trickster, dweller on the threshold. They occupy their own dimension, yet occasionally visit our own, when it suits their purpose, to give us clues, glimpses, gifts, to play with us their oblique and capricious games. They are profoundly and irreducibly Other, yet many people find that they feel, in the grace of this presence, somehow more *themselves*, in an expanded sense of Self. Why else would seekers spend decades stomping through wilderness, straining after even a glimpse? Many compromise their home lives in hopes of contact, of a moment of ecstasy—"ek stasis": to stand outside oneself.

One of the principal figures in this book describes those moments when you cross an invisible border in the woods, when you suddenly get that *sizzle*:   "You know," he says, "the sense that I've been here before...but I haven't?"   It's the *déjà vu* that lets you into a new, old territory, both intimate and remote, lets you rest on home ground for the first time.   It's as though you're coming face to face with what you once knew, perhaps eons ago, a recollection of the whole story.

Thirty-one months after the woodpile incident, back at Texas #2 in June, 2011, my host and I chat on her front lawn. I'm just about to drive to the airport after a six-day visit, and what happens next I can only describe as the most remarkable moment of my life. I'll share this event at the end of the book, in the Epilogue, "Through the Looking-Glass"; with this portion set off on its own, readers unwilling to entertain the paranormal and to pass beyond consensus reality—beyond even the fresh consensus that Sasquatch *exists*—can more easily opt out. What has just emerged from the Ketchum DNA Study and the Erickson footage represents the pure, fleshly side of the truth—visible, quantifiable, materialistic. But there is a flip side.

Once, seeking to curb this runaway folly of mine, a good friend warned, "Don't forget, this is the only life you have."

I remember.

Titusville Morning Herald
Titusville, Pennsylvania
November 10, 1870

The Wild Men of California

A correspondent of the *Antioch Ledger*, writing from Grayson, CA, under date of October 16, says: "I saw in your paper, a short time since, an item concerning the 'gorilla' which is said to have been seen in Crow Canon and shortly after in the mountains at Orestimba Creek. You sneered at the idea of there being any such 'critters' in these hills, and were I not better informed I should sneer too. I positively assure you that this gorilla, or wild man as you choose to call it, is no myth. I know that it exists, and that there are at least two of them, having seen them both at once not a year ago.

"Their existence has been reported at times for the past twenty years. Last Fall I was hunting in the mountains about twenty miles south of here, and camped five or six days in one place, as I have done every season for the past fifteen years. Several times I returned to camp, after a hunt, and saw that the ashes and charred sticks from the fire-place had been scattered about. An old hunter notices such things, and very soon gets curious to know the cause. I saw no track near the camp, as the hard ground, covered with dry leaves, would show none. So I started on a circle around the place, and 300 yards off, in damp sand, I struck the track of a man's feet, as I supposed — bare, and of immense size. Now I was curious, sure, and resolved to lay for the bare-footed visitor. I accordingly took a position on a hillside, about sixty or seventy feet from the fire, and securely hid in the brush. I waited and watched.

"Two hours or more I sat there. The fire-place was on my right, and the spot where I saw the track was on my left, hid by bushes. It was in this direction that my attention was mostly directed. Suddenly I was startled by a shrill whistle, such as boys produce with two fingers under their tongue, and turning quickly I ejaculated, 'Good God!' as I saw the object of my solicitude, standing beside my fire, erect and looking suspiciously around. It was in the image of man, but, it could not have been human. I was never so benumbed with astonishment before. The creature, whatever it was, stood full five feet high, and disproportionately broad and square at the shoulders, with arms of great length. The legs were very short, and the body long. The head was small compared with the rest of the creature, and appeared to be set upon his shoulders without a neck.

"The whole was covered with dark brown and cinnamon-colored hair, quite long in some parts, that on the head standing in a shock and growing close down to the eyes. As I looked, he threw his head back and whistled again, and then stopped and grasped a stick from the fire. This he swung round and round, until the fire on the end had gone out, when he repeated the manoeuvre. I was dumb, almost, and could only look.

"Fifteen minutes I sat and watched him, as he whistled and scattered my fire about. I could easily have put a bullet through his head, but why should I kill him? Having amused himself, apparently all he desired, with my fire, he started to go, and, having gone a short distance, he returned, and was joined by another — a female, unmistakably — when they both turned and walked past me, within twenty yards of where I sat, and disappeared in the brush. I could not have had a better spot for observing them, as they were unconscious of my presence. I have told this story many times since then, and it has often raised an incredulous smile; but I have met one person who has seen the mysterious creatures, and a dozen who have come across the tracks at various places between here and Pacheco Pass."

Introduction
The Role of "Habituation" within the History of Primate Research

The most difficult aspect of this passive research method is
the interminable waiting: It may take months, even years, of
repeated visits to your research site in order to produce results.
—*Bigfoot Observer's Field Manual,*
by Robert W. Morgan

I am glad I didn't see them until after most of the data were
in. I needed to prove it scientifically to myself first as a
former skeptic before hitting the field and actually observing them.
I had no fear, the ones I encountered were peaceful and gentle. I
keep going back. I know why so many people love doing this now.
I saw one silhouetted between me and a white gooseneck trailer in
bright moonlight at about twenty-five yards. It was about ten feet
tall as it walked by. I was awed at the appearance, so graceful and
silent and so tall. You cannot appreciate all that they are until you
see for yourself. I hope that when our data is out, it will afford
protection for our hairy friends. They do not deserve to be
hunted or captured. Everyone needs to step back and take a Jane
Goodall approach.
—Dr. Melba Ketchum, Facebook,
January/February 2012

Late in 1960, in Nairobi, Jane Goodall experienced her first close encounter.

> For over half a year I had been trying to overcome the
> chimpanzees' inherent fear of me, the fear that made them
> vanish into the undergrowth whenever I approached. At first
> they had fled even when I was as far away as five hundred
> yards and on the other side of the ravine...[But now,] less
> than twenty yards away from me, two male chimpanzees
> were sitting on the ground staring at me intently.   Scarcely
> breathing, I waited for the sudden panic-stricken flight that
> normally followed a surprise encounter between myself
> and the chimpanzees at close quarters. But nothing of the
> sort happened. The two large chimps simply continued to
> gaze at me. Very slowly I sat down, and after a few more
> moments, the two calmly began to groom one another.
> —from *In the Shadow of Man*

Three years later, having recently set up a gorilla research station in the mountains of Rwanda, Dian Fossey experienced an initiation as well.

> I shall never forget my first encounter with the gorillas.
> Sound preceded sight. Odor preceded sound in the form of an
> overwhelming musky-barnyard, humanlike scent. The air
> was suddenly rent by a high-pitched series of screams
> followed by the rhythmic rondo of sharp *pok-pok* chestbeats
> from a great silverback male obscured behind what seemed
> an impenetrable wall of vegetation....Most of the females
> had fled with their infants to the rear of the group, leaving the
> silverback leader and some younger males in the foreground,
> standing with compressed lips.
> —from *Gorillas in the Mist*

"During the early days of the study at Kabara," continues Fossey,

> it was difficult to establish contacts because the gorillas were
> not habituated or accustomed to my presence and usually fled
> on seeing me. I could often choose between two different

kinds of contacts: obscured, when the gorillas didn't know I was watching them, or open contacts, when they were aware of my presence.

She learned that the best way to habituate these creatures was simply to act like them.

> Open contacts…slowly helped me win the animals' acceptance. This was especially true when I learned that imitation of some of their ordinary activities such as scratching and feeding or copying their contentment vocalizations tended to put the animals at ease more rapidly than if I simply looked at them through binoculars while taking notes. I always wrapped vines around the binoculars in an attempt to disguise the potentially threatening glass eyes from the shy animals.

Jane Goodall, too, took a humble and consistent approach in order to familiarize her subject with her daily presence.

> Because I always looked the same, wearing similar dull-colored clothes, and never tried to follow them or harass them in any way, the shy chimpanzees began to realize at long last, that after all I was not so horrific and terrifying.

Famously, of course, through years of devoted patience, both Goodall and Fossey gained acceptance by their respective primate study groups, and it was this high threshold of immediacy and intimacy that allowed their research projects to break new ground.

Since the mid-1980s, researchers have found increasing success in making contact with Sasquatch, too, progressively refining their methods. For the most part, these methods have featured *acoustical* overtures—"wood knocks," "whoop calls," etc.—designed to elicit responses; when a colloquy does take place, it usually occurs late at night, quite often well past midnight. Like Goodall and Fossey, Sasquatch researchers have come to rely on such imitative behavior in order to play upon the animals' natural curiosity, and in the darkness, imitation means *sound*. Species interaction in this mode has now reached the point at which it can be achieved on a regular basis in many locations throughout North America. Regular, yes, and even predictable, yet by no means frequent. Perhaps five percent of the time, an overture will receive a recognizable response. But even this seemingly low figure far outweighs what was possible before.

Rarer still, during expeditions, sightings have taken place, an individual Sasquatch lured into view—again, mostly at night, and mostly very fleetingly, such as a head peeking from behind a tree—by these humans' oddly non-human behavior. Expedition-goers have caught glimpses through night vision infrared binoculars or scopes, but only quite recently has the gold standard of night-vision technology—hand-held thermal imagers able to record video—come within financial reach of some researchers or, more accurately, of generous sponsors of researchers; and still, a good one costs nine thousand dollars. Thermal imagers are such a gold standard, in this specialized area of primate research, because 1) they are an entirely *passive* instrument, emitting nothing, able to read the "heat signatures" given off by objects, especially living organic objects, whereas most other night-vision devices are *active,* giving off an infrared beam that can, it seems, be seen and avoided by this animal, and 2) thermal imagers can "see" even in the thickest dark, when the Sasquatch feels most comfortable and will often draw nearer.

As "shy" as Goodall and Fossey found their chimpanzees and mountain gorillas to be, Sasquatch is a hundred-fold more evasive, and smarter; otherwise, such a creature never would have been able to survive alongside human beings for millennia, and to avoid our increasingly weaponized dominion.

Jane Goodall tells, for instance, of the chimp she called David Greybeard becoming brazen enough in time to simply stride into her camp and take bananas from her hand, his example soon persuading other members of his troupe to follow suit.

Dian Fossey, also, was eventually able to touch, even to groom and be groomed by, her subjects.

In the case of Sasquatch, however, this level of physical contact and interaction does not fall within the researchers' range of rewards.

At the same time, the Holy Grail of Sasquatch research does remain consistent habituation, this concept taken, though, in a more attenuated sense than in the case of other primates. The situations described in detail in this book represent the furthest advances toward genuine contact and interaction yet achieved. Or, to be more precise, these are our furthest *documented* advances, for it must be assumed that many times, over the vast stretch of human/Sasquatch co-evolution, interaction has occurred, some of it no doubt rising to the level of familiar regularity. But this must always have represented the rare exception, when, under the right circumstances, they will indulge in a highly textured—albeit still exceedingly cautious—degree of contact. While we may place the following examples in the category of "play," the implied intellect behind these gambits is much more nuanced than even the clever chimp or wise gorilla will manifest.

One of my neighbors in Vermont is a woodsman. Sylvester has been interacting with Sasquatch for years, though he has never laid eyes on one. That may sound like a naively credulous statement, until you realize that he has heard wood knocks and distinct—yet unintelligible—voices in the middle of nowhere, and found many of the simple stick and tree structures that have been reported throughout North America in close proximity to well-documented Sasquatch sightings. These pieces of evidence by themselves would not, I think, be compelling enough in Sylvester's case, were it not for the added layer of game-playing.

> I put two quarters on the ground and put them about a foot apart. Right out in plain sight. My idea is that no one could resist a couple quarters. If they disappeared then I know I have people in my woods and should keep an eye and ear open for them. (I fear people in the woods.) I also had them facing up and pointed them to face north. Nothing happened the first few years...till last year. Then a quarter was gone, and other was rotated to go east/west. I examined the area and found in place of the quarter a cute little arrangement of feathers. Each a different color. And spread out facing east. If it

> were a person they would have taken both quarters and
> would not have left such a beautiful little arrangement.
> That is just like the games I played with the thing in the
> [Town Name] Woods. I would put sticks or stones next
> to the trail in various positions and they would be
> rearranged when I returned a few hours later. I am a
> very observant person, especially out in the woods. At
> one time it put a broken arrow into the ground so I
> took the two pieces and placed them on a stump next to
> where they had been. I faced them north. When I
> returned only one piece was there and the other piece
> was stuck in the ground again.

Thousands of reports, continent-wide, of such quiet, sly pranksterism share an undercurrent of strangeness, humor, and a kind of tacit empathy.

A fellow researcher in Upstate New York wrote me of an ongoing situation he experienced at his remote trailer, which culminated in the following series of events. Having very recently undergone a painful break-up from his girlfriend, one afternoon Kevin started crying. He had brought a load of firewood back home.

> I left the rear hatch of the Jeep open, because I intended
> on going back out to finish unloading. I lay down on the
> couch with the cat and just kept crying. I am not sure
> how much time passed, but Wayne W. knocked on my
> door, screaming my name. He is a friend from Oneonta,
> who had heard on the scanner that a sheriff had driven
> up my road, found my Jeep, and seen what he thought
> was a bear in the backyard. Now, that same sheriff, two
> state troopers, and the fire marshal came flying up in the
> snow. I went outside, with Wayne, and the sheriff
> said that he saw a bear trying to get in my Jeep when he
> came around the bend down by my property. He said it
> went into the creek, then when he stopped behind my
> Jeep, he could hear it breaking branches up that steep
> mountain to my west. Finally, everybody left except me
> and Wayne. When we went to unload the rest of the

wood, the truck was empty but for three logs, and the
wood was piled up near the burn barrel, out back.
Earlier, I had only just begun the process, myself, the
truck had been full. Odd as it sounds, I began to suspect
that something was trying to help me, though I definitely
didn't want its help. There are many old apple trees on
my property. I thought that if I left an offering at the
northeast corner, where my land meets state land,
whatever it was would leave me alone. So I left a
big Tupperware container, with no cover, filled with
apples, and nutty power bars, on a platform, about five
feet up a spruce tree.

Next morning, gone. OK, maybe deer, or some animal.
Next day, same thing, four or five apples, nutty bars,
chocolate sugar cookies—gone.

At the time, part of me is saying, "What is wrong with
you, Kevin?" The other part is starting to feel relieved,
like everything is going to be OK. Still, I'm afraid to tell
anyone, and it could still be animals.

Third day, I had dinner with my friend, then stayed at his
house. I didn't get a chance to walk up the mountain to
load the bait container. The next morning, 5:00 am, I
left his house, and drove up to my trailer. The container
is sitting on my back stairs, with this frozen, dried-up
little bush: lemon mint. Pulled up by the roots. I
unlock the door, go in, and the window by the couch
where I'd started sleeping is open, and another three or
four dried-up mint branches are lying on the back of the
couch. I really lost it at this point. The cat is nowhere to
be found. I start to call the sheriff, but what the hell am I
going to say?

The next day, after I'd left another "gift" in the bait
container at the corner of my land, more mint leaves, and
the whole plants, appeared in the seats of my Jeep, all
pushed through the space I'd left the windows open.

The nature of the habituation experiences that people undergo depends heavily upon context; the quality of the interaction seems conditioned most by the posture assumed and the attitude projected by the *Homo sapiens* involved. This is a lesson well learned, in their own research, by Goodall and Fossey, who had to teach themselves an ever-increasing level of patience and good will, which the primates eventually returned in kind. When they erred, they often paid the price, as in this incident recounted in *Gorillas in the Mist.*

> On a slope gorillas always feel more secure when positioned above humans. I never relished climbing up to a group from directly below, but the thickness of the vegetation compelled me to do so. Once…just about twenty feet below the gorillas, who could be heard feeding above, I softly vocalized to make my presence known. A number of curious infants and juveniles climbed into trees above to stare intently down at the unaccustomed equipment [my bulky tape recorder] ….Just as expected, the [adult male] silverbacks instantly led the females, all hysterically screaming, in a bluff-charge to within ten feet. Because of the intensity of the screams…I tried to bend down to adjust the machine's volume, but the slightest movement incited renewed charges from the overwrought animals. Forgetting all about the microphone, I whispered to myself, "I'll never get out of this alive!" Only when the group eventually climbed out of sight was it possible to turn off the recorder.

The "Siege at Honobia," in 2000, presents a darker side to both human and Sasquatch behavior. It all started when residents of a rural Oklahoma property began leaving fresh deer meat in a freezer in their backyard. On January 17th of that year, the Bigfoot Field Researchers Organization website received the following urgent message:

> Too many incidents to mention here, please have someone contact us. This is no hoax and my brother is afraid for his

family. This creature is getting bolder every time it returns. This thing is huge, walks upright, smells like musky urine, burned hair type odor. He repeatedly comes back in the early morning hours after midnight and harasses them until just before dawn. It has on more than one occasion tried to enter their home. We don't know where to turn.

Everyone thinks we are crazy when we mention it. Please, we don't know what to do but I do know that something needs to be done! There are stories we could tell that would make the hair stand up on your neck.

"The message went on to explain," writes Matthew Moneymaker, Founder and Director of the BFRO, "that the family was having problems over the past two years with one or more nuisance animals that were prowling around outside the home at night. The animals were stealing deer meat from an outside shed. The situation had escalated when the animals tried to get into the home. At one point the father went outside to confront the animal. He got a good look at one, and took a shot at what he claimed was a Sasquatch running back into the woods.

"We contacted the family after receiving the report," Moneymaker continues. "The man we spoke with first was the brother of the father of the family. He insisted that they were not kidding around. At least one Sasquatch was coming around the homestead almost every night. It was coming onto the porch, messing with a window, wiggling the door knob as if it wanted to get in, and even stealing deer meat out of a freezer that was kept in an open-sided outbuilding. Whatever it was wasn't alone. The family could hear chattering and screaming from the hills when the prowler(s) were near the home.

"The wife was too fearful to remain in the house. She and the kids were relocated temporarily while the men armed themselves with assault rifles and prepared to defend the homestead against the nightly prowlers."

Moneymaker dispatched a regional BFRO Investigator to the scene, and then monitored events by phone. Here is his account:

Tim [who shot at the intruder] wants us to take care of his problem. He doesn't want the Sasquatch coming back to his house anymore and he doesn't care what it takes to make it stop. He will not move and not hold back from shooting at it if it returns.

[The BFRO Investigator and two other men] are at the location setting up. I spoke with Tim's wife briefly. She reiterated how frightened they were of this thing and described some of the incidents. Far from jumping to conclusions, she said she and her husband had denied the whole thing to themselves for a few years. It wasn't until after the deer meat (three complete quartered deer) had all disappeared from the large, chest-high freezer in the outdoor shed that the intruder started trying to get in the house at night. It didn't just scratch at the window, she said. It had pulled off parts of the window and was getting bolder in its attempts to get in the house. The recent deer kill found outside had not been shot. One of its legs was violently twisted and broken. It had clearly been carried, not dragged, to the spot where it was found. The most interesting thing was how the predator pulled out the internal organs. The belly of the deer had not been opened. The   opening was up between the neck and rib cage. The predator made a hole large enough to stick its arm in and apparently reached down from above the rib cage and pulled out the organs.

The loud vocalizations, tree thrashing, chattering and whistling outside the house at night are the most noticeable, recurring features. There was considerably more noise during the night the deer was killed.

[Twelve hours later, more details:]
I was on the phone with the people at the house last night for a few hours. I was asking questions and listening to what was happening. Things got very hectic at one point. These guys were actually shooting from the porch while I was on the phone. From my conversations

yesterday and early this morning with the residents, we think we figured out why this situation is so extreme. The underlying cause seems to be that lots and lots of deer congregate on Tim's property. He's got thirty acres in the mountains and he plants Austrian snow peas all over the property, especially near the house, because deer go crazy for them this time of year. People plant these plants specifically to attract deer. It makes it easier to hunt.

Many deer come to feed on his property. There's a deer overpopulation problem in the area to start with, so his property is apparently an effective magnet for deer. There are so many deer that he doesn't even have to get off his porch to go "hunting." He bags lots of deer on his own property and has been doing it for a few years now. He said that on some occasions the deer carcasses were snatched away by something.

A few times Tim ran out after it, but it would always flee into the woods. The first time he got a good look at it was the night he shot at it–a few nights ago. The most baffling thing for all of us was why these things weren't running away after being shot at. They'd pull back a bit in the trees, then move to a different part of the hillside and could be seen through the brush when the spotlights reflected off their eyes.

I asked Tim if he ever spotlights deer from his porch. He does. Then we established that indeed, MOST of the time when he's spotlighting the woods and shooting from his porch is when he's shooting at deer, not Sasquatch. So if the animals who aren't running away from the loud gunshots are some kind of predator that's been in the area for a while, then those predators may have noticed that sometimes after those spotlighting-gunshot incidents, a wounded deer would be struggling up the hill trying to get away...and will be much easier to catch. Deer will always take off running when they hear gunshots, especially within fifty yards, that's how they know they weren't seeing deer's eyes while the shooting was going on.

Tim sounded stunned when I explained the deer connection. He slurred out a long steady "oh my God," as if it finally all made sense to him. The Sasquatch might be hanging around the property waiting to grab a wounded deer. I explained that these predators might not understand that they are the intended targets now, because all they would see is a spotlight shining through the trees toward them, then a very loud BANG from an assault rifle. The animals may be expecting to see wounded deer running toward them up the hill. They may have watched that pattern for years. It's possible they either don't realize that there are bullets whizzing by them, or they've gotten used to it. At that range the shot is so loud you wouldn't hear a bullet hitting the trees next to you. And they wouldn't see when the guns are pointing right at them because the spotlights would be in their eyes at that moment. It may appear to be business as usual with all the shooting going on.

Eventually, the situation de-escalated when the residents simply stopped killing deer; over time, the visitations waned and then ceased altogether.

A polar opposite approach is advocated and practiced by Robert W. Morgan, Sasquatch researcher for more than half a century, and is pursued as well, each in her or his own way, by all the researchers profiled in this book. "I had my first encounter in 1957," Morgan recalls.

I had just gotten off a cruise in the Pacific with the Navy. I headed for the mountains. I was in Mason County, WA. I heard something coming down in the brush behind me. It was rustling around, and as I moved to one side, I started seeing black patches of hair, and naturally thought it was a bear. So I stepped out and I yelled, and everything went dead silent. I yelled again, and it started running at an

angle, and it got up the slope to me. And finally it got to a
point and turned around, and I saw it from just above the
navel, up. And I'm looking into the eyes of a Bigfoot. Being
a kid from Ohio, I'd never heard of this, so to me I was
looking at a gorilla, but it was the most expressive, humanlike gorilla. His face looked much more like a man's than a
gorilla's, but he was real hairy all over, so that was all I could
think. The look on his face was almost comical, because he
was as surprised as I was.

Morgan's *Bigfoot Observer's Field Manual* lays out "sincere
counsel" for achieving "passive contact" with this species. Never carry a
firearm, never even raise a camera to your face, because "most of them
have observed this same behavior in hunters."

Once you have chosen a research site, it's time to create a
provocative routine. Your objective is to be non-threatening
enough to be tolerated, yet so different from the scads of
usual hikers as to warrant investigation. Cultivate that
difference in your own way. Be creative, but never be loud,
intrusive, disruptive, or flamboyant. Make yourself and your
routines familiar to the Forest Giants. Find a way to gently
announce your presence even while hiking. Try whistling or
singing a tune now and then. Walk casually enough to allow
your own observations but don't bother trying to sneak
around because your actions will remind them of hunters.
The reason to do all this is to deliberately come under their
scrutiny. The most difficult aspect of this passive research
method is the interminable waiting: It may take months, even
years, of repeated visits to your research site in order to
produce results.

To be a gracious host to a Forest Giant, you must first design
the party with careful attention to detail. Consider your
invited guests' requirements: only a friendly and mutually
curious atmosphere, the absence of loud noises, quick
motions, and sudden lights. Your invitation begins the
moment you drive down your first tent peg. However, do not

imagine that you will be present the first few times a
Forest Giant drops by. While the Giants are nosey
characters, they are considerate, ghostly visitors. They
can appear and vanish in a heartbeat. Unless you are
sharp, you may not know they have visited in your
absence unless you set your stage with precision. Your
observation camp must be neat and tidy to an extreme
approaching anal retentiveness. Prepare to set out some
passive lures that will give you a perceptible sign that
they've been "inspected."

Your lures should be too subtle to be noticed even by
[human] experts because they will consist of items that
are commonly found in camps. Instead of being cleverly
hidden to snare your guest, your harmless lures   will be
even more cleverly placed *in the open*, yet the slightest
touch will be easily detected. For example, I routinely
place on a stump or a flat rock my steel signal mirror, an
open plastic case containing aromatic soap, toothbrush,
toothpaste, dental floss, and my razor, each arranged
with its tip touching a curved line that I faintly etch onto
the rock or the stone with the point of my knife. I
sometimes leave a book or a magazine, anchored by
stones, open to a page that might catch a Giant's eye. I
use *National Geographic* or similar publications that
contain images of gorillas, chimpanzees, or orangutans
in gentle contact with humans. I prefer photos of Jane
Goodall or the kindly folks at The Gorilla Foundation as
they work with Koko.

If you play recorded music, be prudent: Make it soft
enough that no human being outside of the immediate
perimeter can hear it; you must not attract hikers. Also,
never succumb to playing popular music because that
will place you in the same category as the usual campers.
Avoid that comparison at all costs. Why are you doing
this? Because that music will serve as your trademark
with them, and when they hear you play it, they'll

know who you are. Remember, you are involved in a protracted, meticulous chess game in which nobody ever scores a checkmate and no pieces are lost.

As I will describe, I myself have taken the opportunity to apply some of this advice in my Vermont Project, and have reaped exciting results.

First, though, we'll take a look at the work of the research group that has managed to coax this creature out of the realm of popular myth and into the light of consistent, empirical study, learning how—throughout North America—to communicate with it in a preliminary, very simple manner. Attending expeditions with the Bigfoot Field Researchers Organization became my avenue to learning the basics of Sasquatch habitat and behavior, and, more importantly, to discovering the remarkable existence of habituation sites.

The stage has been set, finally, for a deeper-level interaction, and mutual education, between our two primate species—*Homo sapiens* and Sasquatch—in the tradition of the decades-long, exquisitely detailed projects of Jane Goodall and Dian Fossey. The latter writes:

> Peanuts…was feeding about fifteen feet away when he suddenly stopped and turned to stare directly at me. Spellbound, I returned his gaze—a gaze that seemed to combine elements of inquiry and of acceptance. Peanuts ended this unforgettable moment by sighing deeply, and slowly resumed feeding.
>
> Two years after our exchange of glances, he became the first gorilla ever to touch me.

Nevada State Journal
Reno, Nevada
July 16, 1924

Clue to "Gorilla Men" Found—May Be Lost Race of Giants

"Mountain Devils" discovered at Mount St. Helens, near Kelso, are none other than the Seeahtik Tribe, said Jorg Totagi, Clallam Tribe editor of The Real American, an Indian national weekly publication, in an interview here today.

The Indians of the Northwest have kept the existence of the Seeahtiks a secret. Partly because they know no white man would believe them, and partly because the Northwestern Indian is ashamed of the Seeahtik Tribe, said Totagi.

"The 'mountain devil,' or 'gorillas,' who bombarded the prospectors' shack on Mount St. Helens, according to the description of the miners, are none other than the Seeahtik Tribe, [who were] last heard of by the Clallam Indians about fifteen years ago, and it was believed by the present Indians that they had become extinct. The Tribe made their home in the heart of the wilderness on Vancouver Island and also on the Olympic Range.

"They are seven to eight feet tall. They have hairy bodies like the bear. They are great hypnotists, and kill their game by hypnotism. They also have a gift of ventriloquism, throwing their voices at great distances, and can imitate any bird in the Northwest. They have a very keen sense of smell, are great travelers, fleet of foot, and have a peculiar sense of humor," Totagi added.

"The Seeahtik Tribe are harmless if left alone. The Clallam Tribe, however, at one time several generations ago, killed a young man of the Seeahtik Tribe and to their ever-lasting sorrow, for they killed off a whole branch of the Clallam Tribe but one, and he was merely left to tell the tale to other Clallams up-Sound.

"Henry Napolean of the Clallam Tribe is the only Indian who was ever invited to the home of the Seeahtik Tribe. It was while Napolean was visiting relatives on the British Columbia coast about thirty years ago, that he met a Seeahtik while hunting. The giant Indian then invited him to their home, which is in the very heart of the wilderness on Vancouver Island. Napoleon claims they live in a large cave. He was treated with every courtesy and told some of their secrets.

"Some Indians claim that during the process of evolution when the Indian was changing from animal to man the Seeahtik did not fully absorb the tamanaweis, or soul-power, and thus he became an anomaly in the process of evolution. It is generally their custom to frighten persons who have displeased them by throwing rocks."

The Helena Independent
Helena, Montana Territory
October 28, 1882

A Wild Man in Idaho

Two cowboys who just came in from Camas prairie relate an experience which will probably go a great way toward re-establishing the popular faith in the wild man's tradition. On the first day of this month two cowboys, searching for cattle lost in the storm, passed over some lava crags and were startled by suddenly seeing before them the form so often described to them. They were so terrified that they sat upon their horses looking at it in dread. Mustering courage and drawing their revolvers, they dismounted and gave chase, but the strange being skipped from crag to crag as nimbly as a mountain goat. After an hour's pursuit both young men were so completely worn out that they both laid down, seeing which, the wild man approached them and stopped on the opposite side of the gorge in the lava, from which point he regarded the cowboys intently. The latter would not shoot, as they considered it would be unjustifiable, though they kept their pistols ready for use, while carefully returning the compliment thoroughly inspecting the phantom of Snake River.

The wild man was considerably over six feet in height, with

great muscular arms which reached to his knees. The muscles stood out in great knots and his chest was as broad as that of a bear. All parts of his body were covered by long, black hair, while from his head the hair flowed over his shoulders in coarse, tangled rolls and mixed with a heavy beard. His face was dark and swarthy and his eyes shone brightly, and he acted very much as a wild animal which is unaccustomed to seeing a man. The boys made all kinds of noises, at the sound of which he twisted his head from side to side and moaned— apparently he could not give them any "back talk" so, wearying of eyeing him, the two boys fired their revolvers, whereupon the wild man turned a double somersault and jumped fifteen feet to a low bench and disappeared, growling terribly as he went.

It is supposed that this is the same Apparition so often seen before. The man, no doubt, does as the Indians did for subsistence and lives on Camas roots, and he no doubt kills young stock, as many yearlings and calves "disappear" mysteriously and nothing but skeletons of them are ever found.

Chapter One

Listening at the Tree Line—
Sasquatch Field Research Hones its Methods

There's this American chauvinism, this sense that we're well in control of our own country, thank you very much. That *nothing* like this could get away with it…in *our own backyard*.

It's as if you're trying to make contact with a lost tribe. You approach them with great respect, with the attitude that you know they're smart, and that you want to let them *know* that you know. And that you understand you are trespassing on *their* territory.

I think they've seen human activity that seemed endearing or sympathetic.

You've probably watched people having fun somewhere, from a distance. And you wish you could go and have fun with them too. I think they watch us and probably plenty of times they wish they could just freely walk among us. But they know they *can't..*

—Matt Moneymaker, Founder and Director,
Bigfoot Field Researchers Organization

1. BFRO Expeditions—What It's Like to Go

It's elemental. Hard, cold ground. Distant outline of hills, of trees. Wind through grass. Breathing humans nearby. Ferns. Silence that pulses, then gradually inflects itself with insect and animal signals. You listen.   You try to remember when you've listened more emphatically. Probably not since childhood—since that closet door.

Nor have you been awake this late in years, not happily anyway, not without chewing over anxieties in bed or soothing a frantic baby.

It is 2:16 AM.

During a brief, hushed walkie-talkie exchange between your small group and Matt, the expedition leader, you dare to crunch, gingerly, your last handful of peanut M & Ms, and then it's back to the task at hand. A task that you still can't believe you're actually undertaking.

In certain moods—and your moods shift minute to minute—you think you might as well be awaiting the Mother Ship. Sure, a few people have come equipped with night-vision goggles, GPS, thermal-imaging devices, but not you. No, you prefer to go with your very own low-tech ears. You shut your eyes and listen harder. You're sitting hunched and cross-legged in the chill on a tarp at the edge of a cold-dewy field. You're in a bowl-shaped formation, surrounded by those hills, their ridgelines. No moon.   Starlight sufficient to show only dim contours of other group members, breathing.

Matt has divided the expedition members into five groups of three or four, and now he radios that it's your group's turn to make a series of "wood knocks" against the nearest tree. You stand stiffly and take up, of all things, a baseball bat. The slam against the oak terribly stings your hands. You send a series of three—BAM! BAM! BAM!—out into the night. Like a message in a bottle tossed into a vast sea.

And then, you resume your seat.

(These early expeditions I'm compositing here occurred nearly six years before the popular television program "Finding Bigfoot" premiered on Animal Planet. This show is highly produced and edited for maximum pace and punchy drama, employing audio and video evidence "enhancements"—even outright "simulations"—with no time set aside to represent the sort of leisurely exploration and campfire conversation that occur over a three-or-four-day expedition in real life. For beginners passionate to learn about Sasquatch, nothing can come close to this time spent with veteran researchers and other like-minded seekers, this total immersion in nature and the nocturnal world. I can also highly recommend the new expeditions being offered by The Olympic Project; see olympicproject.com.)

You recognize the luffing call of a barred owl; the chorus, far up on the ridgeline, of a coyote pack; bullfrogs; insects; small animals crackling leaves or twigs in nearby foliage. You have become expert already in factoring out such sounds. What you are waiting for, the whole reason you have traveled across several states to be here tonight, much to the bewilderment of family and friends, is the unthinkable. A reply-knock from deep inside the forest. It may come a moment from now. It may take two more hours. It may never come at all. What if it never comes at all and the joke is on you?

Ten minutes. Nothing. Some kind of bird sounds off to the north. Five more minutes. Matt asks the next group down the tree line, a hundred yards away from you, to knock. You can hear their bat, their oak, though you hope your radio will crackle suddenly with the news, "That wasn't us!"

The idea is to do what *they* do. They vocalize. They make loud "whoops!" and screams. But more often, to communicate amongst themselves in the dark, they knock. They bang thick sticks or logs against tree trunks. We want to sound just like them, to lure them, to *appeal* to them from the other side of this timeless gulf. Because this is how they seem to locate one another across miles in the night. Matt has told us that he and countless expedition-goers have heard such distinctive wood knocks throughout North America. "They make them in Florida, in West Virginia, Ohio, New Mexico, California, Oregon, British Columbia. So since they're not getting together to *plan* this behavior, this must be behavior that's *ancient.*"

He is talking about Sasquatch, a species of enormous primate that has, apparently, been able to elude our capture and domination—even to elude human *belief*—for eons. He is talking about none other than the animal that has captured *your* imagination since, at age ten, you first saw the Patterson/Gimlin Film.

One reason, you have figured, that many find it difficult or impossible to believe that Sasquatch can be a real creature surviving in our forests is that they radically underestimate the nocturnal world. It is at night that the animal is most active, and especially between the hours of midnight and dawn, when there are approximately 1% as many people out of doors as during the other eighteen hours of the day. And of this 1%, how many of us stray off of roads, yards, public spaces? Well, you finally have found an organization that does exactly that.

It is 2:37 when, sure enough—and never has this common phrase, *sure enough*, seemed so ridiculous, or so right–you hear, if not as clear as day then half as clear, maybe a hundred yards off inside the forest, a responding series of knocks: two, a thirty-second pause, and then two more. After everyone takes a couple beats for absorption, all five groups quickly call in, reporting that yes, they have heard the knocks too, and that no, none of them is playing a trick on the rest. This hardly needs asserting, since the knocks came—you need to keep reminding yourself—from *inside* that forest, way up the side of the hill toward the ridge, and all people are accounted for here at the edge.

As per instructions, then, everyone falls into radio silence. "If you hear wood knocks, that means he's curious," you've been told. "Just keep quiet and give him time to come closer."

After some six minutes, the longest six minutes you can remember, from another ridge beyond and above the opposite side of the bowl-shaped field comes a responding knock, just a single one this time, and softer, farther.

Nine more minutes pass, and the next sound you hear is a heavy footfall through underbrush, approaching down the long incline. You warn yourself not to jump to conclusions, that it could be a deer, a moose, a bear, but the steps are unmistakably bipedal, a *stamping* that makes no effort to conceal its power. Quite the contrary. CRACK! A hefty tree branch is split, and splits the night, and you abruptly recall others' reports of hearing such displays in the woods. Intimidation. Reprimand for territorial encroachment. And…it works. You back away from the forest like you're playing crab soccer. You feel like you might faint or have a coronary. Mike, to your left, breathes, "Hoe. Lee. Fuck."

But your equilibrium is restored by Matt's calm voice over the walkie-talkie. "Okay, folks, this is a *good* thing. Don't be afraid. This is normal behavior." He has been doing this for twenty years, and never gotten closer than forty feet; this underscores the idea of an inviolable barrier, maintained by our enormous cousins. "Whoever thinks they're closest, go ahead and try to talk to it. Show it something it's probably never heard before from people, which is a little sympathy and understanding. Remember, it's never known humans to act like we're acting. It is not going to hurt us."

Your mind boggles—you can literally *feel* it in the *processes* of boggling—as you ask it to accept the premise that a seven- or eight-foot-tall, nine-hundred-pound *primeval ape creature* is actually standing in the woods over there. Inhaling and exhaling the neighboring air.

All you want to do is to train a piercing spotlight in there through the trees. But you don't have one, nobody does. They're strictly prohibited on BFRO expeditions, because bright lights are adversarial, that's what hunters do, or mere campers. "If we don't make any aggressive moves," Matt has taught everyone, "then the animal will not quite know how to categorize us and will be curious. It'll be more likely to hang around."

Jonathan, in the group a hundred yards to your south, radios that he'll give talking a shot. He has been on several expeditions; you even shared franks and beans with him earlier tonight, at his campfire, and he related past encounters. He seemed so happy back then, poor doomed fella. You can't hear his exact words from this distance, but his tone is very friendly, veryveryvery friendly.

(The next morning, at late breakfast, he'll tell you, rather sheepishly, what he said. By the light of day, the whole incident seems, of course, positively absurd, dreamlike, instead of like any dire showdown. "'Hello,'" I said. "'Hi there, sir. How are you tonight? We're just here to learn about you. We respect you.' At one point, I think I actually might have said, 'We come in peace.'")

Jonathan receives no response. Minutes pass, and intermittently he tries again. And then, just when you're ready to assume that whatever it was has stealthily departed, or, more accurately, that it was never there to begin with, was instead the result of some sleep-deprived collective wish-fulfillment hysteria, comes the belated reply in the form of the leaf-ripping flight of some object, and then a thud onto the sod, not fifteen feet from Jonathan's group. A rock has been pitched a long way through the forest, and it's the size of a basketball. (Barbara finds it on the way back to base camp, and you all claim it as your prize, put it front and center in your group photo.)

You hear footsteps retreating up the hill for half a minute—this time just stepping lightly, crunching in dead leaves—and then nothing more, so the small groups reconvene and head back to base camp and your dry sleeping bags, exhausted, freaked out, and deeply honored.

Later tonight—and yes there is room for a "later" squeezed in before dawn—one couple in their tent wakes at 4:34 AM to approaching footsteps, but this time they're entirely different, not aggressive and heavy but sneaking near the vinyl wall, stealthy, delicate, though clearly bipedal. And then something grabs and shakes the rain fly for twenty or thirty seconds.

In the morning, over breakfast, Matt calms the couple by explaining that what they experienced is normal behavior. Often, first, the Sasquatch attempts to intimidate the humans, to oust them from territory where, long after dark, they don't belong. Second, once the people have gone deeply to sleep, and are blatantly snoring, incapacitated by slumber, between, say, 3:00 and 5:00 AM, the Sasquatch's native curiosity can afford to supplant its fear and affront, and so it can investigate.

Other middle-of-the-night stakeouts follow, and you experience nothing. Nobody does. Nothing at all. The nights ring back at you with hollow silence.

The quarry has either moved on or decided it is unsafe to play. The expedition members, though, draw together and become close. You find in one another kindred spirits, people who have endured years of being the butt of jokes but possessing, nonetheless, the necessary wit and imagination to grasp the very possibility of Sasquatch, to take in and take seriously the extensive physical and anecdotal evidence. How can you *not* appreciate such   folks, so bold and wide awake? And what an ancient, potent archetype you're co- and re-creating together, too: humans versus "the monster."

Over the next several expeditions, you learn that in fact the majority of the time group overtures go unanswered, even the great majority. Because in order for acoustical contact to occur, the animal or animals must be within earshot *and* be in a mood to communicate. After all, they are in their element, behind trees at the pitch-black core of night. You come to think of it this way: Here is a species whose survival strategy, vis-a-vis *Homo sapiens*, has been virtually 100% effective for eons. And even when they do sound off, occasionally, they are simply not going to come close, not going to commit that kind of fatal error. If they did, we'd all know about it; the case would have been closed long, long ago. There are researchers who have spent their entire adult lives in this pursuit, such as Grover Krantz, John Green, Rene Dahinden, and never caught a glimpse. And here you expect to witness a breakthrough equipped with your $250 SONY "nightshot" Camcorder and a fistful of peanut M & Ms?

But two months later, in May 2006, on the Ohio Expedition, in the early afternoon, Florida-based legal secretary Caroline experiences a daylight sighting, rare beyond rare, while standing on a defunct railroad bed, looking up to a ridgeline.

> At the top of the hill, you could see blue sky, and
> then you could see all the saplings, and you could
> see between the saplings and the blue sky a figure

walking. I thought it was a person, but then we told
Patty to go in the same place and I could see the
colors. I could see the color of her face, I could see
the color of her clothes. And this was just all one
color—torso up, dark... Matt and Patty, when they
were standing up there, you could definitely see the
difference between where their head stopped and
their shoulders began. This thing had shoulders, but
it wasn't a definite neck.

Twelve hours later, at 1:41 AM, you produce an impressively
sustained moaning howl (emulating the sound recorded in 1994 in this
same county; Google "Bigfoot Ohio Howl") and receive a response howl
from the ridge high above. This is, to put it mildly, a kick, and you
entertain the fleeting fantasy that you could now simply charge up that
slope and meet the source of that glorious call. But then of course you
realize such a climb would take you two hours, by which point the caller
him- or herself, having recognized the first few *moments* of your heroic
ascent, would have exited to the neighboring county.

Nearby, the same night, Onil (a Toronto S.W.A.T. team member)
and three other expedition-goers walk along a slow-flowing river, at a
place called "Gretchen's Lock," named after a small girl who died of
malaria and was buried here back in 1838. Her ghost is said to have
haunted this spot, making her presence known these 168 years since. Out
of nowhere, Onil's group hears the great plunging impact of a rock thrown
into the water less than ten feet from where they are standing. Judging by
the sound, this object was about the size of a volleyball, and based on the
direction it must have come from, was heaved more than eighty feet,
across the wide river.

Such incidents, as well as those of stick- and log-throwing, are
commonly reported in areas with a long history of Sasquatch encounters.
With remarkable consistency, these projectiles land close to people but do
not strike them; it seems a good way to spook us, to chase us off Sasquatch
turf. And it generally works wonders. Some of the locals, whom you talk
to, seem to prefer a different explanation: Little Gretchen's ghost has

always been credited with a particular mischievous penchant for hurling rocks at interlopers.

The next morning, on a trail system above Gretchen's Lock, you're in a party of four who comes upon an extremely impressive "tree structure" in the forest. It's made of seven trees, pushed over from where they grew, averaging ten to twelve inches in diameter. These trees intersect in a neat cross-hatch fourteen feet off the ground, leaning into the crook of a larger, upright tree. Choosing a tree of the same thickness, growing nearby, burly, six-foot-five-inch Mike from New Jersey finds that he is unable even to budge it, much less to topple it over and add it to the formation.

Throughout North America, such stick and tree structures—most much smaller and less elaborate than the one you found in Ohio—have appeared in the vicinity of reported Sasquatch encounters and acoustical evidence. Researchers speculate that they serve as some sort of marker, rather than as shelter, but it's not possible at present to be more precise. Given that they are often found near roads and trails—and often thirty to forty feet off of such routes—one possibility is that they are built there by the older ones to warn the younger ones to avoid human areas. They may also represent aesthetic expression, or play, or the simple statement: *We were here.*

On the Arizona Expedition, while exploring along the steep wall of a rugged box canyon within the White Mountain Apache Reservation and just two miles from where Apache rangers found massive five-toed tracks in the mud, you and three other members discover a horizontal cave thirty-five feet deep, shaped like a keyhole. Its first fifteen feet, the narrow stem of the keyhole, is an entrance corridor in which large rocks have been cleared away, moved to either side, leaving a smooth floor for crawling. Bears, according to Lynn, a wildlife biologist attending the expedition, have never been known to do this in their dens; they simply clamber over such rocks.

This corridor then opens out into a round room twenty feet in diameter. Back here, the floor is covered with a uniform eleven-inch-thick layer of soft organic material, mostly dead grass and leaves (deeper, this has decayed and disintegrated into dust), that has been carried in here and spread out as though for bedding. Lynn can think of no animal capable of dragging hundreds of pounds of soft organic material far into a cave, no animal without *hands*, that is.

Nowhere in the whole place is there any sign of human use—no fire ring or soot on walls or ceiling, no beer cans, cigarette butts or a single scrap of litter. The rounded chamber at the back of the cave could easily sleep a family of three. And it would be temperature regulated: In winter, the body heat would make it nice and toasty, and in the summer, one could duck in here to beat the heat.

Furthermore, this cave is located strategically perfectly—thirty feet beneath the rim of the canyon, its mouth entirely hidden from up top, and overlooking, three hundred feet below, the confluence of two rivers where the elk cross, and come to drink.

It's actually quite homey inside here and, reveling in your discovery, you lie down, curl up, pretend to be many times your own size, in which case the walls would curve neatly against your spine.

I can now shift from second to first person and tell you that all of the above did occur to me personally, or to credible others around me, during eleven BFRO expeditions between September 2005 and October 2008. For instance, I took the pictures of the large tree structure in Ohio and explored the cave in Arizona.

(See YouTube: "Suspected Sasquatch Shelters: Arizona.")

Though moments of close approach are few and far between, the mere fact that these expeditions *ever* yield genuine contact at all, even from a distance, is remarkable enough, representing as it does a quantum leap over previous efforts, especially during the second half of the Twentieth Century, when "expeditions" were little more than hunting or scouting trips, poking around in promising areas during the day. Before the BFRO began finding success in the mid-1990s, researchers did not employ the subtle approach, making consistent nocturnal overtures, attempting to elicit response.

For example, I once drove eleven hundred miles round-trip from Vermont to an expedition in southern Pennsylvania, stood in the woods with fellow members at multiple propitious locations in the middle of the night, making wood knocks and whoops, attempting to emanate a maximally peaceable attitude into the pitch blackness, and heard nothing back from across the divide for the entire three days. Yet I reminded myself that this outcome is, after all, part of the *point.* Theirs is an entirely strategic lifestyle, and it is, of course, thanks to this very fact, this foundational cold shoulder, that Sasquatch has been able to persist into our own time.

2. Fostering Mini-Habituations

Unlike the case of chimpanzee and gorilla research, the field of Sasquatch study affords, as of yet, no luxury of protracted witness and interaction; thus, it remains in its infancy—that is, the field *as a whole* does. Many avid and committed individuals have, however, interacted with Sasquatch *in* the field, at certain forest locations or in their own backyards, but have kept these interactions strictly *entre nous.* I learned this important truth only gradually.   Even at habituation sites, any interaction with this species is a glancing one, oblique and capricious, though developing a relationship with an individual or a family, over months and years, is the surest way of shortening your odds.

In terms of evidence officially documented and reported, the best that had been achieved before the mid-1990s was the chance wilderness or roadway encounter, in which both human and Sasquatch are startled and so neither party is acting naturally. And thus, the person almost never has the presence of mind to wield a camera. (Notable exceptions are Roger Patterson, 1967; Paul Freeman, 1994; and Lorrie Pate, 1996.)

So Matt Moneymaker spends a lot of time during each expedition educating participants on what to expect, rehearsing outreach strategy, going over dramatic encounters from expeditions past—none of which culminated in a proximity closer than fifty feet, much less a face-to-face encounter—all in an effort to help quell that primal interior voice that tells us we're dealing, here, with a monster. He frames the issue this way: "It's as if you're trying to make contact with a lost tribe. You approach them with great respect, with the attitude that you know they're smart, and that you want to let them *know* that you know. And that you understand you are trespassing on *their* territory."

He encourages us to clear aside the confusing clamor of apprehension, to quietly explore and tune in to our intuition, to become alert to the subtle sensations that may arise. Sometimes, one can actually feel something in the air, a shift in quality, becoming aware of being watched or receiving what he describes as "a *sizzle.* You know, the sense that I've been here before...but I haven't?"

Expeditions last three or four days, occasionally longer, and there is a reason for this. "If they're around they can obviously be very cautious and very coy at first, and you won't hear much. And they'll come around and check you out and you won't even know they did it. But after a couple of days, they may just begin to let down their guard. One night, and you're showing good behavior, and they're still playing it cautious. Then the next night you're still making their sounds, and you're not grabbing spotlights, and you're not pointing guns and going out after them every time you hear something. After a few days, they may begin to let down their guard a little and let you hear them, and even see them, usually at night."

In North Carolina, once, I was sitting beside Michael Greene from Pennsylvania when he spotted, through his thermal vision scope, the shape of a massive figure, like a tall football player with shoulder pads, walking among the trees at about seventy feet. He turned his upper body toward me and the others, said, "Our friend is here," then took a moment to switch on the record function (limited battery life prevents him from recording constantly). When he turned back toward the trees, the figure had already receded from view. Michael was despondent. A veteran North Carolina tracker commented, "Them buggers is slick." The thermal scope resembles a gun.

That same night, our youngest North Carolina Expedition member, the fifteen-year-old daughter of an attending couple, had the traumatic experience of being "zapped." She was just sitting at her family's campsite, near the campfire, fifteen feet from the edge of the woods, pretty relaxed, when suddenly she was overcome with anxiety, felt nauseated and weak, with an intense pins-and-needles sensation in her arms. Her parents helped her walk over to join the rest of us, to help give her perspective on what had just happened to her. It was a warm night but she felt profoundly cold; I brought her a blanket from my car.

Certain species of mammals, such as whales, elephants and lions, can emit "infrasound blasts," pulses of sound at a frequency too low to be heard by the human ear. They will use infrasound to communicate over long distances, or to overwhelm their prey; the pulse affects the central nervous system. Lions have been documented disabling gazelle in this manner. There is abundant anecdotal evidence that Sasquatch, too, sends out infrasound blasts, and researchers often refer to receiving such a pulse as being "zapped." Perhaps, in this instance, the Sasquatch decided we had been encroaching on its territory (walking in the dark late at night outside the campground, where human beings are not *supposed* to venture), and so targeted our youngest, and most vulnerable, group member.

People can become so profoundly disoriented that they "freeze up." In 1995, I met a man in British Columbia who told me that when an adult male Sasquatch crossed the road in front of his car, then looked in at him, "It pretty much lock-jawed my whole body." While thus paralyzed, victims of infrasound often find that their perception of time is distorted, such that minutes can feel like seconds.

And yet, "What we may discover in this whole thing," Matt conjectures, "is that there's always been this kind of unquenched thirst on their part to interact with people and they just couldn't. Because you know how people react when they see these things. We're not friendly.

"They've seen human activity that seemed endearing or sympathetic. You've probably watched people having fun somewhere, from a distance. And you wish you could go and have fun with them too. I think they watch us and probably plenty of times they wish they could just freely walk among us. They know they can't."

The way to habituate Sasquatch, even during our brief visits to a given site, is to play upon this desire for interaction, and to attempt to walk a tightrope—both emotionally and tactically—between over-eagerness and timidity. If we get a knock response, for instance, we will often refrain from following up immediately with another overture. If they're knocking, they're curious. They may not be sure of the source of the sounds, whether human or their own kind. Best to let this uncertainly ride for a while, see if they will approach for a closer listen and look.

In southern Pennsylvania, Matt and Steve Willis (U.S. Army, Retired) were standing by the woods after midnight, making occasional vocal overtures. "Before they actually came up on us," Willis reports,

"Matt said he thought he could hear a faint response to his whoop call. We stood there for five, maybe eight, minutes, and we could hear something coming through the woods, coming toward us. So we just stayed quiet and it kept getting closer and closer. It was just like this, the dark of night, we didn't have any night vision with us, and all we were doing was just listening. At one point, Matt whispered to me, 'If these are 'squatches, we'll hear one go around behind us.' Sure enough, pretty soon that's what happened. The steps started separating into two distinct sets, two pathways that they were taking. There was one group that went directly across the front of us, and it probably wasn't more than fifty to sixty feet away from us. It was an adult and a young one, you could tell, because every once in a while the trailing one would have to run a couple steps to catch up."

"See, you want to have the attitude," Matt tells us, "that you're so sure they're civilized and decent that you can fully surrender yourself, put yourself out there. And that's going to be expressed in all kinds of ways. There's the way to express it mentally, if there's anything to that, and again, you've got nothing to lose by trying. It projects also through your body language, and then just everything that they can sense about…is this guy afraid? Have I got this guy scared?"

3. The Kentucky "Pancake Eater" Footage— The Erickson Project is Born, June 2005

While I traveled around the country with the organization, eventually rolling up a total of nineteen thousand miles, I began to pick up a few details from other expedition members about an astonishing situation currently unfolding in Kentucky.

It seemed that a woman had succeeded in establishing a reliable routine of feeding a young female Sasquatch. This woman had contacted the BFRO and, in the early summer of 2005, Matt had flown down there to investigate, and her story checked out. He managed to obtain some late-night infrared video footage of the creature coming for a plate of pancakes, eating them with its back to the camera.

Naturally, upon first learning of this Kentucky situation, I became fascinated by this whole new notion of a habituation site. That such a thing existed at all was quite a revelation to me, transposing the spotty tune of Sasquatch research into a rich new key and tempo, and I set out to learn as much as possible.

In the spring of 2005, a young, female Sasquatch began making repeat visits to a particular rural residence in Kentucky. She'd be enticed there by the woman of the house, whom we will call Sissy. She'd spotted the animal several times from a distance and had then begun calling out to it in a high, sing-song voice: "Come here, my little man, Mama's got something good for you! Come here, my little man!" (Later, the woman saw the creature squat to pee, and understood it was female.) The Sasquatch was not very tall, no taller than the woman herself. It was hair-covered and bore a large, rounded head with lots of frizzy, flowing hair running down beside the face. It was barrel-chested but immature, with no obvious secondary sexual characteristics.

During the day, she had no luck in getting this startling primate to approach. But late at night, she'd sing her little song and leave a paper plate of pancakes and syrup on a low dirt hill, near the forest, at the edge of her backyard catfish pond. Remarkably enough, twenty minutes or half an hour later, the individual would consistently emerge from the densely wooded valley and accept the offering. Sissy could hear it down there, and in the morning, she'd find its footprints, impressed into the dirt. These prints went far deeper than her own, or even those of her husband, at more than two hundred pounds, confirming how robust the visitor was.

"Of course it makes sense that the subject was a juvenile," says Matthew Moneymaker, "because she hadn't learned the ropes yet. She let down her guard." The organization's website, BFRO.net, has received many thousands of reports of encounters from all over North America, has interviewed the witnesses, assessed their credibility, and concluded that Sasquatch species distribution is much wider than formerly contemplated, even by those who believed it existed. But never before had he stumbled upon a case remotely as promising as this one.

On the 2005 New York Adirondacks Expedition, my first, Matt

showed a few of us, gathered at base camp, the infrared footage he'd obtained in Kentucky three months earlier. We could see the figure of Sissy herself, inching along unsteadily in the inky blackness (humans cannot see by infrared light), setting down the paper plate of pancakes, and then withdrawing. Twenty-one minutes later, another figure enters the frame, reaching a thick furry forearm toward the plate. The hand even scoops up a couple of pancakes that have fallen off, replacing them. (Apparently, these eyes *can* see by infrared.) The subject then picks up the plate and sits down on the dirt hill, turning away from the camera. It has a disproportionally large head surrounded by wisps of flowing hair, but aside from this, it also reminds one of the rear view of a mountain gorilla—that same thickset frame, that stiff straightness to the back, that air of power in repose.

From the movement of its head and from the elbows projecting out on both sides, one can then infer that the animal is eating. And the head looks strange, definitely *not* resembling a gorilla's; it is huge and round, like a pumpkin haloed by wispy hair. A gorilla's skull bears a conical shape or "sagittal crest," as does the figure seen in the 1967 Patterson/Gimlin Film, a female Sasquatch retreating gracefully from the camera. But juvenile gorillas do not yet sport such a crest. So when it comes to the creature on this Kentucky hill, either we are talking about a similar state of morphological immaturity, or else the Sasquatch species features regional differences, like races or breeds. Indeed, Kentucky lore about wildmen in the forests sometimes referred to them as "Ole Pumpkin Head."

This initial footage is quite dim and would never convince any hard-core skeptic. Luckily, though, more and better was to come. Much better. It was not long before real estate developer and Sasquatch researcher Adrian Erickson came on the scene and inaugurated The Erickson Project. He purchased this Kentucky property and installed qualified researchers at Moneymaker's recommendation—Leila Hadj-Chikh (Princeton PhD in Ecology & Evolutionary Biology) and BFRO Investigator Dennis Pfohl.

Interestingly, Erickson neglected to stipulate contractually that the former residents relocate a certain distance away, so they simply bought another home two miles from the first, Sissy resumed her sing-song calls in the night, and her "little man" promptly began visiting the new place instead.

With Erickson's encouragement, though, Sissy did soon succeed in obtaining the close-up facial footage that has since made history. He purchased it from her and kept it tightly under wraps for six long years, while his Project continued patiently gathering evidence here in Kentucky and at several other habituation sites in both the United States and Canada.

After learning of all this, I'm lucky enough to form trusting relationships, over the next several years, with other habituators. In the next chapter, I try out some of their veteran advice, and BFRO methods, in Vermont, my home territory; and then, in Chapters Three and Five, with their permission and in their own words, we'll plunge into the lush symphony of the habituators' experiences.

If the world can become more familiar with the subtle, civil, and wily ways of this species, can come to recognize just how widespread is their distribution across North America and elsewhere, then perhaps the "Sasquatch fever" that has spread with the release of "Shooting Bigfoot" and the Dyer specimen can become tempered by humane wisdom.

Man or Gorilla?

The Extraordinary Character Who Is Scaring Canueks

Ottawa, Ontario, Aug. 1—Pembroke, about one hundred miles north of Ottawa, has a lively sensation in the shape of a wild man eight feet high and covered with hair. His haunts are on Prettis Island, a short distance from the town, and the people are so terrified that no one has dared to venture on the island for several weeks. Two raftsmen named Toughey and Sallman, armed with weapons, plucked up sufficient courage to scour the woods in hope of seeing the monster. About three o'clock in the afternoon their curiosity was rewarded. He emerged from a thicket having in one hand a long stone and in the other a wooden bludgeon. His appearance struck such terror to the hearts of the raftsmen that they made tracks for the boat, which was moored by the beach. The giant followed them, uttering demoniacal yells and gesturing wildly. They had barely time to get into the boat and pull a short distance out into the stream when he hurled the stone after them, striking Toughey in the arm and fracturing it. Sallman fired two shots, but neither took effect, the giant retreating hurriedly at the first sound of firearms. It is more than probable that the townspeople will arrange an expedition to capture, if possible, what Toughey describes as a man who looks like a gorilla, wandering about in a perfectly nude condition, and, with the exception of the face, completely covered with a thick growth of black hair.

The Wild Man of the Woods
Wisconsin Democrat
Tuesday, September 17, 1839

Robert Lincoln, Esq. agent of the New York Western Lumber Company, has just returned from the St. Peters river near the head of steamboat navigation, on the upper Mississippi, bringing with him a Living Wild Man of the Woods, with two small cubs supposed to be about three months old.

Mr. Lincoln went out to the north-west as Agent of the New York Lumber Company, in July last, with a view to establish extensive sawmills, on the pine lands near the Falls of St. Anthony, and he has given us a detail of the operation of the Company, and the circumstances which led to the capture of the extraordinary creature mentioned above.

About the 14th of January, two of the carpenters who had been out in pursuit of a gang of wolves, that had proved very troublesome, came into the camp and reported that they had seen a huge monster in the forest, on a branch of the Mississippi, having the form of a man, but much taller and stouter, covered with long hair, and of a frightful aspect. They stated that when seen, he was on a log, looking directly at them, and the moment they raised their muskets he darted into the thicket and disappeared. They saw him again in about half an hour, apparently watching them, and when they turned towards him he again disappeared. Mr. Lincoln was at first disposed to think lightly of this matter, believing that the men might have been mistaken about the size and height of the object, or supposing it might have been a trick of the Indians to frighten them. He was informed, however, by some natives, that such a being had often been seen on the St. Peters, and near the Falls of the Mississippi, and they proposed to guide a party of workmen to a bluff where it was thought it might be seen. The men were all ready for an adventure, and arming themselves with rifles and hunting knives, they started for the bluff under the direction of Mr. Lincoln and the Indian guide. On the way they were joined by several of the natives, and the whole party numbered twenty-three.

They arrived at the bluff late in the afternoon and encamped in a cave or grotto, at the foot of the hill. Early next morning, two of the Indians were sent out to reconnoiter, and in about an hour returned, and said they had seen the wild man on the other side of the hill. The whole party immediately prepared for the pursuit. Mr. Lincoln gave positive orders to the men not to fire upon him unless it should be necessary in self-defense, as he wished if possible to take him alive. The Indians stated that although a powerful creature, he was believed to be perfectly harmless, as he always fled at the approach of men. While Mr. Lincoln was giving his men their instructions, the wild man appeared in sight. He ordered them to remain perfectly quiet, and taking out his pocket glass surveyed him minutely. He appeared to be about eight or nine feet high, very athletic, and more like a beast standing erect, than a man. The Indians had provided themselves with ropes used to catch wild horses, with which they hoped to ensnare and bind the creature, without maiming him.

The instant the company moved towards him he sprang forward with a horrid and frightful yell which made the forest ring; the Indians followed close upon him and Mr. Lincoln and men brought up the rear. The pursuit was continued for nearly an hour–now gaining upon the object of their chase, and now almost losing sight of him. He finally darted into a thicket, and they were unable to find him.

They then began to retrace their steps towards the place of encampment, when within about a mile of the cavern, the wild man made his appearance again. They immediately gave chase again and accidentally drove the creature from the forest to an open prairie. At length he suddenly stopped and turned upon his pursuers. Mr. Lincoln was then in advance. Fearing that he might attack them, or return to the woods and escape, he fired upon him, and lodged a charge of buckshot in the calf of his leg. He fell immediately, and the Indians sprang forward and threw their ropes over his head, arms, and legs, and with much effort succeeded in binding him fast. He struggled, however, most desperately, gnashed his teeth, and howled in a frightful manner. They then formed a sort of litter of branches and limbs of trees, and placing him upon it, carried him to the encampment. A watch was then placed over him, and every effort made that could be devised to keep him quiet, but he continued to howl piteously all night. Towards morning, two small cubs, about three feet high, and very similar to the large monster, came into the camp and were taken without resistance. As soon as the monster saw them he became very furious–gnashed his teeth, and howled, and

thrashed about, until he burst several of the cords, and came very near effecting his escape. But he was bound anew, and after that was kept most carefully watched and guarded. The next day he was placed on the litter and carried down to the mills on St. Peters.

For two or three days, Mr. Lincoln says he refused to eat or drink or to take any kind of food, but continued to howl at intervals for an hour at a time; at length, however, he began to eat, but from that time his howl ceased, and he remained stupid and sullen ever since. The cubs took food very readily and became quite active and playful.

Mr. Lincoln is a native of Boston, and some of the workmen engaged at his mill are from this city. He arrived here on Saturday afternoon, in the brig St. Charles, Stewart, master, from New Orleans, with the wild man and two cubs, and they were all removed from the vessel that evening. By invitation of Mr. Lincoln, who is an old acquaintance, we went down to his rooms to examine this monster. He is a horrid looking creature, and reminds us very strongly of the fabled satyrs, as we have pictured them to our own mind. He is about eight feet three inches high, when standing erect, and his frame is of giant proportions in every part. His legs are not straight, but like those of any four-footed animal, and his whole body is covered with a hide very much like that of a cow. His arms are very large and long and ill proportioned. It does not appear from his manner that he ever walked on 'all fours.' The fingers and toes are mere branches, armed with stout claws. His head is covered with thick, coarse, black hair, like the mane of a horse. The appearance of his countenance, if such it may be called, is very disgusting–nay, almost horrible. It is covered with a thinner and lighter coat of hair than the rest of how body– there is no appearance of eye-brows or nose, the mouth is very large and wide, and similar to that of the baboon. His eyes are quite dull and heavy, and there is no indication of cunning about them. Mr. Lincoln says he is beyond dispute carnivorous, as he universally rejects bread and vegetables, and eats flesh with great avidity. He thinks he is of the ourang outan species; but from what we have seen, we are inclined to consider him a wild animal somewhat resembling a man. He is, to say the least, one of the most extraordinary creatures ever brought before the public, from any part of the Earth, or the waters under the

Earth; and we believe will prove a difficult puzzle to the scientific. He lies down like a brute, and does not appear to possess more instinct than common domestic animals. He is now quite tame and quiet, and is only confined by a stout chain attached to his legs.

Chapter Two

A Visit from "Thumper"—
Applying Lessons in my Childhood Forest
(The Vermont Project 2007-2008)

The discovery of an uncatalogued great ape would not
make a revolution in science and would not make
anthropologists re-write the story of human evolution.
The discovery of a *living* hominin different from *Homo
sapiens* would certainly have such an effect, because it's
a long-held dogma of anthropology that *Homo sapiens* is
"the one and only living product of the hominin line."
Unfortunate [are the titles and premises] of such books
as *Sasquatch: The Apes Among Us,* 1978, *North
America's Great Ape: The Sasquatch,* 1998, *Bigfoot! The
True Story of Apes in America,* 2003, authored by the
leading hominologists of North America.

> —from "Thoughts on the Revolution in
> Anthropology," by Dmitri Bayanov,
> International Center of Hominology,
> Moscow

August 2007

I can just make out Sylvester's dim shape in the mist as he maneuvers his kayak. It's 6:30 in the morning and, in a borrowed canoe, I awkwardly paddle toward a man, Ojibwa by descent, who has agreed to guide me to a forest he's been carefully exploring, and calibrating, for more than a decade.

I reach my new friend now and, after exchanging a few words, we paddle together toward the peninsula. We're only halfway to our destination, along a winding beaver canal. The canal divides a wide swamp and is lined by reeds so high that, riding low in the water, one cannot see over them. Given the layout of the topography, and the natural buffer created by the swamp, navigating this canal is the most direct route. There is no sound except songbirds, our breathing, and the gentle swish of water.

"When I find a special spot," Sylvester has told me,

> what I always do is to put something there so an observant person, or whatever, would see it and wonder why or how it got there. I'll put two quarters on the ground about a foot apart. I also had them facing up and pointed them north. Right out in plain sight. My idea is that no one could resist a couple quarters. If they disappeared then I know I have people in my woods and should keep an eye and ear open for them. Nothing happened the first few years...till last year. Then a quarter was gone, and the other was rotated to go east/west. I found in place of the missing quarter a cute little arrangement of feathers. Each a different color. And spread out just like a picture, facing east. If it were a person they would have taken both quarters and would not have left such a beautiful little arrangement, I imagine!

I feel, of course, extremely privileged to be taken in trust by this patient, perceptive seeker. After having logged more than nineteen thousand miles on expeditions with the BFRO, I find it nearly impossible to believe, yet also delightful to contemplate, that my best chance at success may have suddenly announced itself barely five miles down the road from my home.

I first became aware of Sylvester a couple of weeks ago, when he submitted a report to the BFRO website.

> I hang out in the deep woods of Vermont a lot. I was out in the woods the other day and was walking through the area when in the distance I saw a bright patch of ground. I couldn't tell what it was, but as I got closer I saw that it looked like a pile of hair. I noticed that it was covering a layer of...what looked like huge poops. I looked around the area for more evidence, like a carcass, but couldn't find anything. I then very gently sifted through the pile of hair with a small stick for evidence of whatever it was. I didn't disturb the area at all. It was indeed a layer of hair and under it was a layer of poops. The hair was interesting. It looked to me as if someone had shaved the animal, as the hairs were all cut even. So...a bear...with a razor or shears? A weird hunter who poops all over the ground then kills a deer and covers it with the hair?

I immediately contacted him, and that's when he let me know of his extended history playing sylvan games with "someone." Until recently, though, he'd never suspected that this someone could be Sasquatch. He played me a video of the scene, showing that indeed the gray-white clump of hair had been *cut* from whatever body, and nearby, the sharp broken bottom of a green bottle. Sylvester's current theory is that with the arrival of warmer temperatures this spring, the Sasquatch—if this is what it was— sheared off its own winter coat using this makeshift "razor."

The Peninsula

I say "peninsula," because this is its shape, even though the formation rises not from open water but out of swampland.

In our two boats, we finally arrive at the muddy bank where he always runs his kayak aground, at the foot of an imposing, hundred-and-twenty-foot sheer face of pine, rock and roots. He helps me to secure my canoe. "We're in *their* woods now." And we begin our ascent.

After a difficult climb, we crest the ridge and I see that its top is very narrow, twelve to fifteen feet across, and is covered by tamped-down pine needles: a clear pathway, with none of the punctures made by deer hooves. Sylvester's shoulder-length, graying hair and broad, earnest face drip with sweat, and he says with a laugh, "I keep picturing them running along this ridge all night, like a track meet."

After we explore awhile, an odd general feature becomes apparent. This peninsula is probably three hundred yards long and a hundred and fifty wide, and the ridge top wraps around it to create what might be better termed a *rim*. Within this rim, the peninsula dips into a bowl shape to form a hidden valley. I see zero sign of human presence—no wrappers, tin cans, cigarette butts, water bottles, bottle caps, fire rings, etc.—and Sylvester says that in fact, with one exception, he's *never* found any such up here. This place is just too inconvenient to get to. The one exception, in fifteen years, is that broken bottle, and even this was, by his next visit, duly removed from the premises; most of the hair, too, had been cleared away.

Continuing our tour of the hidden valley, we clamber over fallen trees and up and down steep slopes made nearly impassible by logs and limbs strewn everywhere, and by thick undergrowth. "If it's really tough to get to," he says, "*that's* where we should go."

He tells me that by laying low inside certain clefts within this peninsula, before sunrise, he's been lucky enough to hear bipedal footfalls, other sounds he can only describe as "jaw-popping," and what seems like women talking, with distinct syllables but unintelligible words. Once, he says, he was easing along the canal in his kayak and, just as he rounded a bend, dipping his paddle into the water with a slight splash, he heard something huge powering across the waterway and storming up the bank to his left. Then, it sat up there, out of sight within thick foliage, "grunting and grumbling."

This peninsula is less than three miles from where, in 1991, my good friend Tim, an extremely level-headed man, a writer and college administrator, witnessed something bizarre. Late one night, he was driving with a female passenger when they rounded a bend and saw, caught in the headlights, a small figure standing upright. "It was maybe three, three-and-a-half feet tall, no more than that," Tim has told me. His passenger said, "Is that a...*poodle*?" This is the only association she could make, a dog standing on its hind legs. Tim saw, instead, a monkey. "It had a little leathery face, and it was just staring at me, looking at me sort of over its shoulder, frozen in mid-stride. And then, all of a sudden, it ran off the road and into the underbrush and trees."

Stick Parties

Sylvester points out several fascinating formations, some new even to him, altered since last he visited just six days go. Other stick and tree structures have been laid waste in the interim: "Wow, they've totally destroyed these. Guess I got too close..."

And there are shallow trenches covered by little apparent "roofs" woven of sticks and leaves, perhaps a kind of Sasquatch nursery; these he has found before, but now they have been fortified by large leafy limbs set about like barricades. He takes this new construction quite personally. "I shouldn't have touched the roofs."

But by far the most intriguing and useful lesson Sylvester teaches me is to keep my eye out for what he calls "stick parties." These are spots where branches have been snapped into short segments, by the dozens, six, eight, ten inches in length, and in many cases the bark has been stripped as well, often thrown in jumbled heaps as in the old game of "Pick-Up Stix."

I learn much later that other researchers are noticing this same phenomenon.

Photographed by researcher Mike Paterson in Ontario

Once you start spotting these, of course, it's hard to stop, and you can quickly begin doubting your judgment, but then again, it becomes easy to learn to rule out random deadfall/windfall. The sheer number tells the story, along with the fact that the sticks have been broken into short segments. Also, they will often exude an unmistakable quality of *intention*, of having been manipulated by hand...improbably wedged into tight spaces between rocks or trees in what I came to call "stuffing" behavior...

Found in the ravine

...or organized into simple architecture...

From one angle (bottom p. 63), this looks like a messy heap; from another (above),we can see that the branches are thickly built up on two sides against a central "beam," creating a small room inside; photograph courtesy of Mike Paterson (see YouTube: "Sasquatch Roars" and other videos on his channel: Sasquatch Ontario)

...or longer branches/trees will be leaned in a "half-T-pee," as Texas researcher Bob Truskowski calls them.

Found in the ravine

Photographed by Mike Paterson, Ontario

Photographed by Bob Truskowski at Texas #1

Structure found on the BFRO Ohio Expedition, 2006

Two days later, Sylvester writes me all excited, having just experienced a breakthrough. "I used my hearing device [a microphone augmented by a parabolic dish] and what a revelation. I listened to one eating sticks. It was fascinating. I could hear it eating and gathering more sticks. Just munching away. My sense was that it was standing sentry, keeping tabs on me. The sound came from two hundred feet away, or so, and the source of the sound stayed out of sight."

Researching on-line, I find this: "Why do animals eat the bark of trees and fences? They are looking for minerals. Tree roots go deep into the soil to absorb minerals, which are then present in the bark." And then I locate an article (by Ker Than) about wood-eating behavior in Ugandan gorillas.

> After observing mountain gorillas in Uganda for nearly a year, scientists believe they have discovered why the animals eat wood and lick tree stumps, behaviors that have puzzled primate researchers for decades. The answer: for the sodium. Gorillas in the Bwindi Impenetrable National Park in Uganda will suck on wood chips for several minutes before spitting them out. Sometimes they chew on them until their gums bleed. They have also been seen licking the bases of tree stumps and the insides of decayed logs, and breaking off pieces of wood to munch on later. Gorillas will return daily to the same stump and take turns feeding. A new study by Cornell University researchers potentially solves the mystery. The researchers observed fifteen gorillas of different ages and gender as they engaged in wood-eating activities. After the animals were gone, the researchers collected wood samples from stumps and logs that the animals consumed as well as those they avoided. The researchers analyzed these items for their sodium content and found that the decayed wood was the source of over ninety-five percent of the animals' dietary sodium, even though it represented only about

four percent of their food intake.

I eagerly share this new connection with Sylvester, yet he's only mildly interested; I'm coming to learn that he's a fiercely independent researcher, who cares about ideas only if they're generated by himself, and I get the sense that he's quickly losing interest in my contribution.

Crime Scene

Ten days later, we meet up in another forest, several miles from the peninsula. I'm happy because we can drive here, rather than paddle, and we proceed down a very narrow dirt road, just after dawn. Sylvester tells me that he's recently spoken to a local man who says he saw a tall hairy figure crossing this same road late at night, and that everyone around here avoids this area, believing it haunted. There are screams in the night.

I recognize this road from my youth; as a teenager, I used to go running here. "I think a logging road shoots off to the left," I offer, "just ahead." Indeed, there it is again. We pull over, tuck the car out of sight at the trailhead, cross a field, and enter the woods.

We're immediately transfixed. It's like a classic Sasquatch cathedral or playground in here. We see stick parties everywhere, dead ringers for those present on the peninsula: barkless branches and limbs leaned carefully up against tree trunks, or stuffed between them, and high concentrations of stick segments mounded on the forest floor.

Then we find fresh deer bones littering the ground, leg bones, linked vertebrae, an eighteen-inch skull, all representing, it seems, several different kill sites. Near the skull, we are stunned to stumble upon a great heap of *hair*—coarse and curly, brown, like an absurdly heavy-gauge wig dumped on the ground. Sylvester gathers it up, smells it, and is overwhelmed. "It's so musky, so...*animal.*" I smell it too, and he's right. Some of the curls pull out to fourteen inches in length.

We're both feeling graced and giddy by this discovery, and we pack it off home. Actually, *he* pockets it, allowing me just a very limited hank.

Later, when I hold my share up to the sunlight, an iridescent roan red—like henna—clearly emerges, and I'm reminded of all the hundreds of witness reports that describe Sasquatch as reddish-brown.

That Sylvester has kept 98% of the hair for himself does irk me. But then again, he's taken on the role of leader in our relationship, of shaman guide, and I've tried to go with the flow. Certainly, I have learned much from this man.

The next morning, I return to the site to take pictures and video. He was the cameraman yesterday, but hardly captured any shots, so our visit was underdocumented. Also, I'm hoping to recast us, instead, as equal partners, and so I immediately report my photography trip, email him the pictures. Big mistake.

His reply is too angry **to** reprint here, except:

> I go into an area to gather intelligence. Then the whole picture comes to me, gradually. If I need to return to the area I know that the same vibes will be there again. This is like a CRIME SCENE INVESTIGATION. There is yellow tape all over where we have walked.

Needless to say, it is not long before he drops me altogether, like a stone, but now I'm equipped with powerful new knowledge, thanks to his fleeting mentorship. After all, without it, I'd probably never have found out that my own backyard is a "hot zone."

I send several strands of the hair Sylvester and I found to Jerry in Upstate New York (see Chapter Three), and he confirms that it looks just like that of Sasquatch hair he has seen at close range—brownish-red and very coarse.

Taking up, then, my solo local research, I study satellite maps and realize that there is, adjacent to the area with the deer bones and the hair, a steep ravine that bottoms out into swampland. Suddenly, it dawns on me that I *know* this ravine! When I was fifteen, I "discovered" it not far from my home, and explored it often. It always exerted a kind of sacred gravity for me, seeming a realm apart, and I'd return from time to time during my adult life, to replenish myself on its singular atmosphere.

Now I hasten back here, and while it strikes me in the same primordial manner, I'm seeing it through a whole new lens. Over the next two months till snowfall, I spend more than fifty hours inside the ravine, talking and singing to the trees, making wood knocks, discovering "stick structures," and just sitting quietly, as per Robert W. Morgan.

Late Summer and Fall 2007

Less than a mile, as the crow flies, from where I spent my adolescence—occasionally daydreaming of the creature I'd seen in the Patterson/Gimlin Film, wishing I were grown up so I could travel to the Pacific Northwest—I begin, finally, at age forty-six, a long series of forays into the ravine, still undeveloped, rugged and pristine.

On my first visit, I stick to the near side, near the public dirt road and just a quarter mile from a (human) residence. The same old logging road I used in childhood proceeds downward, and here I notice that two trees have been pushed slantwise across, so that I need to duck under them. At the bottom, several hundred feet down, I look across the swamp to the far side of the ravine, the unpopulated side, difficult to access. What's awaiting me over there?

On my second visit, just three days later, something brand new. (I feel like Sylvester!) Two young birches have been sculpted into arches, bowed across the trail and pointed downward, such that their leafy tops dangle in the precise middle of the path.

Upon examination, one tree proves even more interesting, because the dirt beneath is swept clean. I mean *really* clean, starkly different from the rougher texture of the earth surrounding. The least radical interpretation of this is, of course, that the wind has simply stirred the leaves around, which brushed the turf. But down here inside the ravine, there just isn't enough wind to agitate such a tree so effectively. (And why was it bowed over in the first place, between one visit and the next?) And as I imitate the wind with my hand, I realize that it would actually lift the leaves *away* from the ground. More likely, I reason—though, yes, the word "likely" still seems ludicrous in this context—the Sasquatch who bent this sapling all the way into a semi-circle found it necessary, in order to make the new trajectory stick, to continuously yank it down into the ground, to forcefully *thrash* it about.

(See YouTube: "First Ravine Signs.")

At the bottom, I walk farther along the trail than the last time, and here I find that two more trees, six or seven inches in diameter, much thicker than the saplings above, have been snapped cleanly to form twin right angles from left to right across my way, a clear No Trespassing sign.

Trespassing, I find a strait across the swamp to the far side of the ravine. This bank is far steeper, and a tough climb takes me eventually to several tiers. The forest over here shows no sign of human trails or refuse. Soon enough, besides many stick party scenes, again reminiscent of the peninsula, I come across a very obvious and exciting T-pee structure; most of the branches on its right side are stripped of bark.

This formation employs two bowed saplings as well, both still rooted in the ground. One enters the formation, pulled through from ten feet away to become part of the weave at the top of the T-pee, where the slanting sticks converge, and the other, growing within the T-pee's radius, passes up through the structure, and *exits*, bending away through the air.

Compare to this structure photographed by Bob Truskowksi at habituation site Texas #1.

During early trips to the far side of the ravine, I also find three further types of structure, which I learn only later are typical of Sasquatch activity at habituation sites throughout North America.

First, what I like to call RSS—roughly symmetrical stuffing. These range from the very humble (easily missed), to the monumentally impressive.

A small RSS made of branches (near my house)

Limbs and branches shoved in from both sides
(found near where the tree was later pushed down
beside me in 2009; see Chapter Four)

Found in the ravine

Photographed in West Virginia by Robert Cummings

Second, arched young trees whose ends are tucked and anchored carefully beneath rocks, downed trees, or other objects.

Third, "pinwheel" formations.   One afternoon, I glance downhill through the forest and do a classic, comic double-take at a strikingly artful wheel. I slide sideways toward it, heart accelerating, then approach like one of those monkeys before "the slab" in *2001: A Space Odyssey*.

It's constructed of four long, straight trees, crossing at the "hub," two of which are still rooted and have been pulled through in a manner similar to the arched saplings but also different, in that by the time they enter the "wheel" they are not much bent anymore but act as proper "spokes." In fact, it takes time for me even to recognize that they are still growing   and   have   been,   in   effect,   borrowed   for   the   cause.

In the picture above, one can see another typical arched sapling in the foreground, but when I return just three days later and take another picture from the same angle, this tree has been snapped at the top. I don't know how to understand this, except that perhaps my discovery of the pinwheel has not gone unnoticed; translation: "We've been compromised."

Such wheels are far less common than T-pee structures, sapling arches, or roughly symmetrical stuffing (RSS), but they do appear throughout the continent; below is another example, photographed in Upstate New York by Robert Sharak on his property, where he has seen an all-black female Sasquatch on three occasions.

(For more, see YouTube: "Sasquatch Structures.")

The Third Tomato

Emulating Sylvester and Robert W. Morgan, I find my own "special spot" beneath a pine on one of the tiers between the steep lower portion of the ravine and the steep upper portion. One hundred and fifty feet above me, I can see the clean line of ridge through deciduous trees, and I decide never to mount this wall, but leave it for *them*, a strategic overlook, a safe vantage.

My first order of business is to inaugurate my site with a gift, so I wedge three tomatoes from my garden between two close trunks, where they glow nicely in the sunlight.

Apparently, not only do Sasquatch not much appreciate home-grown tomatoes, but neither do other creatures; when I return the next day, nothing is changed; and when I return again, a few days hence, one of the tomatoes remains in place, one has fallen to the ground and split. The third I can't locate at all but assume it must have fallen as well, and rolled somewhere downhill among the old leaves.

After about an hour of quietly reading, I go to pee at a tree I've used for this purpose several times before. Exactly at eye level, I turn to see none other than the missing tomato itself, just inches from my face. It's been slung over a branch, sitting squarely in the crook. I say "slung" because it's much farther along in the decay process than the other two, and whereas their skins are still smooth, this one's is pocked and mottled, seeds visible, the whole thing now pulpy enough to wrap partway down around the branch, sitting a certain liquefaction having already set in. Has it perhaps been inside a mouth before being rejected and left here for me in "the bathroom"? And if so, it's not been bitten into pieces, even two pieces, would say something about the *size* of said mouth.

It feels like I have suddenly, in essence, lost my virginity as a researcher, because this tomato seems meaningful, and *meant*. I've now joined the gifting and receiving ranks of Sylvester and of the other habituators.

(See YouTube: "The Roving Tomato.")

Yet none of what I leave at my site, next, elicits any further such reciprocal gestures. I leave apples between the two trunks, and they are always taken. I suspend an apple from a limb nine feet off the ground, secured by a tight noose of picture-hanging wire, and it too is gone when I return.

Between August 31st and November 2nd, I visit the ravine twenty-nine times, staying for an average of two hours, talking to the woods, reading, making wood knocks and calling "Whoop!" as on BFRO expeditions.

First Night in the Ravine

Not brave enough, yet, to spend the night alone here on the far side of the ravine, I try the near side, closer to the road and houses, closer to civilization. I use no tent, because I don't want to feel cut off. Brave? Not really: I figure it will be tougher to sneak up on me if there's no thin vinyl wall between "it" and my ear. Not only that, but I choose a spot three-quarters of the way up the logging road, so that I might escape to my get-away car, if need be.

I arrive at 10:01 and set up my high-quality, newly purchased audio recorder, hanging the microphone over a tree limb maybe six feet from my head, then settle in, getting warm, telling myself that this whole *fear* thing is a bit ridiculous, after all, since I'm just here on a simple listening mission, to document any action occurring a quarter mile away across the ravine, on the far side, where they seem to spend time.

It's an utterly still night, and I've nearly talked myself into a comfort zone when it happens. From up on the trail a short distance, the way I came in, *between my car and myself*—CRASH!   The   mind   is funny. I am definitely freaked out but I instantly begin the project of believing that the tree could—couldn't it?—have fallen of its own accord; there is no wind but maybe it was just…ready.

Only at dawn, when I wake and pack up my bedding, do I begin to reckon the long odds of any tree falling, with such force, on a still night; that is, if the tree were so weak already, wouldn't it have been toppled by the previous storm?

But even more to the point, on my way back up the trail, I'm confronted by the fact of precisely *where* this thing came down—partway across. Of all the hundreds within earshot, this is the one tree that decides to crash onto a path with a history of barriers. Also, this location would afford the perpetrator a quiet, grassy approach, avoiding the crunch of dead leaves, so that he could take just one step up onto the shoulder of the logging road, reach out, and yank.

In YouTube: "First Night in the Ravine: The Vermont Project 2007," you'll see, too, that directly across from this crash site is a tree whose bark has been removed or scuffed off in distinct patches, to make it a perfect knocking post.

Using my knocking club   This patch is seven feet high.

Exactly one week later, I return to find that another tree, a birch now lies on top of the first, at an exactly perpendicular angle, to form a cross or X.

Yet Another Tomato

One morning in early October, a house guest brings me something noteworthy. At the edge of the pathway leading to an A-frame cabin at the back of my property, he found a tomato. Likely, it came from my garden, out front, but how could it have traveled three hundred feet? I'd have guessed raccoon or squirrel, had the skin been bitten or punctured, the object's shape altered from the round. We examine it carefully: The skin is entirely unmarred.

And even so, I'd probably still have passed off this misplaced produce as some unaccountable quirk of nature, if "tomato" had not recently become a meaningful currency of exchange in this game I seem to be caught up in. I pay attention; after all, my property is only just over two miles from the ravine.

And I have not mentioned that incident to this man. The night before, he argued against the possibility of Bigfoot ("I just can't *see* there being a gigantic primate being able to elude us like that, y'know?"), but this morning, he's ready to pronounce his discovery "definitely odd."

Man oh man, I do like this hobby!

Of course, as with so much that occurs in the realm of Sasquatch study, one does find oneself suspecting an insidious slide into mental illness.

One proceeds.

Summer 2008—Sleeping on the Far Side

This spring, I find the courage to camp regularly at the spot where my tomato was relocated. Each time I arrive, I set my CD player on a log and share for the woods the same Bach melody (Orchestral Suite No. 2 in B Minor: Sarabande), or sometimes the recorded voice of my two-year-old daughter, babbling and laughing. I'm dutifully observing Robert W. Morgan's recommendation to "create a provocative routine...

> Find a way to gently announce your presence. Try whistling or singing a tune now and then. Why are you doing this? Because that music will serve as your trademark with them, and when they hear you play it, they'll know who you are.

On June 9th, I wake in the middle of the night, sometime after 2:00, quite confused and facing an impenetrable wall of darkness. I'm slapping mosquitoes and hearing distinct nearby stick breaks, as well as a hard-to-describe picking or rummaging sound through undergrowth. There begin occasional thumps on the earth, somewhere generally "over there," spaced by long intervals of silence.

Until 2:35, I'm able to pass these sounds off as possibly just my desirous imagination projecting itself onto a neutral background of pinecone falls and small-fry rodents. Maybe a deer snapped some twigs with its hoof.

Suddenly, though: a loud and intricate birdcall from the exact direction of the stick breaks. This is hard to reconcile with the image of a deer. I have heard that Sasquatch mimic birds. I sit up and stare into this blind nothingness, feeling a peculiar mix. On the one hand, I'd expect myself perhaps to freak out, since my car is more than a mile away, reachable only through rugged hike challenging even in daylight. And yet, on the other hand, my worst enemy is, after all, *actual* nothingness, being stranded up here and truly alone (or at least the only primate), on some fool's errand; in this sense, such promising sounds are a welcome affirmation.

Many have asked me, "But aren't you terrified way out there by yourself?" and I've answered, "Well, my fascination always outweighs the fear." This rather glib response has the advantage of being, for the most part, pretty accurate, and never more so than tonight, when, after falling back to sleep, I am rewarded at 3:29 by a double wood knock, maybe sixty feet away, maybe eighty, hollow, concerted and clear: *thwock thwock*! I smile under my blankets, glad to feel included, however obliquely, in some ancient practice. I'm at home here, strangely able to relax. There is nowhere in the world I'd rather be, and tell myself, "Sleep now, it's real."

"Thumper" Night

June 24th, I fall asleep early, partly because there's nothing to look at. It's extremely dark these days, thanks to a new moon and thick leafy canopy.

At 9:51, I become aware that I'm not alone, and that what's with me must have hands. What I hear is a snap-crackle-pop of sticks being deliberately broken, emphatically and close by, maybe fifty feet away. I've got no night-vision technology, nothing but a large hand-held spotlight, and using the latter is of course a well-known taboo among researchers. I've learned this on BFRO expeditions, and from several Sasquatch habituators I've begun corresponding with. The idea is to build up trust.

The sounds go on and on. Sometimes three sticks will be snapped within five seconds. The more I listen, the clearer it becomes that this display is *moving*, slowly circling me. Best I can tell, it's just *one* of them. *Just*?! Unless a person has hiked in here and found me in the pitch dark, when I've told nobody where I'm camping, and has decided to behave like a Sasquatch, this is actually a Sasquatch, and an old suspicion returns to strike me with fresh relevance: We're told that though they may threaten us, they'll never hurt us, that it's not in their nature. Logically, this has always made sense to me, because it would not be in their interest to aggress against us; it would be anti-stealth, would "out" them, make them a target.

And yet, doesn't every species feature individual differences, a bell curve of traits and aberrations? In other words, in the case of any given confrontation, mightn't it be that *this guy* happens to be insane, has a brain tumor, a chemical imbalance, or is a teenager with severe emotional problems?

"Hello over there," I call out in my kindest possible voice. "Hello hello hello, I'm glad you're here. Please stay. What are you trying to tell me?"

From my backpack, I pull my daughter's one-piece pajamas, which she's outgrown. Utterly invisible at the moment, they're white with blue polka-dots. I hug them to me, like some talisman against manual decapitation.

Hours pass, and the message remains the same, though I cannot read it. Occasionally, to the snaps are added light thumps on the turf. I keep talking, anything that comes into my head, whistling, even singing songs such as "Twinkle, Twinkle, Little Star" (my little girl's favorite). And then, shortly after midnight, these thumps become, for a short time, anything but light. My visitor suddenly smacks the ground four times, *pounds* it; half a minute later, three more impacts.

I say, "I *hear* you over there." My tone is casual, jovial, and in retrospect, over the succeeding weeks, I'm increasingly surprised at myself, at this apparent lack of fear. I say, "I'm going to call you Thumper! Would you like an apple? I'm going to roll it over to you, okay?" But doing this elicits nothing further, certainly not the ideal response of the apple being rolled *back* to me.

In fact, never for the rest of this protracted night does my visitor allow himself so much abandon again, thumping that loudly, but luckily, the audio recorder captures the whole six-hour encounter distinctly, including occasional, intricate birdsong...or *ostensible* birdsong.

(Hear it for yourself on YouTube: "A Visit from 'Thumper'" and "Field Audio from my Two Close Encounters in Vermont.")

By 1:35 AM, my composure is slipping. The stick breaks are impressive in their sheer constancy. I have not slept and my tone has gotten downright plaintive: "Well, don't just keep circling me. You're going to scare me. Why don't you just say something, or make a knock or something?" There's no way to discern intent here, but though initially I extended the benefit of the doubt, now I'm no longer quite so sure; I've started to feel menaced. I'm tempted, of course, to turn on my spotlight, but I don't want to fall into that trap and ruin this interaction, no matter what it is precisely trying to accomplish.

Between 2:00 and 3:30, I notice a tightness in my chest and jaw, but can't tell if I'm being mildly "zapped," or if instead these are the garden-variety anxiety symptoms one might expect when being surveilled all night by a legendary ape man.

At 3:57, just pre-dawn, I reach my limit. I stand up stiffly and lurch off into the night, my hiking boots landing on sticks that sound like gunshots going off. I'm holding the spotlight but waiting...waiting, thinking to flush the creature so that I'll know where to aim the beam. (Listening to the recording later, I *think* I can hear footsteps running away.) After twenty seconds, I jettison this tactic and just switch on the damn light. Scanning, I feel like a fool, because the bright circle looks paltry, revealing nothing but trunks and branches. I've just lost the game, and maybe the whole project.

After sleeping half the next day, I reach out to the wise women of the habituators' forum, and I hear from Ammi in North Carolina (see Chapter Three):

Great night!!
>
> They must be getting used to you, to even make any noise to let you know they are there. They can circle yer butt all day, and not make a sound...
>
> You may need to be a bit more gentle, and not have the voice of someone who is working a deadline...
>
> They may not have our technology and tool use skills, but they have had just as many thousands of years, to simply hone the "read people" thing.
>
> Consider them serious specialists in that field... I am sure our concept of body language and voice tone, as a clue to real thoughts is a joke to them. You have to understand, they don't just hide, they hide the fact that they exist, to most of the world. That means they don't make sounds, leave footprints, etc...if they are doing this openly, you have to realize this was their first show of trust. Just to come out around you.
>
> I don't believe they are "stupid curious"...they seem to know just when, with whom, and how much, they can get by with.
>
> I think they test us like that.

Three Gifts

Over the following week, I worry that I have managed to destroy, through ego and lack of respect, all that I've been able to build so far—that *both* sides have invested—in this habituation enterprise.

And then, on three successive mornings, June 30th, July 1st, and July 2nd, I find objects waiting for me in the grass by the passenger side of my car, in the exact same spot each time.

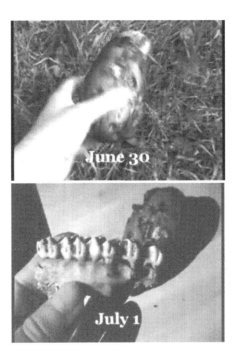

First, a large bulbous…what?   It's shaped like an eggplant but it's partially decayed and lacks the rind.   A fungus?   Later, my neighbor recognizes it as an eggplant indeed; it came from her compost pile.

Second, a two-inch length of jawbone, the back portion, with all teeth still in place.   The teeth are not the flat grinders of a herbivore, such as a deer.   A canine?

Third, a skull, apparently a deer's, with a little curl of greenery (still green) tucked into the brain cavity.

(See YouTube: "Three Gifts: The Vermont Project 2008.")

I do have a dog and so does my neighbor, but what dog carries a rotting vegetable? Also, these two bony offerings are entirely desiccated, nothing whatsoever to gnaw on. Further, this location would make sense as a "gifting spot" because a) my car is the means I take to travel between my home and theirs, and b) the passenger side faces away from my bedroom window, so that the items could have been left by someone crawling across my yard, concealed behind the vehicle.

Okay, so if these *are* gifts, what's their meaning? Am I forgiven for losing my cool the other night? Or is the entire paradigm of the dire taboo against the use of light perhaps an overstatement? Perhaps there is another angle from which to view this important night, rather than as a potentially game-breaking betrayal of a delicate trust relationship; perhaps it is well *within* the rules and the game is more in the vein of a good-natured sparring match, so that what I'm guilty of is no more than forfeiting one round among many. Within this frame, the gifts would seem an affirmation, meaning: "Well played."

Late Summer and Fall 2008

I can group these two periods together because less happens now. Nights in the ravine often come up empty, or contain only ambiguous, far-off thumps and stick breaks, potential footfalls, easy to write off. When I become discouraged, I remind myself of Robert W. Morgan's wise counsel: "It may take months, even years, of repeated visits to your research site in order to produce results." And here, in the infancy of my research process, I've been so lucky, having ample results already.

Yet, what I really want is another visit from Thumper. During that experience, I can remember assuming that I was nestled in the midst of a reliable escalation, that such interactions would only continue and improve. But whether it's because of my spotlight escapade, or because the Sasquatch clan has simply relocated or shifted routine, or perhaps because whoever smacked the turf near me so frankly crossed a line that night and then chose to back off, or was *told* to back off by an elder, my field work reaps precious few rewards for the remainder of the season.

In any case, through August and September, I keep showing up and sleeping in my spot, playing Bach and my daughter's hopeful voice, piping into the night. Sometimes my recorder contains, in addition to my snores, possible faint news of Thumper's re-approach, but again, nothing even 10% as definitive as what I was treated to back in June.

Leaves fall off, making for lousy conditions, because the sort of deep, cloaking darkness cannot occur; even beneath cloud cover and a new moon, ambient starlight filters down through the bare branches.

It's not until October 12th that I finally record, once again, a worthy stick break not far from the mic, not far from my inert body, followed by several promising, earthy thumps. I'd likely attribute these sounds to the hooves of a deer if not for the fact that today, on my hike into the ravine, I encounter something truly wonderful—a dramatic tree twist at the top of the logging road entrance, very near where the two young trees were arched across the path fourteen months ago, and exactly where that other tree was brought crashing down onto the trail during my first overnight, September 2007.

There's no mistaking it. This tree, eight or ten inches in diameter, is bent at a nearly ninety-degree angle so that it now crosses the entire path, three feet above my head. The twisting action has buckled the structure, popped loose the tree's three longitudinal segments, so that now it looks like a huge, woody braid.

Whatever the intended meaning of this gesture—even if the opposite of my interpretation, even if this is no "gesture" at all but something else—I'll go ahead and take it as a healthy pat on the back for me alone, a vote of confidence to tide me over through the long winter.

As Ammi has told me, "Baby steps all the way, but steps nonetheless." Also, I try to firmly lodge in my mind, again and again, the open-ended fluidity of this whole course of research. In Morgan's words, "It's like a chess game in which there is no checkmate and no pieces are lost."

Nourishing me as well is the increasing trust I'm gaining with the Sasquatch habituators, some of whom have agreed to let me share their spell-binding, instructive accounts in this book.

And whenever I drive through my little village, past the baseball field where I played Little League a third of a century ago, past the town's general store and post office, its U.S. flag, the feed store, the two dozen houses, past kids playing catch, swinging, shooting baskets, I think, "If they only *knew*." And then I remember that even *if* they knew, most would find a way to ignore it internally; as No-Bite at Texas #2 says, "It goes into the non-thinking part of the brain." Pets and satellite dishes, barbeques and beer, people mowing their lawns or tending their home grounds, resting on front porches, catching up on gossip. And all of this, all of *us*, not half a mile from a cleft in the Earth where another race shares our taproot primate practices, playing and chatting, too, conducting their ordinary business—a whole culture thriving on the graveyard shift.

Woodland Daily Democrat
Yolo Country, California
April 9, 1891

An Unheard-of Monstrosity Seen in the Woods Above Ramsey

Mr. Smith, a well-known citizen of Northern Capay Valley, called on us to-day and tells us the following strange story which he would be loath to believe were it not for the fact that he is an old acquaintance of this office, and has always borne a spotless reputation. Several days ago, Mr. Smith together with a party of hunters, were above Ramsey hunting. One morning Mr. Smith started out early in quest of game, but he had not gone far when his attention was attracted by a peculiar noise that seemed to come from up in an oak tree that stood near by. Looking up Mr. Smith was startled to see gazing at him what was apparently a man clothed in a suit of shaggy fur. Having heard of wild men, he was naturally placed upon his guard, but thinking that he would see "what virtue there was in kindness," he called to the supposed man to come down. The speech did not have the desired effect, rather the opposite, for the strange thing gave grunts of unmistakable anger. Our informant went at once in a bee-line for the camp. After placing some distance between himself and the strange creature, the hunter turned around just in time to see it descend the tree. Upon reaching the ground, instead of standing upright as a man would, it commenced to trot along the ground as a dog or any other animal would do.

Smith then realized that it was no hermit he had seen but some kind of monstrosity. The hunter stood amazed and spell-bound for a moment, but soon gathered his scattered senses again and was soon making his best speed to camp, where in a few breathless words, was telling his companions of what he had seen.

They were disposed to laugh at him at first, but his sincereness of manner and his blanched cheeks soon proved to them that he had seen something out of the usual order of things.

A hasty council was held, and the party decided to go in search of the monster, so taking their guns and dogs they were piloted by Mr. Smith and they soon came in sight of the unnamed animal. In the meantime it had commenced to devour the contents of Mr. Smith's game bag that he had dropped in his hasty retreat. The creature would plunge its long arms into the bag and pulling forth the small game, transferred it to its mouth in a most disgusting manner. An effort was made to set the dogs upon it, but they crouched at their masters heels and gave vent to the most piteous whines. This attracted the attention of the creature, and it commenced to make the most unearthly yells and screams, at the same time fleeing to the undergrowth. The whole party immediately gave chase and soon gained upon the strange beast, and it, seeing that such was the case, suddenly turned, and sitting upon its haunches, commenced to beat its breast with its hairy fists. It would break off the great branches of the trees that were around it, and snap them as easily as if they had been so many toothpicks. Once it pulled up a sapling five inches through at the base, and snapping it in twain, brandished the lower part over its head. The hunters seeing that they had a creature with the strength of a gorilla to contend with, beat a hasty retreat.

Mr. Smith describes the animal as being about six feet high when standing, which it did not do perfectly but bent over, after the manner of a bear. Its head was very much like that of a Human being. The trapezie muscles were very thick and aided much in giving the animal its brutal look. The brow was low and contracted, while the eyes were deep set, giving it a wicked look. It was covered with long shaggy hair, except the head, where the hair was black and curly.

Mr. Smith says that of late sheep and hogs to a considerable extent have disappeared in his vicinity and their disappearances can be traced to the hiding place of the "What Is It."

[For these newspaper articles, I wish to thank Scott McClean, whose impressive collection, "Big News Prints," gathers together many hundreds of such historical accounts of human-Sasquatch contacts from the 1700s to the late Twentieth Century. The CD Rom is available at McClean.org]

Chapter Three

Playing Hide and Seek with
"The Monkey Kids"—
Six Families Get to Know the Neighbors

In his taxonomy, published in his *Systema Naturae* (1758), Carl Linnaeus included not one but two living species of man: *Homo sapiens* (man the wise) and *Homo troglodytes* (the caveman). The latter term was not coined by Linnaeus— he borrowed it from ancient naturalists, and he described *Homo troglodytes* as *nocturnes* and *sylvestris* (*nocturnal* and *forest-dwelling*). He wrote in his dissertation *Anthropomorpha* (1760): "Is it not amazing that man, endowed by nature with curiosity, has left the *troglodytes* in the dark and did not want to investigate the creatures that resemble him to such a high degree?"
          —from "Thoughts on the Revolution in Anthropology"
            by Dmitri Bayanov, International Center of
            Hominology, Moscow

The people who are habituating already know what they have living on their land, so really aren't trying to convince others. The satisfaction they receive when they capture the shadow folk in photos is just a bonus for them and just convinces them that what they saw and heard was a real creature. Generally the only telltale sign the shadow folk were there will be foot tracks left in the early morning dew. Occasional sounds or some stick signs. On rare occasions a glimpse of them moving about.

—Anonymous

An Historical Habituation: 1835-1850

It all began shortly after Sam Houston and his army had secured independence from Mexico for Texas. Settlers who had fled from the advancing Mexican army now returned to their homesteads and were starting over. It was about this time that odd tracks began turning up near various settlements and homes along the Navidad River. There were usually two sets of tracks, one pair larger than the other and always barefoot, so it was widely assumed the prints belonged to a male and a female. Sometimes they appeared in the sweet potato or cornfields where the pair helped themselves to some of the bounty secured by the labors of the sod-busting settlers. No one ever saw this pair. It seemed they took great pains to avoid detection and, other than helping themselves to some of the crops, avoided mischief of any kind. Speculation ran rampant as to who the mysterious barefoot couple could be. Some thought they were runaway slaves while others posited they were children, a brother and sister perhaps, who had been separated from their family during the war for Texas independence and had gone feral. Of course, many assumed they were a pair of wandering Indians. There were holes in all of these theories but it didn't keep many a lively debate from being enjoyed by the locals who defended their position regarding the possible origin of these two mysterious visitors.

A couple of years passed and the barefoot tracks of

the larger individual ceased to be seen, but the tracks of the smaller individual continued to appear in the potato fields of the area unabated. In fact, the visits seemed to increase in frequency. The people of the community wondered if this might not be due to the fact that the "woman" was not as adept at finding game as her mate had been. For various reasons, ranging from a desire to help this recluse to mere curiosity, a plan was hatched by several of the young men in the area to lie in wait and capture the wild woman. One night, as they hunkered down in a potato field, she came. The night was dark but the men claimed they could discern the figure of a woman, apparently unclothed, cautiously approaching their location. When she had drawn near to them they sprang in an effort to capture her with their bare hands. They drew nothing but air, however, as the woman, exhibiting impressive agility, dodged, ducked, and quickly bounded away without their ever laying a hand upon her. No sign of the wild woman was seen for several months afterward.

At length, the wild woman returned, though her tactics changed a bit. She continued to visit the potato fields but became more bold and started entering the cabins of the settlers on her visits. The settlers thought that this must be a sign of desperation as she was risking her life by entering homesteads at night while the occupants slept. In addition to owning firearms, nearly all the settlers kept two or more large and fiercely protective dogs. The dogs were the alarm systems of the day and were kept to protect the families from interlopers be they man, big cat, bear, or something else. The wild woman, seemingly, was able to step right over these dogs and enter the premises. Once inside, she would take only what she needed. It was widely reported that she would tear a loaf of bread in two and take only one half. Her motive always seemed to have been hunger. Several

times the wild woman had the opportunity to take
gold watches, silverware, guns, and powder but never
did so. She only took some, never all, of the food.
She would make off with a pitcher of cream and then,
days or weeks later, return the pitcher, washed. She
would steal tools – handsaws, hammers–polish them
to a high luster and then surprisingly return them to
their workbench.

Her most spectacular caper was swapping a feral
piglet from the woods for a giant hog a farmer had
fattened up.

 All the while, nary a settler awoke during her
intrusions nor did a dog so much as whimper upon
her trespasses. This ability to sneak in and out of
occupied homes gave rise to much superstition
regarding just who, or what, the wild woman actually
was. The slaves in particular were greatly disturbed at
the prospect of receiving a nighttime visit from the
wild woman and took to calling her "that thing that
comes."

It was soon discovered that the wild woman would
often enter a crib, or storage building, in the area that
housed harvested corn. As always, she took only a
trivial amount; but the curious felt this was just the
way to catch her. All that need be done was have
someone hide within the crib and shut the wild
woman inside once she had entered. For several
nights the watch was kept to no avail. The locals
were not discouraged, however, and their patience
was rewarded when the wild woman returned to the
crib. The man on watch that night was lightly dozing
when he heard the soft rustling of the cornhusks. All
he needed to do was close the door, slide the bolt, and
call out to his friends; however, he was overcome by
an unexplainable dread and could not bring himself
to stay even one more second inside the crib. He

cried out in his fear before making his move and the creature tore out of the door with blinding speed. Another opportunity had been lost.

Years passed and the wild woman of the Navidad continued to haunt the fields, homes, and animal pens of the settlers. It is said that she began to take things other than food: a chain, a hacksaw, forks, a pitcher, etc. What she might have done with these things is not clear. One thing remained constant, however, and that is that during all her comings and goings never a bark, growl, or whimper was ever raised by even a single dog when she paid her visits. This baffled the settlers and began to weigh heavy on their minds. Just what kind of being was this "thing that comes"?

All of this had been going on for roughly eight years when a crude camp was found in the heavily wooded area near the river. Many of the items that had come up missing over the last year or so were found there. No clothing was found and the only bedding was a pile of moss and leaves. Once again, pity for this wretched creature welled up within the hearts of the settlers. How could they just leave this poor woman alone out in the wilderness? It was resolved then and there that this mystery had to be solved. A new plan was devised by the locals that was more systematic and sophisticated than previous plans to capture the wild woman. A number of hunters would form extended lines and drive through the woods with leashed hounds. Other mounted men, lassos in hand, would take "stands" outside the brush line in the hopes of roping the woman once she had been flushed out of the woods and onto the open prairie.

The plan was implemented without success several times. The hunters got a break when a settler found fresh sign of the wild woman and took up positions that very night in the area. Their quarry was, indeed, in the area. It is generally known that hounds bark, bay, and cry in different ways depending on the animal whose scent they are following. That night under a bright moon, the hounds raised a cry that their owners had never heard before. Shortly after the hounds were on the track there came a rustling of brush near one of the lasso men who was waiting outside the timberline. Suddenly, there she was, the wild woman of the Navidad. The creature sprinted out of the brush at an amazing rate of speed. She was attempting to reach another heavily wooded area several hundred yards across the open prairie. The rider spurred his horse to full speed in an attempt to catch the sprinting figure. To his amazement, the rider had to push his mount to a full gallop to get within range of the fleeing woman. He pulled to within lasso range several times but each time his horse, obviously afraid of this strange creature, shied and his throws came up short. Within moments the wild woman reached the safety of the woods and the chase was over.

The disappointed hunters regrouped and the rider who had pursued the wild woman gave his account. He had drawn close to her several times before his horse shied away and had gotten a good look. She had long hair, almost down to her feet, that flew behind her as she ran. She wore no clothing of any kind and was covered completely in short brown hair. The rider had not been able to get a very good look at her face as she only took a few frightened glances over her shoulder at him. The rider said that initially she had been carrying an object of some kind but had dropped it during the pursuit. The hunters spread out to look and found what was described as a club, roughly five feet long. Additional searches were made with no luck. The wild woman of the Navidad had vanished.

—TexasCryptidHunter.blogspot.com

As of today, I am aware of twenty-three active habituation sites, of which I have permission to share the accounts of six, below, in the habituators' own words. The handful accessible to me represents merely a narrow, self-selected cross-section of habituators—those intent upon comparing notes with fellow habituators and with certain outsiders. Given this, and setting aside the vast number of similar cases that must have accrued over centuries, over millennia, these twenty-three can well be multiplied many-fold to estimate at least several hundred such situations now unfolding across North America. These involve both reluctant "hosts" (such as the settlers above and, at times, the frightened contemporaries below) and the more intrigued, receptive folks who interact with Sasquatch within a self-contained economy of trust, and who will never risk exposing their private experiences, or their visitors, to the world at large.

Of course, all identities and locations of those contributing to this book have been kept in the strictest confidence.

1. North Carolina

The speaker is a forty-eight-year-old woman whom we will call Ammi. Her husband "hates" what has been happening on their property for the past five years, but her son, now twenty-two, has worked with her to learn more. Beyond their yard is extremely thick forest and a vast swampland that extends seventy-two miles northeast. Occasionally, her six-year-old granddaughter visits and talks to "the hairy kids in the woods."

From 2002

It was back when we were living somewhere else, five years ago, and out here remodeling this house every day. Very first thing was a god-awful, gut-wrenching scream that came from our woods one day. My son and I both thought it sounded like a young child being raped or torn apart. There is an elementary school near here, and we believed someone was hurting a child in there. We both ran into that area of the woods, and looked, but saw nothing. I went back to the field, to make sure someone wasn't getting away, and my son continued to look around in that area of the woods. He said he never saw anyone, but it looked like someone had been there, because a lot of plants and grasses were laid down and flattened. We heard the same scream, in the same area, a few days later, but same results, on searching. There was an obvious path we hadn't noticed before, so my son checked the area off and on, at random times for about a week.

Then, from different parts of the woods over different times, we'd hear what we thought was humans trying to break into the place or coming up here. We weren't staying over here all the time, like I said. We thought there were people running through the woods. We shot at them. We've called the Sheriff's Department out here several times, too many times. Nobody ever found anything. My son chased them, never could catch up with anybody. And that went on for a long time.

What really brought it to a head was, we rented a backhoe and went to dig the ditches, and when I did that they started throwing stuff at me. Mud and sticks. I really didn't know what was going on, so I had some BFRO investigators come out. They came out three different times and did an overnight. The first time they came out they found footprints and they did some hollers and got some answers, did some wood-knocking and got some answers, and that kind of blew us all away. We were like, Oh okay, we got Bigfoots. I mean, we kind of thought the place was haunted for years. But then once we found out, my son and I just really got interested in it. We started trying to study them. Daily. We started going out there and trying to communicate with them, and basically just went from there.

I've got one group on one side of the house that's pretty receptive and friendly and we've come quite a ways. On the other side, behind the barn, they're mean. I've only been doing this about three months.

They hide really good. Even right in front of you. How would I know that? By taking pictures behind my back. I can hear them, and know they come very close, and from the sound of movement when I turn around, I suspected they may show out behind me. So the thought came to do the backwards camera trick.   I pretend I am shooting in another direction, and just turn the camera backwards. Then I compare these shots to the ones I take straight on.

I also know by hearing them, all the sounds they make, but hardly ever seeing them. By watching my woods change here daily. In all these years I've only ever seen them three times.

You would just have to experience the thickness of my brush. You could hide an elephant in there. The pictures I'm taking now are winter pictures. In the summertime, those vines, you can't see from your waist down. They could crawl around under your feet and tickle your toes and you wouldn't know it.

I believe what makes them stay here is that our area is very quiet, with a good source of food and water. There's not a lot of traffic. We don't go out in the woods a lot. They've been here before we were here. It's not that they moved in, they just didn't move out.

The nice ones, when I feed them, sweet potatoes and apples and bananas, they sometimes leave me gifts. I keep them all in a small bowl. Pretty rocks. One of the rocks is studded all through with large garnets. One looks like some kind of petrified bone...maybe a hip and part of the socket, from some little animal. The rest are lots of quartz, and some is just plain rocks. I also got a civil war grapeshot cannon ball, and half of some kind of old metal bullet mold. And I got a little ceramic duck that looks like it has spent some time in the swamp.

The mean ones, out behind the barn, they killed my dog and left me his skull and some bones on the work table over there. He must have been bothering them.

It was very hard to accept, but we moved on. I have had worse times. You get over stuff, and move on.

I want to let people know that there are some down sides to this too. I will study them while they stay, but if they moved on tomorrow, I would just get back to a "normal" life here. I wouldn't go looking for them anywhere else. Some days I don't want to deal with them here. But I try to keep it steady, so I can learn more.

It's a whole game of building trust with them, and it doesn't just include handing them food and walking away. People would probably think I was crazy. I go out there and I talk to the woods. I walk around, I speak to them, I sing to them, my son plays guitar for them.

My son is twenty-two. He and I are the only ones doing the study here. He occasionally brings in one friend, and it took repeated visits, but now they come close and vocalize when he is here also. He is eighteen.

I definitely know they know when I'm there. I think they know every time I step out this door because I hear them whistle. They give little whistles to I guess kind of let each other know that you're coming out. From area to area in the yard they whistle the same way. Different little whistles different places.

They imitate my son, and say, "Mom!" loudly, they can sound just like him. I thought he was playing tricks, until they did it when I was here alone, and then when he was with me talking to me.

When Rita [BFRO researcher] was visiting here, the one who tries to imitate me followed us from the house, to the swamp side, and kept whistling to us. I've been trying to teach him the tune from *Kill Bill* (when the nurse is walking down the hall). He is really trying to get that tune down, and gets quite persistent with it, if I don't do it back for him. He was back out there again today with me, and trying again. He has the first part down, and is getting pretty good at the second part. He is only about two notes off now, and he whistles the two, but not in the right tune.

(You can take a brief video tour of the property, shot by Ammi herself, and listen to the Sasquatch attempting to whistle this tune, at YouTube: "Faces in the Foliage: North Carolina Habituation Site.")

It is so amazing to hear it, because it is so different than any other sounds of the woods. At times, he just keeps repeating it over and over, like I do to teach him. They are such mimics! I always wonder if he is the same one who follows me around and does the "babbling brook" noise. Rita has heard that one.... and she can explain it to you, because she got such a kick out of it here.

From Rita, BFRO member and Ammi's research assistant; she first visited the property in December 2007

Poor thing. She was taking pictures with a 3.5 MP camera with no zoom through a pair of binoculars. That just tugged at my photographer's heartstrings. You know, if she's got Bigfoot in her backyard, she needs a decent camera.

She pays close attention to her swamp and monitors it daily for every little change. When she shares a photograph, she's already compared it to reference photos, so she knows that the figure in the shot is worth a closer look.

I saw this for myself today. Imagine seeing a large form of deep inky blackness behind some brush. So dark that it absorbs all light--like black fur would do. And then suddenly, silently, it's gone and you see browns, tans and greens where it once was. Someday, we'll get a great shot, or a shot that becomes great with the right enhancement. And it may take a long time to get that great shot. Or it may be tomorrow.

I saw more than one dark figure that disappeared after we spotted it; I heard knocking, whistling, bad dog bark mimicry, two incredibly loud and angry thumps, and other odd noises. I had one mimic my whistles. I saw tons of stick structures, trails blocked, trees snapped and in some cases huge logs that had been moved from place to place for some unknown purpose.

It's my opinion that through situations like hers, and with her determination to study these creatures in a peaceful setting, we will learn more about them than we could through other means.

A zoomed-in crop from one of Ammi's photos. The resolution is poor because the original shows a much wider field, and the figure is at least 150 feet away, sitting in the swamp, nearly impossible to pick out, virtually the same color as its surroundings.

So, we sat around and chatted for a little while, and then we went outside. She feeds them fruit and sweet potatoes. She called them, and I actually heard them walk toward us. There was a group of about six or eight walking toward us and you could hear the leaves just crunch crunch crunch crunch. You couldn't see them. They started walking from a distance of I'd guess fifty yards or so, and approached probably as close as about sixty feet. But the entire time they were behind this screen of evergreen, brush, and vines. They have actually built screens in her swamp made out of these vines and trees.

You could clearly hear them approaching and that was just a fantastic experience. I mean, I was blown away, and I thought I'd be able to get a picture of them because there was a break in this screen, and I thought, Okay, when they walk across that I got 'em, I'm gonna get a picture. But oh no, they stopped just as they got to it. They were just too smart to come out in the open. And we heard some whistling, and we heard the chit-chit-chit-chit-chit of maybe rocks or Ammi was thinking walnuts, being clicked together. And they imitated the sound of a babbling brook. I found that actually kind of humorous because babbling brooks don't start and stop like you flick a light switch. And they also don't move. And during the course of the afternoon, as she was showing me around the place, the babbling brook followed us, which I just thought was funny.

So she basically threw the fruit and the sweet potatoes toward where they were. I think they just see where stuff lands, and then they come later and pick it up when she's not around or when nobody's looking, or possibly wait until dark.

We walked around a little bit and I was trying to get some pictures, and it was really interesting because you could actually see dark fur appear behind the brush, and then it would disappear. And of course she's got several photos that look like that, it's just a dark form that you can see through the brush. And it's challenging from a photographic standpoint because it's hard to photograph anything black anyway, because black is black because it absorbs all light, so if you're talking about dark animals in shadows, you're just out of luck. But that doesn't mean we don't try.

One of the more profound experiences I had that afternoon was getting "zapped," twice.

This was over on the other side of her yard, where they're not quite so friendly. It's where they had put the skull of the dog that they had killed on a work table. The table is strong. You know, it's one of those old-fashioned tables that a farmer would have put together to work on outside, really hefty. We looked at the table and thought, Okay, so this is where the skull is. And then we walked down into the woods there. All of a sudden I felt nervous, I felt a little nauseated, my head was bothering me. I felt very unwelcome. She started some similar symptoms. We stayed down there a few minutes, took a few pictures, and then we came back out.

We walked a little ways further down and ended up with some very thick brush between us and the barn so we could not see the barn. And we're poking around, trying to take pictures and stuff, and all of a sudden we hear this THUNK! up at the barn, and we're like, What was that? And then we heard it again. So we figured that we had upset someone that came up and pounded on the table.

I walked up there, with my video function on my camera running, and didn't see anything, that I *remember*, because once I got over there and I turned off my video camera I got another infrasound experience. It's like when you're about to put your hand on a TV screen, you get that tingling all over the surface of your hand, it was like that all over my whole body, and worse on my arms and legs. And I said something to her about it, and then I stepped backwards.

In my mind, it only took two seconds. But she informed me later, "Oh no, you were frozen and staring straight ahead for about twenty seconds." And...I didn't take her seriously, but I happened to have an audio recorder in my hand, so I played it back and you could tell by the beep when I turned off the video function on my camera, and when I spoke to her. I actually spoke to her twice, and then you hear when I finally do step backwards. It was a total of thirty-six seconds.

It's very interesting to me that I only remember it taking a couple of seconds. So when you hear about some people becoming disoriented and possibly losing time when they have an infrasound experience, I feel like that was an example of it. It was a very profound feeling, I've never felt anything like it. And it was a little scary too, I'll be honest, it was kind of scary. And she didn't go over to that area until a couple of minutes later, and that's when she discovered that one of the boards on the table had actually been broken and bashed in. Somebody down there just was not happy that we had walked into his woods. And we only walked in about forty feet, we didn't go far, but I think that evidently was too far.

Back to Ammi

Yesterday, when Rita and I went out, she stayed closer to the edge of the woods, and I really wasn't going to venture that far back in there but my curiosity can get a little better of me and there was some stuff I wanted to look at. I got down in the area and took me some pictures and I didn't feel too welcome. Just a little uneasiness, so I decided I'd come out, call the dogs. When I started walking back out, that's when it hit me in all the large muscles in my legs and in my rear end. My legs pretty much just buckled. I just kept going. I got real disoriented. At one point I left the little path and was walking through brambles and Rita had to holler at me and let me know which direction to back off to get back on the path. It was very visible in there. I could see her, she could see me, we could converse pretty easily. I wasn't that far from her. But my legs didn't really want to work. The best way to describe it is, I've lived in the northern states and if you've ever tried to walk through a three-foot snow drift, or running in water, that's pretty much how it felt to try to move them legs. By the time I got up to where Rita was, it started easing off a little bit, and the thing that was really weird was when we hit the edge of the woods, as soon as I stepped out of the woods into the field, it disappeared, the whole thing just disappeared.

There are so many little things they do that have nothing to do with collecting hard evidence of them, but is just fun and lets me see and hear the behaviors. That is my main focus here...I want to know all about them. Having the young ones so close here is a delight most of the time. In the same way for me as I loved watching and hearing my own kids play, and grow up. I tend to get comfortable with them being playful, and am reminded with a not so gentle zap, or growl, that I am too close, or somewhere they don't want me. Then I back up for a day, and get right back out there and try again. I am trying to come up with different ways to do things, to see what works.

When my grandchild was here last year, at age six, she used to walk near the woods and talk to herself constantly. She would take her toys and play there too. I would be gardening, and ask her who she was talking to. She would say the hairy people in the woods, or the hairy kids in the woods. I thought she had a good imagination. I didn't know anything about the Bigfoots back then.

She was walking near the "nest." This is a long strip of land, next to the swamp, and bordered by the wood area, until it hits my yard. It is made up of loads of evergreen brush, vines, and stick add-ons. There are two and in some places three "screens," along the side towards me. These are made of vines with added sticks, logs, brush and leaves. They have been built up even more near my house, daily. The one near the back of the pumphouse used to be easy to take pictures through, and is now almost a solid wall of debris.

I would say the nest ranges from ten to thirty feet wide, in places. It is at least fifty yards long because that structure is not all vines there, it is also laced with a lot of small sticks and branches.

Other people, habituators that I talk to who do this at their places, and do have kids, say that the Bigfoot are always watching the kids play, and they get a lot of the best pictures when they are doing that. They are the ones who told me the Bigfoot love the stuffed toys they put out, and will keep them. Other toys are moved and scattered at night, or taken, but are always returned eventually.

So I am going to try that. I will be leaving them near the feeding and nesting area, and see what happens.

I was also told they like plastic flower pots, and that explains why mine are always ending up in the woods here. I do have three boxes of old toys in the barn. And they get scattered a lot, and stacked on each other. I hadn't thought of it being them. I just blamed the dogs.

January 23rd, 2008

Tonight, they have been playing games on my roof, since it got dark. The porch roof is right by a tree, and then they climb onto the house roof. They've tossed rocks and a branch down my chimney, in the last few minutes. I went out into the cold twice, but of course they are gone, or ducking over the roofline.

My dogs have been going nuts, and judging from the new branches in my walkway they must be throwing at them too.

Last time they did this, they tossed pieces of bricks down the bedroom chimney and woke hubby up, then a handful of live lizards came down...freaked him out...he hates lizards...made me catch them all.

This has made me think of something, though. They do seem to be very active in the colder weather. Thinking back on my days before I knew it wasn't humans trying to mess with me here, it happened more in the colder days than in the summer.

So far, it has been smaller ones up there. I think the juveniles play those games. I hope none of the big guys ever take a notion to go up...could damage my dome.

I have floodlights on the house, and turn them on when they climb up there, or pound on the house. I turn them off after a couple hours, and it has stopped them before, did tonight also.

I do tolerate the tapping on windows and at the electric box. That is done more gently, and for attention, so I treat it as such, and just tap back from in here, or talk to them loud enough for them to hear me. It is a game that is played for a while, then I usually have to be the one to stop it.

My husband refuses to believe, as in, everything can be explained by deer or owls. Yep, we had a fun debate about who dropped the bricks and lizards down the chimney. He has heard them, and refuses to go behind the barn at all. He used to say there was nothing out there, but now he slips up, and he talks about them some. He just hates the whole thing, and would rather I do what his mom's family did when they were living here in the past, and just ignore and deny them. He really only gets mad when his mom starts in on him about me studying them. But she doesn't say they are not here, just that I shouldn't "mess around with things I don't know about."

When Rita came and brought the camera here, as soon as she left, he started to move the couch from in front of the window that faces the swamp. I asked him what he was doing, and he said, "I thought you could get the best shots from here."

I said, "Shots of what?"

He got mad and said, "I was just trying to help!!"

I just laughed, and helped him move the couch.

February 4ᵗʰ, 2008

I had an interesting day here. I had a half-frozen lizard on my kitchen steps, rare, because they usually are under something in this weather. It was thirty-five degrees out today. And this little guy was so cold he couldn't move, thought he was dead at first. Hubby had just come in that same door, not long before I went out and found the lizard. Maybe it was meant as a little gift for him?

I saw in front of the door the bag I'd left chips and Cheetos out in, near the woods, so I went to check the pumphouse, where it had been hanging, about six feet up inside. Gone from there. I went around the pumphouse to look, and found some small footprints, about the size of our six- or seven-year-old grandkids'. One was almost perfect, so I got pictures. Still don't have casting materials here.

Went and picked up the bag, and took it, and popped the lizard inside, so I wouldn't be shunning a "gift." (I later snuck him back out and tucked him under a pile of leaves.)

I put the bag on the big table, behind the barn. While I had my back to the woods, the dogs went nuts towards the woods, so I turned to see one of them chasing after something that I couldn't see, into the nest area. The pups were looking at something hard, just under where the stuffed teddy bear is hanging, so I went to check that out. The ground had been dug up and dirt was all over on top of the leaf litter, so I went in closer. Ewwwww! A fresh deer leg, no skin, half of a pelvis, the thigh, knee, and part of the leg. Still all connected, and half full of meat, the other half chewed off. The hoof had been broken off. The whole thing was still warm, even though it was freezing out.

This was only about five or six feet from where I had picked up the bag, so I couldn't believe I hadn't seen it then. (Later checked the pic I took of the bag, and nope, it wasn't there then.) I don't want to turn down "gifts"...and know they have "gifted" other habituators with deer, so I made a big deal over it, and giving it to my dogs, who wouldn't touch it at first, but then one finally grabbed it and ran off with it.

I thanked the wookies out loud, and headed inside.

I want to study behavior, share what I am doing so others can have some idea what it is like to do this, and mainly have me and the critters here, left to live in peace. I do bring some people in, for the study, who have the skills needed to try to get some evidence, but it is done quietly, and not in crowds. The BF react to different ones, different ways. I note that, and try to figure out that also.

They are most active if I am alone and tend to hang back more if even my hubby is out there. They do favor my son being out with them, at times, but he has a pretty strange way of playing with them, and will go out alone to do that at night.

I get more good reaction with the younger ones, and the mammas and day ones. The night ones scare me at times. My son gets reactions at night, good and bad, but he is twenty-two and "bullet-proof," so he takes more risks than I do, and enjoys doing so, or can at least run back inside quicker. I can, however, sit quietly for hours, and just listen, and look for them. I can go out and sit close to the area, and sing, hum, whistle, play "Peek-a boo," use myself as entertainment, like you would for a toddler, and make a total fool of myself, just to try to get a reaction from them. And then sit there even longer, ignoring them, to try to make them get me to react, which gets me movement, and vocals, and maybe a picture. That is what I do the most, and it seems to be working, as far as getting them used to me, and accepting me being there some. I push it too much at times, and then have to back off a few days. It goes on like that.

I have learned that if I ignore them totally, don't raise my blinds, and don't go outside at all, by around noon or one pm, they will come up and tap on a window near me...easy....or jiggle the tag on the electric box, next to where I sit here, on the computer. I always have rewarded that, by pulling up the blinds, and taking them out a treat. They know that now, so it is a regular thing, if I do that. No, I am not going to jump up and run snapping a camera, it would totally mess up what little trust they have, which is more important than a "great picture right now." If I can build the trust more, I will have much greater chances for a very good close-up shot. I have that kind of patience.

March 17ᵗʰ, 2008

Today, I spoke to my neighbor on the other side of my swamp. He had called me over there to take some pics of his pups...he has no computer or camera. He wants to have me help find them homes. I went over and took the pics, and was getting ready to go, and he asked me if I had ever heard or seen anything "strange" in the swamp, since I had been here. I told him, "Yes, plenty," and he went on to describe all the sounds. He has had two sightings, believes they are "a people, and not devils," and described being paced, and zapped. He asked me if I ever heard one whistle a "funny little tune," and when I whistled the *Kill Bill* song, he said, "THAT'S IT!!!"

I told him I had taught it to them, and he now wants to see if we can teach them "Amazing Grace," if we work from both sides on it. So I'm game for that one!

2. Oklahoma

The speaker is a Native American woman in her late forties. She is a medically retired police detective with a bad back that has required several surgeries. Her daughter and grandchildren are frequent visitors.

1954

One of my very first memories of a Shadow Person was on a foggy morning. The time of year was early summer. I was about four years old. My brothers and I spent hours in the woods near Ma's house. In those days families didn't worry about kids being taken. Hours were spent outdoors.

I recall Ma was cooking breakfast, as I slid out the front door headed for the woods. The woods were thick with locust trees, grasses, and moss. This particular morning the fog was thick. I wanted to see what it looked like in the woods. As I walked up the road to the entrance, I saw them, all four of them, four tall shadowy figures. They looked like an Indian family. The difference was they were all gray. The father and mother were standing behind two children. Their faces looked Indian to me, like Ma's. They were the tallest people I had ever seen. I stopped a few feet in front of them and looked at them. Their expressions didn't change as they looked back at me. To this day I still remember it felt like a dream staring at them. They had grayish hair from head to toe. There was no hair on their faces, hands and the bottoms of their feet. The hair on their bodies was probably two inches pretty much uniform in length. It lay flat against their bodies. The hair on their heads was more ruffled. As if it needed to be combed. They stood for probably only seconds. The largest one, the father I assume, turned to his right and walked away with the others following. They never made a noise. Everything was muted. They disappeared into the fog and the woods.

I walked up to where they had been standing. I remember wondering why the edge of the bank there was crumbling. I was never afraid while standing there looking at them. I was more curious than anything else. I felt lost.

Then, I turned and ran all the way back to Ma. When I entered the house I was confused. I remember telling Ma about them. She told me those were the Shadow People, leave them be. She was very adamant never to follow the Shadow People. There was a possibility if you did you would never return. Ma said that children that did follow them often get lost and confused.

For several years we ran and played in the woods always under the watchful eye of Ma. She never allowed us out to play until she checked for signs. She always checked the scents on the wind and the tracks in the sandy road. Once in a while she would not allow us out to play until late morning. She never told us exactly why, just wouldn't.

Over the next few years Ma would occasionally mention the Shadow People. After I, her persistent grandchild, insisted on it, she explained they were ancient people. They didn't bother anyone nor did they want to be bothered. There were several tribes of them. They were all people, just different than us. Ma explained they avoided people like us.

One summer day, Ma called me to her and read me an article from Readers Digest. This article was about some men that had filmed a Bigfoot [the Patterson/Gimlin Film]. Ma showed me the tiny pictures in the article and told me that was a Shadow Person. "Never bother them, it's bad to hurt one," she told me. "Leave them be." They wouldn't hurt me, I should just leave them alone.

When asked to share with others the knowledge I have obtained over the years, I realize it's not as easy as it once appeared. It's complicated to talk about the Shadow People. Through the years they have been labeled with every imaginable tag—mythical, imaginary, monsters, monkeys, apes, hominids and of course unknown primates. There have been many who have chased them, begged and pleaded with them to appear.

I do not care if you question my credibility. I do not have to prove who I am or what I am. I have simply agreed to share old and new things. I cannot prove to anyone what I am sharing. You will either believe or not believe. Whatever you decide will be up to you. All photos and video were taken by myself or my family.

I only care that the Shadow People remain in peace to rear their children and live their lives.   At this moment it appears many wish to murder one or a family for science.   Killing one is murder. These are the ancient people of the world. Call them what you will, they have survived much and adapted to remain in the quiet areas of our world.

As I grew, every few years my path crossed with the Shadow People. Each time it was a different place, several years apart.   Each one appeared different in color, shape and size. Each one was in an area I would characterize as the fringes of civilization.   Never have I been threatened or harmed.   Each time the Shadow Person was the one who disappeared into the shadows.

Years back, after relocating my family to a rural area, I discovered that those Shadow People were again close at hand. They are as interested in us as we are in them. They will if the opportunity arises peek in your window.   They will stand back and watch you.   They have never approached any member of my family or myself. I do talk to them. I always respect the personal space that we each need to maintain our relationship.

On many occasions one of the kids will be outside and come running in asking, "Did you call me?" I have been working in the gardens or sitting outside and have heard a child's voice call, "Mom." It sounds just like one of my kids. This has happened many times over the years when I was home alone. They are known to knock on houses both day and night. Why they do this is anyone's guess. I suspect it's a form of communication, checking for a reaction.

I will never be able to answer for myself or for others all the questions about these wonderful, gentle creatures.

Summer 2007

My nine-month-old grandson Squirt was sitting in the sandbox at the time of "the monkey-chase," as the kids called it. He was reaching and laughing at the bushes where they burst out. It was his behavior that got my attention at first. He was cooing and laughing as he reached out in that direction. I thought wow he must see one of the cats.

A split second later the first one burst out of the brush and ran bouncing across the yard. I am convinced Squirt had spent several minutes watching the monkey-kids in the edge of the brush. We call them that because they look like the drawings from the rise of man or the hobbits.

Actually I knew they were coming around for years. I just kept it to myself until about five years ago and told my husband and dad. I finally had good prints to show them.

It was when I realized that so many want to kill them that I stepped forward and met others who were looking for them. I believe them to be hominin and not apes. Sorry, that's the way I was raised. I have gradually begun sharing things I have seen and heard with others. It's hard to learn to trust anyone. I decided it was time to teach the kids and grandkids the old ways also. As I was taught.

This summer just brought it all home. My little five-year-old grandson is the one, besides the nine-month-old, who can spot them hiding in the brush when no one else can. Taking pictures of the areas he says they are in generally shows shadows shaped like humans. I don't want the kids to fear these guys, I want them to learn to respect them.

But back to the monkey-chase. Just before dark, I saw three of them. The grandkids say there were five altogether, plus the babysitter. She was about the color of this little guy in the picture I took, maybe a bit more auburn.

I saw one very dark one, mouse-colored, and one red. The grandsons said there was actually three very dark ones and the two lighter ones. They were everywhere in a matter of seconds It was one of the most amazing things I have ever had happen. They burst out of the bushes, ran all around us, and the kids gave chase like a game of hide-n-seek. They won hands down. Then they were gone. They were between two-and-a-half and three-and-a-half feet tall, rail thin and fast as the wind. Along with a female about five-and-a-half feet tall hiding in the shadows and holding a baby. The babysitter kept reaching out from the brush as they

would run by. She ran up and down in the brush. The most amazing thing
is they never made a sound. None of them. As soon as it was over my
grandchildren put out a pizza and P&J sandwiches. Which disappeared
right after dark.

Here's how I got a picture, on a different night. I usually just point
the camera in the direction I hear noise, and if I can tell which way it's
moving, I'll point it just ahead, where I think it's going to be. This night,
we were sitting outside and then I heard some rustling and I started
walking around the yard. It was well after dark. My daughter and I made
a big circle around the yard just snapping pictures, and when we got over
by the bench, we couldn't see him, we could just hear him moving around.
I ended up with forty or fifty pictures and they were just dark. A friend of
mine, another habituator, has a program where she can lighten them up,
and she called me and said, "Guess what you got! You got a three-foot
teddy bear walking around." I couldn't believe it. Then she asked me,
"Does it look like he's holding something?" I'm thinking it's one of the
teddy bears, they're about ten inches long.

Juvenile Sasquatch photographed in nearly pitch dark, August 2007.
The right hand holds a "borrowed" teddy bear; the left arm is in front
of the dark body and thus not visible (don't be fooled by the bench frame)

I have lived here sixteen years and they have always traveled through back and forth a couple times a week. Year-round. This year the lake came up and they hung around a lot more than in years past. However, this year the grandkids converged as a group more than usual. Generally, the kids are here one or two at a time. Plus the baby was here a lot.

I have always fed the wild animals. It's a hobby as much as compassion for the creatures the Creator has given us. This is a way of giving back to the Creator. We have so much and the little fur balls have so little. The more you feed the more they will come.

Years back we built a small garden pond, more of a frog sanctuary than anything. Stocked it with minnows and goldfish, which were promptly eaten. This was an ongoing pattern. Stock the pond and see how quickly the fish disappeared. A garden pond can be a great source of entertainment, also much work, depending on how you wish to handle it. Building an ecosystem takes time.

As each spring came and went more was added to the pond. It was during this time that the prints began to appear around it. The first bare prints measured fourteen inches by five-and-a-half inches. They appeared on the garden path beside the pond during the winter. They also appeared *in* the pond. As the footprints appeared the fish disappeared.

Each year the fruit would ripen. Just as it was ready to pick it would disappear overnight, never in the daytime. The bare footprints were different sizes. They ranged from a mere four inches long to nineteen inches long. The amazing thing about footprints: Often they are beside the paths, in the grass, as if to avoid detection.

Since the beginning of the year I have started to organize and keep a brief record of the Shadow People in my world. After the ice storm last winter we emptied two freezers of food. No idea how many pounds were placed by the habitat area. All disappeared overnight. During this time the bird feeders would often empty overnight, also, as would most of the feed on the ground.

About a month later, during the night, someone jerked on the back door. Several times, this actually broke the bottom hinge off and sprung the door. My thoughts were that the Shadow People were hungry and knew that there could be food in the freezer. Over the years we have actually lost food from the icebox and freezer, never giving much thought to it.

As the ground began to thaw there were faint tracks appearing. They once again were different shapes and sizes. We purchased a trail camera to use and play with. It isn't for serious hunting, it's merely for the enjoyment of catching our nighttime visitors. I was hooked on trying to see more.

As the winter began turning to spring, I was recording audios and some videos, never catching a Shadow Person on film. Although I believe they did walk by chattering as in a conversation. This audio was shared with several others, including researchers, for evaluation. I have hope that someday there will be an answer to what sounded like a foreign language being spoken in my yard at two AM. I have had cameras moved, picked up, set down, and turned over. I have had only shadows to show for hours of video.

We have some neighbors. I don't know most of them. They moved out here from the city and tried to make country like the city. I don't think country agrees with them that well. They are putting up cameras, lights and fences. For whatever reason!

I suspect the neighbor right next door has seen them. He is an older guy and carries a big pistol on his hip and a rifle slung on his back to walk around his yard. There for a while he creeped around in a ghillie suit. Built a brush blind and just crawled around the yard. He had an alarm that was hooked up to an air raid type siren. Imagine what fun that dang thing was. Every few minutes it was like WWII around here. Some of the other neighbors finally called the law on him.

This year, I began putting out snack food for the Shadow People. I tell them when I am putting it out that it is for them. They often are hiding in the woods nearby and I am certain they can hear me as I talk to them. This food is not in the same areas as the critters' food. I separate the food out of respect. I would not serve a guest food from the dog dish nor will I share snacks for the children of the Shadow People with the raccoons on the ground. My quirk. I was taught to respect them. At first they didn't touch the snacks. In fact nothing touched the foods. Which was very odd. This continued for several weeks.

Then one night the snacks were taken. An audio recording of this indicated that during the rain the container the snack was in was lifted out of the tree and returned. This container was approximately eight feet from the ground.

Thus began the game of "snatch the snacks." Certain nights the snacks would be taken. Soon, I began attempting ways of catching the Folks on video. Never have I gotten more than a shadow moving or sounds that I have come to associate with the Shadow Family. On occasion I will have one container moved to another tree. Sometimes it will be higher or lower in the tree. Sometimes, I will need a ladder to take the container down to refill it.

I also leave gifts of beads, toys, balls, and other interesting objects. Sometimes, toys and balls will disappear for a period only to reappear months later. Sometimes the reappearance will last for only a day or two and then the objects will disappear again. The working assumption is that it's the Shadow Folks moving the items. At this point I have doubts that possums and coons want trinkets.

The toy house is a playhouse filled with abandoned toys not played with any longer. As the main house overflows with toys they are crated up and moved to the toy house. Only to be forgotten. This year I checked the toy house and found that most of the toys were no longer there. On occasion, I find small toys scattered over our acreage. Based on the behaviors I am observing, the Shadow People never take anything they know belongs to some member of the family. It appears they only take what is ignored. This not only includes toys. At times garden tools will disappear and reappear months later in an odd place.

We leave stuffed toys on the bench in the backyard. Sometimes by morning they are scattered all over the lawn, but sometimes they are only slightly rearranged. Or just one will be turned over, like a trick or a game, seeing if we'll notice. One morning, we found that the toy dragon was flipped.

While playing with my grandchildren one evening, I noticed a change in the birds singing. There was a snapping of tree limbs and soft noises in the brush. I started snapping pictures within the area. There is no panic feeling. No fear. We continue about our business. I firmly believe that no harm will come to anyone who has a relationship with them. I will say never leave small children alone. Not because they will be harmed. Children can and will try to follow these guys. A small child in the bush is never a good thing.

It is truly a blessing to have even a glimpse of these wondrous people. Now, that being said, there are many reports of these creatures being frightening and dangerous. Yes that is probable and possible. I am always puzzled by these reports. What makes a creature, any creature, become aggressive? What makes a killer a killer? I will not dispute anyone's claim of aggression by a Bigfoot. I refuse to argue this point with anyone. I suspect that if there is aggression there is a reason for these actions. My thoughts are perhaps that aggression is due to getting too close to the young. Most animals, including humans, will protect their young by whatever means are at hand.

I have never witnessed aggressive behavior from the family unit that often visits us in the night. My family and I spend time out there at all hours of the day and night. Never while we are outside do we feel threatened. Watched, yes. I don't know how to describe it other than just that. Somewhere close by someone is watching.

It does, however, seem that the children and women more often have that feeling. There are possibly several reasons for this. One, the creatures watching are more interested in or entertained by children and women. Or possibly they withdraw further back when it's males about. I personally think that it's because men have a different air about them and are often the ones in the woods with guns.

Often the feeling of being watched is accompanied by soft sounds of movement. Sometimes sticks breaking or being pushed aside. It's at these times I try taking pictures of the area the noise is coming from. I have tried to school myself not to put a camera up to my eye or make a quick movement. Looking at photos taken at such times, I feel it is safe to say that most often what you will see in a photo is partial facial features. The eyes are what I notice most often. After finding an eye then I look for the other features.

I am not making a claim that the Shadow People live, reside or dwell on or near my property. What I do know is that they wander through at times. There have been several occasions in which we have gotten glimpses of them. Never the prized face-to-face.

There are times, especially at night, when I can tell the Shadow Folks are about. What can be said is if there is a whistle or click and it's verbally answered it will become quiet. Almost like an embarrassed quiet. The Shadow People have had millennia to perfect their camouflage. Like any creature, they adapt to the area they live in.

Until the last few years I had never tried to have a relationship with a giant creature. If you were to ask us to describe how we feel, knowing big hairy guys/gals are wandering the area, well you would get as many answers as there are people in the family.

The problem with a relationship with the gentle creatures of the forest, especially the larger ones, is a basic fear factor. It's built into each and every one of us. There is the fight or flight reaction. I would tell anyone who wants to know more: Take it slow and easy, there is no other way. This is a trust that slowly develops over time. We are talking about a creature that our Creator placed here with us. This creature to my way of thinking is on the same level as those of us without the constant hair shirt. My ancestors believed that to a certain degree if they come forward to you they have a reason, such as an immediate danger to you or your family.

At this point in my relationship I believe that may well be the case. They remain elusive and silent. Habituation any way you want to present it is in fact a relationship. Started by one side or the other, for whatever reason. If you want a relationship with the Shadow People, remember they are intelligent. They are masters of hunting, camouflage, and probably fishing.

I see no harm in gifting, but boundaries need to be established in habituation for the peace of mind and comfort of both sides. Never give what you do not want to be taken. Never set boundaries that you cannot live with. Remember, setting them may not work with intelligent creatures such as the Shadow People. They have had thousands of years to roam about. Just because you don't want one at your back door doesn't mean you have not encouraged this behavior. Think before reacting. Overreaction will not help with any relationship.

I didn't start out to form a relationship with any animal in particular. I certainly never expected to have a tribe visit me in the middle of the night. I do feel that this is a very special gift from them to me that they have chosen our home as a respite at times.

Here's an example of a reaction that I can share. Recently in the middle of the night I was awakened several times to the sounds of scratching on the windows and sides of my home. Annoying to say the least. This continued for several hours throughout the night. And what did the guys want? I have no idea. The scratching noise came to a halt with what sounded like a firm smack and a wounded baboon yelling and running away from the house. What I believe it to be was an errant child "pranking" and Mom becoming tired of this behavior and correcting it.

My reaction was getting up and actually taking the time to try to guess where it was coming from. Each time I turned on a light the noises stopped. As soon as the lights were turned off the noises began again. Did I see Bigfoot standing looking in the window? Nope! I do believe it was the family wandering about. I had left gifts of fruits and nuts for them. I believe they were about because of faint odors that had been detected by my family earlier in the evening.

Our youngest is now eighteen months old. He has a thing he does every chance he gets. He goes to this spot and talks to the window and/or the bushes outside. He doesn't get into anything or bother anything here. He just sits and talks in baby talk to whatever is out there. He waves to it and motions for whatever to come to him.

At first I thought that it was a fluke. Then I started paying attention to him. He does this quite often. He acts the same way he did the night the monkey kids blazed through the yard. He sits and talks and motions to something. He did this that day at nine months old also. Even stranger is when I approach he stops and acts like he is caught doing something he shouldn't. He will not, as long as someone is watching, continue with the baby talk and motions.

I did notice one of Squirt's toy guns is laying out there on the ground. There is a well-worn footpath outside of that window. The interesting part is we rarely us it. The path goes right along the side of the house and out back to the brush and chicken house now. I looked here on Google Earth the other day and you can actually see the footpaths. One of them to the chicken house. Which we have not used in several years. Over three years to be exact.

As I started actually trying to communicate in some manner with the local Shadow People here I tried many things. I have read many on-line conversations with many ideas on communicating with or "baiting" the big guys. A lot of these I dismiss as silly. The silly ideas generally are people who assume that these guys are of lower intelligence than us and must be treated on the level of a child, or a pet.

I fall back on treating the local Shadow People as I would want to be treated. I hate pushy know-it-alls. I avoid them myself. Using how I feel about neighbors and being a neighbor, I started with food and little gifts, which were often taken. I began to add other things: pebbles, feathers, ribbons, all of which have been moved around, relocated or taken.

Then, one day, I wondered how roses would be received. I picked several rosebuds of different sizes and colors and included them with the other items. I found the buds the next day nearby where I had placed them. They were taken apart petal by petal, and left.

A few days later, I awoke and went out to have coffee. I found a trail of pink rose petals to the area where my chair was. At the time I thought, hmmmm, that is odd. Later, I questioned my family about this. No one had done it.

On another morning we found red roses lying on top of the car.

Several weeks after this, I again found a trail of rose petals from the door to the patio. All in all on three different occasions I found a trail of pink rose petals scattered from the front door to the patio.

Our household is taught: "What is done to the least of these is done unto me."

In 2009, researcher Pat Rance visited this site and obtained middle-of-the-night eyeshine video at the edge of the yard. This footage is included in "A Figure by the Bench: Oklahoma Habituation Site," posted on YouTube, as is the toy dragon that was flipped over, and the habituator's voice describing her photography practice.

3. Iowa

Bonnie is sixty-one years old and has lived in the area since birth. Three generations of her family have experienced Sasquatch encounters here. Like many other habituators, she has long suffered from health trouble, including severe respiratory problems. Feeling chronically unwell can predispose people to a more vigilant attitude, a certain stillness, an outsider or misfit status, and more awareness of their surroundings, perhaps because they are forced to slow down, to live one day at a time, and not to get so caught up in the average person's busy, distracted stream of existence. Fair warning: The incident involving the horse in February 2005, below, is very disturbing to read and demonstrates that, as is true in our own species, certain Sasquatch—particularly young, unaffiliated males—are capable of violence.

1957-1966

I was seven years old and taking my four-year-old brother to the outhouse. He ran on ahead and then came back saying there was bear in the outhouse. When we got there, there was no bear inside, so while my brother was using the toilet, I was swinging on the door and that's when I saw it, standing behind the outhouse. I remember thinking it was a really big one, whatever it was. It was a male and just stood there looking at me.

I never heard of other sightings in the area and never told kids at school what I was seeing. Heck, my half-brothers saw them too but we never told our parents. We knew better: When my little brother told our father that he'd seen a bear in the outhouse, he got whooped. Our father would knock you through the floor if you said anything like that.

I was never scared of them. I didn't think of myself as lucky, either. They were just there. I've always whistled, for the animals, and young Sas would come closer.

We'd go berry-picking with Grandma. We'd start out in the morning, and pick berries till night. Gallons of them. And they'd be lying nearby and we never talked about it. But she knew, you could see it on her face, but she'd act like they weren't there. She never once acknowledged them. Well, once she did say there were old Indians around, and to be careful of them. I *never* felt threatened.

I used to walk on top of the barbed-wire fences. And so I think that's where the hairy kids learned it, from me. I'd see them walking on the barbed wire. Their feet are real thick and calloused.

The time I heard one scream I was sixteen, and I wondered what was going on. I walked around till I found some men wearing sheets and sacrificing animals. I figured they were KKK. The scream was very high-pitched and loud, and you could tell the men had heard it too because they were looking around nervously. There was just the one scream, though. I lay there in the grass for a while and watched them sacrifice a dog, but I was smart enough to know that a young girl should not show herself to these men.

One time our neighbor's bulls got into it. There was a Hereford bull on one side of the fence, an Angus bull on the other. And one got to shoving the corner post and it come loose, so the rail come down and the two bulls started going at each other, really seriously, biting and stuff. At about that time, a Sas come out of nowhere, in the woods, and come up to where they were at, maybe fifty feet away from the bulls. I saw it. It opened its mouth and screamed at them. It sounded like a monkey, like that loud chimpanzee scream. It got their attention to where the bulls took off, it scared them. I think the Sas was saying, "Okay, I've had enough of this." Then he just went back into the forest.

1994-Present

My husband has never seen one but somehow he seems connected to them in his mind. Once, he told me exactly where they stay at. And seven or eight times, I've heard him talking in his sleep, having a conversation, and I'll go look out the window and sure enough, there one will be standing in the yard, twenty feet away. Michael will just be talking like a normal conversation, sometimes mumbling that I can't make out, and sometimes...you're not going to believe this...but he talks like the

Sasquatch in the "Sierra Sounds" audio. Sometimes the next morning he'll tell me he dreamed he was talking to one, and I just say, "Oh really?"

He doesn't seem to have a burning desire to see one, and so it don't bother me one way or another. It's like he's got two different minds.

One night he was sleeping and said, "They run my dog through with a spear." I found out later from his sister that when they were kids they found their dog with a thick stick all the way through him.

The alarm on his truck will go off every night at about two AM. He always leaves goodies in there. They tried to open the door and the alarm would go off, and one of us would have to go out and shut it off.

The little ones will come up close to the house at night. I've put out pieces of granite for them to sit on, two foot by two-and-a-half foot, because they always used to break the wooden benches. They'll come up and harass us some. I've put wind chimes up, so if I hear a wind chime I'll know what it is. They'll tap on the glass or touch the screen. I have one that hollers, "Bonnie! Bonnie! Bonnie!" And I'll shout back, "Be quiet!"

They will follow my daughter-in-law and my son everywhere around this place. He's forty-one. He's been seeing them since he was a kid. The first time he was in the fifth grade and he told me about it. I told him it was a bear, even though he said it was walking on two legs. I didn't want to scare him. When he was older, he had one grab him while he was splitting wood. It just come and grabbed him, hugged him. This didn't last very long. He screamed and it run off.

I think this is the same one that put his hand on my daughter when she was fifteen, on her back. She said the hand stretched from the base of her skull to halfway down her back. She and her brother were out checking traps, on a Friday night after he got home from work. When he turned on the flashlight to go down the hill to the river, it quit working. So she stayed there at the top and he went down, he didn't need no light. He wasn't gone but fifteen minutes, and when my daughter felt the hand, she thought at first that he was playing a trick on her, but when she hollered he answered from way down by the river. She'd seen them before, but she was like in denial.

One time her brother, my son, went camping out in the winter, and the next morning I go down to check on him and there were Sas tracks all around him.

At first I was scared for my grandkid. Down the hill we have what's called a junk pit, and I remembered seeing a Sasquatch down there. I said to my five-year-old grandson, "Stay away from there or the Junk Pit Monster will getcha." Then one day he come up and said, "I went down there and I talked to the monster and he told me he wouldn't hurt me."

My daughter (the same one who got touched) was still kind of in denial, but she come over for coffee one morning and left about ten o'clock, and I heard that whistle and I knew they were up close to the house. My daughter gets down the road and calls me on her cell phone, and tells me she saw a big old red one on the other side of the barn. I'd seen him before. They're so common, it's like seeing dogs.

I used to leave them sweet feed all the time, but then things got tough and we couldn't afford it anymore. So I told them I was sorry but that we could hardly get what we need for ourselves and the horses. One morning, I went out to the barn to water the horses, and there was a deer leg.

I always leave stuffed animals out and they move them around. The car keys from my son's truck were moved into our boat one time. Stuff like that. I have a little wagon to haul firewood, and I never know where I'm going to find that wagon.

They mimic our voices too, all the time, to mess with us. The grandkids'll say, "We heard you hollering for us," and I'll say, "Oh...yeah." Again, I don't want to scare them.

We used to love to ride horses in the moonlight, but then I had my knee replaced and it hurt to ride, so I started riding my ATV. One night it was a full moon and I wanted to go out. I stepped off the porch and felt "the fear" that everyone talks about, and this was something I'd never experienced before. So I just stood there looking around, and all of a sudden across the field it looked like a whole bunch of bicycle reflectors moving along, and evidently they wanted me to stay out of their way.

Once, I bought this homemade doll with buttons sewed on for eyes, and I thought, I'll take it down there, because I knew where the little ones were at, at the mouth of the creek where it feeds into the lake. First day, nothing happened, I went down and checked. Second day, I went down there and the eyes were gone and the material, like nylon, looked like it had been cut in two circles. Their fingernails are very sharp. And the two eyes were laid inside a fish carcass. Looks like they thought they belonged on a fish instead of a babydoll. They do lots of little funny things like that.

We left out flutes, little recorders, first showed them how to play it. And pretty soon we heard them being played in the middle of the night, down in the cornfield.

One Sunday afternoon, my three grandkids and I was out behind the barn a bit and lying on some big bales of hay that were lined up next to the fence row. The two girls and I were on one bale and my grandson on the other. We were all watching a mama fox and her babies with the binoculars. As the girls and I were watching the fox my grandson says, "Hey Grandma," and hands me the binoculars. "Look, another Junk Pit Monster is catching deer." As I put the binoculars up to my eyes I seen five deer standing over by the junk pit grazing on the clover pasture. I seen this large sorrel-colored Sas coming out of the tree line. I watched this critter run up alongside that deer and grab the deer by the underside of the neck and bend the head back to its butt. Must of broke its back. He carried it off into the timber without missing a step. It was all done and over with, within two minutes. As the thing ran up to the deer it was on all fours. After grabbing it and bending its neck back then it walked off on two feet carrying the deer on its right shoulder.

Last part of October 2002

I had decided to go for one of my early morning walks and I headed out across the pasture. Following me were four horses, two dogs and a cat. They go on most of my walks as they are my buddies. Now I was talking to them and we were walking along having a good time when we come upon the edge of the timber. All of a sudden the horses spun around and took off with the cat and one dog with them. All that was left was Boss and me. He was looking over at the timber and did this low growl thing. I looked and all I could see was a shadow. Huge shadow on the timber. We were about thirty-five feet from the edge of the timber. I hadn't remembered the shadow being there before and as I looked down at the dog with his hair standing up and back to the shadow it had moved ways to the right. I decided it was time to go back as Boss wouldn't if I didn't and this thing was too darn big to mess with even for him.

That evening it was almost completely dark and I was at the gate out by the barn and petting the old mare and talking to her. The mastiff mix was up close to me and Boss was not far from the front porch. All of a sudden this huge thing ran by me after the dogs. As I turned Boss was gone and this big hairy thing was right on the other dog's tail, close behind. They all disappeared in the timber. Fifteen or twenty minutes later Boss showed up and wanted in the house. The other dog was never seen again.

Mid-February 2005

It was about 11 AM and I was washing my back door window panes. It had been a very warm winter and not much snow. Not typical of Iowa in February. It was about forty to forty-five degrees outside. A few days before, it had snowed a light dusting. There is a lot that I call the feeder lot out back of the barn. At the far end of it there is a gate that you go through into a little patch of timber that is about sixty yards long and on into another pasture. Now back in July of 2004 I had rescued a filly that was almost fifteen hands tall and weighed in at about a hundred pounds. She was just walking bones. Now as a new-comer she was the low dog on the pecking order. I had a big four-year-old gelding, an older mare who ran things, a year-old filly, and the rescued filly. I was just washing those windows when the old mare came to the gate and screamed at me. It was a high-pitched shrill noise is why I say screamed at me. I threw on my coat and grabbed my camera. I thought Big Cat. As I get out to the feed lot I see the gelding walking on his back legs and biting at the air with his nose holes flared bigger that I knew they could ever be flared. The year-old filly was just running around in circles and making high-pitched noises. I noticed the rescued filly wasn't in sight. As I walked into the feed lot the mare gets on my left and the gelding gets on my right. I wasn't walking but not full-out running. Now those two horses stayed right with me and never got more than a few inches from my body. We are heading down to the gate that leads into the timber patch looking for the missing filly. Just as we got to the gate there in the timber part about twenty feet in was what I called the Monkey Man. It had that filly and was raping her.

She was on her front legs but her butt was pulled to this Monkey Man and she was almost in a sitting position. The Monkey Man had ahold of her shoulders. As it seen me and looked me straight in the eyes for a good three or four seconds it let her loose making three scratches down each of her sides from chest to hips. She had been trying to get loose and when he let her go she stumbled and could hardly get to me and the other two horses as she was shaking too badly. Then the smell came and I started coughing. It was like an asthma attack. Those eyes were very small and black, mean and wild-looking. It felt that he looked to my soul. That's when I started shaking like the horse. I did not move until he did. He just casually turned and strolled off, taking big strides and swinging his arms.

I turned and the two horses were standing right with me and the rescued filly had made it a little farther past them. She stood there and waited for all of us. Still shaking, the both of us. I started talking with her and got ahold of her and took her inside the barn where I kept all my meds for the horses. She had blood running down the backs of her legs almost to her hooves. She had the scratches down both sides. I took a rag and a bucket of water and washed and dried her down. I took the tube of triple antibiotics that was in a tube and squeezed it into a syringe then put that in her vulva. I put another kind of salve that my grandmother taught me to make on the scratches on her sides. Gave her a shot of penicillin, some food and water, and went to the house. I could not quit shaking myself. I thought, Who the hell do I call that would believe such a story? So I called the bird watcher. He and his father came out within fifteen minutes.

I was sitting on the front porch, shaking and making a sketch of what I saw. I was coughing and having a hard time breathing. I took them down to where the crime happened and told them I was going to check on the horse and go to bed. I went to bed and slept for the better part of three days. My husband said I told him it felt like I had been poisoned.

When I woke up after the third day I thought it had been a dream. So I went out and looked the horse over and sure enough she had scratches all the way down on both sides. She seemed to be ok and we went on as usual.

Two weeks later my son brings a girlfriend to visit and she had a twelve-year-old daughter who had short dark hair like the Monkey Man. Up until then none of these horses seemed to have a mean bone in their bodies. That girl tried to pet the gelding and he bit her, almost biting her ear off. Much more and he would have. I still was having problems breathing and went to the local doctor. They gave me antibiotics and said I had bronchitis. They gave me three rounds and it still wasn't any better. Then I went into the hospital with pneumonia. It took me a good six months altogether to get to feeling better. Though my breathing has never gotten back to normal.

By granddaughter Kimberly, eleven years old, September 12th, 2006

Last year about eight o'clock in the evening when we were staying in my grandma's camper, I was going to go to her house on the other side of the barn. I had just came out of the camper and was behind the barn when I looked up to see a Bigfoot. He was standing just on the other side of the fence and was slightly turned though he was looking right at me. He was about ten yards from me. He had dirty gray long straight hair and big lips. He had a big wide nose. I wasn't scared but I was freaked out. He smelt weird, a nasty rotten smell. Part of his hair was messy and part of it wasn't. He was as tall as my grandma's walls in her house. He seemed to just say Hi to me but it wasn't in words. He looked like a monkey he was so hairy. But also like a man with a beard. He didn't seem mean at all.

But I just turned around and went back into the camper and told my brother if he wanted to get a movie from Grandma he would have to go get it himself. I didn't tell anyone because at first I thought I had imagined it. Besides that, my mom and brother don't believe in the Bigfoot and they would have made fun of me or Mom would have said Grandma is brain-washing me. My birthday is September 21st so I was ten years old at the time. I finally told Grandma last night as I know she is telling the truth. She showed me a drawing of another Bigfoot on a book and mine looked like this only his face wasn't as dark. It was only half that dark.

Kimberly continued, August 14th, 2007

My grandma, me and my cousin Brenda went out to talk with them. My grandma yelled "Whooo!" It didn't take long before four of them came up to the front of the house and we stood on the porch and talked with them. Grandma told me how there would be a dead zone (all quiet) and there was when they came up. One chirped at us, one popped his teeth at us. I did not feel scared at all. We watched one play with the barn door and make it squeak as it opened and shut the door for about a foot. Grandma then asked them if they were hungry and if they would like a treat. One said yes. Grandma said it was a male. Me and Brenda heard him say yes. Since it was so late, about midnight, Grandma said she wasn't making pancakes at that time of night for anyone. She went in and took four slices of bread and laid them on a plate and poured maple syrup on the bread. She told them to eat it and if they wanted more they would have to leave the plate on the porch. She set the plate on the top of her jeep right in the middle of the top. Grandma, Brenda and me sat out on the porch and just talked to each other. We saw shadows of two feet on the other side of the jeep only it was from underneath the jeep. The plate disappeared. We could see it plain as it was a white plate. Grandma's other car was sitting behind the jeep and we saw a shadow block out the light that shined on the hood of that car. So we got tired and went into the house and this morning found the plate back on top of the jeep but it was at the other side and at the back of it on the roof. They ate the whole piece that was the heel and part of another only it was just picked out in the middle. They must of not liked it as they didn't put the plate on the porch.

Back to Bonnie, August 2009

I have granddaughters who visit here, and I'm very careful when they're on their monthlies. They all know that they aren't to go out by themselves after dark. There's one that I call Baby Boy, he was obsessed with my granddaughter Brenda, and you could hear him calling "Brenda...Brenda" from the woods. Day or night. He left her gifts in this one spot, and she left little colored rocks that she bought at the Dollar Store. All my kids have done gifts with them. So he left seven of these magnetic stones, I have no idea where he got them. They weren't like the polished ones you see. These were rough in places and rubbed smooth in places.

Closest I've ever been is about four or five feet away. This was in the summertime. I was talking to my girlfriend on the front porch deck, and I'm talking on the phone and all of a sudden he just popped up in front of me, the old gray one. The deck is about eight feet off the ground, and I could see his head and shoulders and chest. He looked silver in the moonlight. His hair was really fine, like a collie dog's. I couldn't mention it to my girlfriend, so I'm talking to her just like normal but looking at him. He was cocking his head back and forth, listening, looking at me like "What are you talking into?" He was so close and the light was so good I could see his pupils, and they were like cats' eyes.

I have no desire to shoot video of them. I wouldn't want someone taking pictures of me without my permission.

Horse Mane Braiding
A Widespread Phenomenon in Areas with Sasquatch Activity

From *Backyard Bigfoot*, by Lisa A. Shiel

One of my horses [in Michigan], a thoroughbred gelding, turned up with strange braids in his mane. The braids consisted of locks of his mane interwoven and twisted together in a complicated pattern similar to a French braid, though vastly more intricate, with a tight knot at the end that was woven back into the braid. Studying the braid, I noted several extraordinary features. First, individual locks were twisted. Next, these twists were woven into a larger braid encompassing coiling, interlocking twists. Finally, the whole braid was finished off by tucking the end up inside the braid and tying a tight knot around it.

Photos by Lisa A. Shiel, BackyardPhenomena.com

In Texas, I found similar braids in the thoroughbred's mane on numerous occasions. Back then, I was content to dismiss them as the handiwork of my neighbors. But the braids reappeared several times, during intervals when no children had visited the rural neighborhood. After noting identical braids in the horse's mane here in Michigan, where I have no neighbors, I can no longer blame the plaiting on visiting children — at least not children of the human variety. While horses generally fear hairy hominins, they can become acclimated to any creature that at first frightens them. In Texas, my horses became accustomed to the wolves and cougars. Here in Michigan, they seem to have adjusted to the presence of hairy hominins, at least somewhat, as they now express a guarded interest in the areas where I've found stick signs, stone tools, and footprints. Lately, they have even behaved as if they enjoy interacting with the hairy hominins. One morning, my quarter horse mare showed up with a braid in her mane. Usually aloof, she acted excited and cheerful that morning, as if she'd had a grand time overnight. The delicate work required to weave the braids implies small fingers — such as those of a child, or a juvenile hairy hominin.

And here are braids found by the habituators at Texas #1 and photographed by Bob Truskowski

4. New York State

Jerry is a thirty-year-old man who lives with his parents. As a teenager, he was hit by a car and suffered a brain injury that still affects him. He has been having experiences with Sasquatch since childhood. I have been corresponding with him since November, 2006, and was able to visit him twice, in June and December of 2007.

May 1985

He was six years old the first time.

"When I met them I had peanut butter and jelly sandwiches," Jerry told me, "and as I remember it they stayed close to me but divvied the pieces up between them. Remember we were way back in they woods so there was nothing for them to run and hide from, it was just me. When they finished what was my lunch but gave to them instead they wanted more but that was it. So [the main male] Miget and his woman—I call her Momma—seen that I gave them my food and fed me some of theirs like some berries we went foraging for. They tasted good from what I remember but I knew I was going to have dinner waiting for me when I went home."

For the next twenty-four years, Jerry has kept up consistent and loyal contact with this same group of Sasquatch. Because they live in a severely limited tract of land, boxed in by suburban residences, he has steadfastly kept their secret, knowing that any leak could cause their ouster, if not their destruction. They have subsisted here, in fact, since before Jerry's great-grandfather first interacted with them in the 1950s, and these accounts were passed down through the generations.

The more he has come to trust me, through our correspondence, the more he has felt comfortable in sharing with me of his past with these *people.* "I like to refer to them as people, not animals." He thinks there were "many races of *homo sapiens* roaming the Earth at one time but many of them went extinct. I just like to think that this is one race that slipped through the cracks and remained on the wild side of things."

He has also long known that he'd like to find a trustworthy

researcher to take along to the site, to help him to officially document their reality (without exposing their home territory), to establish it definitively within mainstream science, and thus to get the wheels turning toward legal protection for the species.

I agreed not to breathe a word of their location, and I have not. That they have managed to survive without discovery in a constricted stronghold of forest—a forest that, albeit thick, comprises just seven square miles—speaks better than any other case I know to their uncanny stealth and adaptability.

"I mean, lots of people know they're back there, even my great-grandpa knew about them and told me about his experiences with them before he passed. He even called them his friends. I just think it's kind of weird how I got to know the same family I like to call the Migets. And it's not certain that they just stay in [name of forest]. I'm sure they go other places, but I know they like to stay close to the stream for water.

"I can't say how many are back there but there are at least five or six that I know of. There can very well be more because they are too unsure or bashful of us men. When I first met Miget, the patriarch or leader, his father was still alive and he was very old but didn't look like it through his actions. They are a very peaceful group of people but very curious of us and at the same time even more scared of us. They are caring of each other and protective of things they take care of. They are even more curious of our foods and simple luxuries like hair combs.

"One time when I was fly fishing, Miget's boy—I call him Junior— walked up behind me and scared me because I didn't hear him till he was right behind me and he was all fuzzy because it was March so he still had his winter coat, but he was only four to five feet tall I guess you could consider him a little guy. He was very uncertain and a little offensive but very curious and just like that he disappeared when I turned my back to check my line.

"The few times when they vocalized for me, I could make out some of our words strangely enough. I hate to sound like a delusional crazy person with all the info I've come forward with but it's what I know. These are wild people we're dealing with and with all their humanness they're still very wild. It's kind of spooky when you think of it or when the situation occurs.

"If someone don't have the right look they won't trust or understand what you say through the simple sign language along with slow talking. They also understand when you speak like them, it comes natural when the moment arises, it's weird. There's no need to practice. The feelings they feel conjure up in you are like a link to our common past.

"One time, I brought my friend back there when cutting school and we were walking about a quarter mile back and I looked to my side and there was Junior. Just sitting there with a grin on his face looking at me like an old friend being reacquainted. My school friend started shaking uncontrollably and ran back to school. After Miget came into sight with his brother we had a visit for a while and I went back to school myself. When I ran into my friend in the hall he was so shaken up he forgot what happened. Which is good because I think that happens to a bunch of people because it is so unbelievable that their brain doesn't register it. Just like the Indian folklore they say that they have magic and control you.

"I'm not really out for self-glorification, but want the truth to be known before it's too late or introduced in the wrong way. But you want to know what my theory is? These people are going to be here after man is extinct. They'll be using our structures in a simplified way. Like a highway overpass would be their idea of a home, for instance, and so forth.

"Among the Migets, the female has something beautiful about her. You can tell she's a woman by her figure of course plus the way she walks and by the look in her eyes, it's gentler. It's definitely different than the guys. That's once you get them to feel comfortable. The guys have a build that will make the world's strongest man look like a little girl. The ladies are built and strong too but different if that makes sense.

"They are like us but they groom each other and they got wild eyes if you look them straight on at first, then they relax. They're like a married couple, they bicker and everything. Plus I didn't want to share this because I didn't feel you would believe me, but they had a baby. When I was a kid. I seen him the second time I was taken back in the woods. I might be the only human to see a baby Bigfoot. Very cute, he looked like a newborn maybe a foot and a half from head to toe or two feet maybe.

"They had him in a piece of cloth they scavenged from somewhere. I forgot to tell you when I seen Missy [a younger female] the first time, Miget came out of the woods about fifty feet away and called for her like *come on let's go you*, that was the tone. So there's Miget, Momma, Sissy, Junior, and Little Brother. Plus Miget's brother who I call Uncle Bugout, because he loses his temper. I'm just amazed how those little ones do alright in the winter. This particular family is lucky they have our pollution and waste to pick from for a baby blanket if that's what you want to call it. It makes you feel bad when you think how poor they are but happy.

"Oh, Miget. He was a very big boy since I first knew him. I can remember standing in front of him and having to tilt my head totally back towards the sky to see the top of him. It's still like that today. Miget has been at least ten feet for as long as I've known him, and three or four feet wide, a true powerhouse. He can clear a path running full speed."

Visiting Jerry

We meet on warm June afternoon teeming with goldfinches and deafening insect life. Our plan is to spend the day and the night in the woods, though I must confess that even after months of copious email exchanges, of apparently sincere testimony from this man, I'm still feeling only about 50/50 on his ultimate credibility; after all, what he is asking me to buy into—in terms of his childhood experiences—seems far too good to be true.

Add to this, now, the fact that although Jerry spent his youth (and knew "the Migets") *downstate,* he claims to have made contact, over this past winter and spring, with yet *another* family group up here, hundreds of miles from the first.

This fact does not, however, strike him as remotely strange; his contention is that these people live in most forests, but that human beings do not, as a rule, have the foggiest notion, much less any aptitude for outreach.

Jerry is just about my height, six feet, heavy-set, with bad knees that cause him to sway back and forth a little when he walks. He works in a machine shop, where he puts together transmission housings.   On weekends and occasional days off, he is free to spend quiet hours inside the forest, just two miles from town.   What strikes one first is how soft-spoken and down-to-earth he is; nothing mystical or rash passes his lips, and his body-language is understated, facial expressions even humdrum, the opposite of what one might expect after hearing his mind-boggling stories.

As he leads me through tall grasses on top of a high clearing, he's more interested in agriculture than in Sasquatch, pointing out the various farmers' fields, telling me their names, and whether or not they've fallen behind schedule in the season's first haying.   He clearly enjoys the look of these swatches of land arrayed below us in the valley.

On the downslope, we approach and pass through the tree line, leaving the goldfinches and bright sunlight behind.   It takes us no more than ten minutes, once inside the woods, to make our way over roots, fallen trees, and along informal fernways to Jerry's hide-out, a simple but effective lean-to he's constructed out of sturdy branches and pine boughs.

The very moment we arrive—and I mean the *very* moment, even before we can sling off our backpacks—a single, distinct wood knock pierces through the thick trees, coming from our west, maybe seventy yards away. Jerry looks at me. "I told you so."

I have to laugh, from pleasure in hearing this, and because he certainly *has* told me, in great detail. We set up a sparse camp—thermoses of coffee, collapsible chairs, candy bars, a candle set on a rock—and then spend four hours alternately talking and meditatively listening.   It's breezy, my heart's bruised from a fresh, treacherous breakup with the mother of my child, and sunspots swirl over the forest understory.

What follows is a blend of Jerry's words from our conversation this afternoon and from his emails to me over the past six months.

I start by conceding that during all my BFRO expeditions, and certainly in my solo time in the woods, I've never gotten such an unmistakable overture as the wood knock we just heard.

"Maybe you're not listening enough once they know you're there. They'll give you one really soft knock. That means you're in their sight and you don't even know it. It sounds crazy but you have to become an animal in your head.

"Remember, you're going into *their world*. They have super senses as it is, so you shouldn't have to over-extend yourself to get their attention. Keep it simple. I feel the BFRO might be too loud when they're on expeditions. When you think about it they already know we're reckless and loud as a race. That's why they stay away altogether. The researchers stay in a crowd out there. Why fill the woods with a bunch? Simple sounds, little whoops go a long way too. That's why they aren't yelling out more as well. They don't have to, they already got great hearing. I'm the kind of guy that sets off in the woods by myself. I don't like talking out here unless I try to talk with one of them, like last week when he threw a rock at a tree by me. Then I talked calmly but excited. Yup, keep it simple. They get spooked about people to begin with.

"They can feel when a person's spirit is good and means good, that's why I've gotten this far. They're just watching out for themselves right now, that's what's happening. You know this all seems simple but the biggest aspect of this besides them is to share good information for their sake and not to let people see them the wrong way but to love and respect them as the fathers of the woods."

Again and again, he stresses the indispensable importance of sincerity.

"Once they know who you are they aren't offended or threatened. I think I just lucked out or maybe I have a peaceful look in my eyes or maybe it's because I am a big guy or I look and act like them, ha. I do enjoy spending lots of time in the woods too, maybe I'm being checked out from a distance and their curiosity brings them in.

"I have to tell you about my experience in the Poconos. When I lived there ten years ago sometimes there would be a thump or tap on the wall of my house on the wall behind my TV at night. I would be wondering what it was so I went outside one night with my dog and out of the woods came a seven-to-eight-foot teenage male. My dog Jack got between us, and it almost attacked him but I walked up to my dog and started petting him and saying good boy, with a calm voice. The male looked in amazement as

Jack calmed down, then I started to play with my dog and he seemed to understand. I could swear that he said 'Jack' too in a pleased voice after I introduced him."

This is the type of thing, of course, that stretches one's credulity. Jerry relates the anecdote as if he's telling me about some innocuous street-corner encounter.

Another such: When he was a kid, he was once able to touch the lower back of a female before she moved off. "I remember her hair was coarse and real *oily*. I guess that's how they stay dry in the rain, the water runs right off."

Winter Work

He writes me near daily updates on his careful process of outreach to the Upstate locals, when he first established their presence.

January 12th, 2007: "I had a gnarly day out in the woods my friend. I went for a walk four or so hours ago and just got home. I brought my homemade club for wood-knocking. I was knocking the whole way back on that road I was telling you about where I seen the bear, they're asleep now I'm sure. But I also know there are Migets in the area because of the deep woods and past experience.

"Well, I went down this path leading deep into the woods. I gave a power pole a good crack before I left into the woods. I wasn't too far when I heard it, a huge thud coming from across the valley in a deep patch of woods I could pick out. Along with another crack far deeper and more powerful than I could ever make. Well I kept on my way out there into the wilderness. I kept on finding things to beat on and finally found a nice rock with a good flat side. I stayed in one spot so I could listen with a vantage point over two valleys to hear and see over the woods and farm fields, and so they could hear me. I was getting responses now only with far-off knocks in the woods. I was knocking my club on the rock and gave it a rest. Then I couldn't place it but there was definitely something on two legs walking around me somewhere with big feet. I could tell from the sound the snow made when it packed, it was so cool. I made contact, not how I wanted though.

"I wanted to stay out there and make a visual and even a close-up encounter. Oh yeah, I also seen some foot prints on the seasonal road on my way back. I couldn't say how big or how fresh because they were wind eroded, but they sure did look big."

I pointed out, by email, that most people wouldn't be able to stay out for hours with their face exposed.

"No, I like the cold. My jaw was hurting when I got back. With the wind it was like a sandblaster out there. But about the knocks. I couldn't believe it at first. I figured someone was chopping wood. But that was a thud. I also heard a vocalization, a whoop with a little monkey chatter. It didn't last for more than a few seconds, twice.

"At first, the knocking came from my east then after a while it came from my west. Which means it was trying to locate me. Then the footsteps packing the snow put it in stone for me. The steps sounded like they were within fifty feet of me. That means he or she could see me but I couldn't see them. In that state of mind looking around to figure out where the sound was coming from, you could easily overlook a perfectly camouflaged figure in a dark woods, plus I was down in the ravine. It might have kept back once the wind really started up and blew my scent toward it and it figured out I was a man. Otherwise it might have just walked up to me until I came into its vision. I was hidden in the ravine good enough to not be seen. There were snow banks tucking me in."

January 21st, 2007: "I spent about, oh, three or four hours out there today and just got back five minutes ago. I headed down the hill on the dirt road and went east by the pond. I was only on that path a few seconds and seen a set of tracks come out of the woods and head down the path, I couldn't tell what direction, they weren't fresh. They didn't have a big stride, so I figured it was a young one. If it was a human what were they doing out that far and why coming out of the deep woods like that? Then again what was I doing out that far? So I said to myself, this is the spot to try today. So I took a good swing with my Bigfoot club three times. It was a few minutes before I got a response far away but I did, ha. Once again the knocks got closer than a mile and changed location. They were trying to find me, oh shit. Then from the next tree line over a half mile away I seen a head poke out from behind a tree and look from side to side I seen its shoulders too. That was north of me. I gave another good set of knocks and got a response right away, no vocals just knocks today. Then I started to think about the pine forest behind me and the fact that they like sneaking up on you. I remember this from [downstate location].   Even when you do see them it's always like the first time you met, you always get spooked because they just appear or sneak up, it's just a weird feeling. They stare at you with those wild eyes and neither of you know what to think of each other.

"Anyway, back to today.   I knew this young one from the ridge across the way seen me so it was a matter of time. It was only a six- or seven-footer by the looks of it.   I kept on knocking at least every five minutes.   Now I knew I was in the middle of a family, because I was hearing knocks all around me in at least three or four locations.   Then I heard a knock maybe shit at least within a hundred yards, with the limb he was using snapping. I knocked right away and just like I figured they were surrounding me from behind so I kept looking over my shoulder once in a while playing along. Then I had to turn around altogether because I heard him break a tree limb off a tree. I studied for a second and there he was, a big boy. You know Chris maybe you're right I might have some magic in me they're drawn to. Well there he was very still now because I had my eyes set on him almost like he was hunting or stalking I should say. He had a look on his face like what the hell does this guy want, it looked kind of pissed off in a studying kind of way. I started making humming sounds, then I surprised him with a whoop. His face changed altogether like oh that's who has been whooping outside of town. Then he looked to the west in the forest, a thick forest I might add. So he was with a buddy, making facial expressions in a calm manner like it's ok he's a friend or something like that. This guy is huge, at first when I glanced his way I thought it was a fallen tree or a stump, then I made out the face. He was crouched up, hunched over. (Solid.) He has a wide black face and fur. A tall forehead and a cone-like dome on top. Big shoulders and huge legs from what I could make out. He was pretty far off, maybe five hundred feet. He was looking around him now a lot. He had no reason to run I was in the middle of nowhere on his turf. So I started eating some peanut butter crackers I packed in my pocket and offering to him. So I ate the whole pack and said mmm every bite, while smooching kisses. Everything understands smooches. I left an open pack in two tree limbs high up for him to get.

"I wasn't that surprised by what happened today, a major milestone. I figure little steps now that they know who I am, I'll be back. The crackers just helped to tell them I'm a good guy.

"So I took a piss and left swaying my arms and looking back every couple of hundred feet, waving back. I knew they would be looking or eating the crackers. I feel all giddy inside when I think of it now. Now that I give it a good figure in my recollection, he had to have been five hundred to eight hundred feet away. I should have left more crackers. Well there's always tomorrow."

January 25th, 2007: "I went out there at 11:00 am and back to the same spot. Again, it only took about fifteen minutes to get a knock response. I think I found their winter hangout, a nice thick spruce forest."

"Still," I say today, the following summer, long hours since we heard that first welcoming knock, "fifteen minutes can feel like an eternity."

"Two things that keep people from making contact," Jerry instructs me, "are impatience and disbelief.

"Okay, so I started out at the top of the hill whooping my way in. I got there and was knocking. The knocks started back and they weren't just tree trunks expanding with the coldness. A big knock out a half mile followed with one close to my east. The sound of thumping snow pack again around me. I couldn't see Buddy run but I knew it was him by the sound. Branches crunching now and again by mistake or just a spurt of quick movement. But today he wasn't where I seen him last time so that means I wasn't seeing things last time, just checking myself. I looked north and seen a head and shoulders that moved between vertical tree trunks maybe a half mile across the field up the hill."

"Wow," I say, "a half *mile*?"

"Yeah. People don't look far enough, hell they don't even look a *quarter* as far as they should when they're out. It happens a lot. You just have to know what silhouettes to look for and be able to tell the difference between tree trunks and legs, arms and fur. I tell ya, Man, we're dealing with the Abominable Special Forces. These guys are good at what they do.

"So I started humming very nicely. The knocks continued but only north of me after the ones to the east and west within a few hundred feet. Then a while later I heard a hum grumble very low in tone in the woods behind me followed by a big knock to the right of me which was where he was. Big knocks deeper in the woods a half mile to the northeast going deeper and closer. I finally caught on. They wanted me to go deeper in the woods, too, so I did. I went west on this path a half mile out of sight of the other area when I heard a burst of movement from where he was to keep an eye on me. I found a stream and stopped and hung up a bag of apples and crackers and a banana, since I found a peel a while back. Oh yeah he only took one cracker from the other day, you could see he ripped the bag open and dropped it in the snow. Also, I found a set of some tracks with an at least a six-to-seven-foot stride downhill. I had to do a split to make one step.

"I was hearing something behind me, thumping, no reason to worry they're just checking you out. I had the feeling that if they could only draw me out deeper they could attempt to approach me. It felt like at least six individuals around me. One kept knocking and would go deeper, knock, go further knock, and then come all the way back and knock in the same area. I would whoop and get a single knock in return immediately. I was in my chair and looking north towards the food bag knocking my chair leg.

"When I heard something over my shoulder I took a look and out of nowhere a huge knock came from in front of me when I wasn't looking. I instantly responded with a loud (nice) whoop and got out of my chair, and a rock was thrown at a tree a hundred feet in front of me. That means you're not welcome I've heard, but they just don't know me yet. I feel they're testing my reaction, so I stayed friendly. Then there was a vocal from what I thought was a youngster who couldn't hold himself back out of curiosity. Not a big one just a bleep or a boop. It's funny because when I'm home thinking, I get a bit spooked about what could happen with a nine-hundred-pound wildman, but when I get out there that all changes. It's like we're both playing opposite sides of the same game board, both very curious and very unsure."

Jerry points to a branch that forms part of the lean-to opening. "I came back here one day to find a single blade of green grass just hanging there. And remember, this was *February*."

It's twilight now, and it comes to our attention that we're famished, unwilling to follow our loose plan of fasting all night. Hiking back out to town, though, our dim foresight suddenly turns to luck. A ridge above us, probably two hundred feet away across a green and yellow field, begins to ring out with voices. Just two, but nonhuman, calling back and forth. It's a cross between a howling and the long sustain of great big bells, and since there are no wolves (or, okay, *virtually* no wolves) in Upstate New York, and since this vocalization contains, anyway, zero of the yipping uptake or the group-choral quality of coyotes, nothing but the high song portion itself, and since it comes from the very area where this straightforward young man has claimed to see and hear "them" for months, I feel my belief level shoot from 50% to 85%.

"Captivating, isn't it?" says Jerry. "I think it's a female and a juvenile, a couple hundred yards apart. That's what it seems like to me. Hope you're getting this," he says, gesturing to my video camera.

To the unaided ear, able to extract the remarkable from the weave of usual summer sounds, this serenade could not be more plain, and would have made the two-hundred-and-thirty-mile drive worthwhile by itself. But my camera's mic picks up way too much foreground, too much buffeting breeze and trilling finches, so that the soaring background voices in the forest, when I play the footage back the next day, are vanishingly faint.

This acoustical visitation feels generous and primes us, of course, for the night ahead, but after we eat—Jerry's mother fixes us a pasta dinner—and find our flashlit way back down to camp, the show is over. Jerry sits up by himself for a couple hours, hearing nothing, then he listens while I sleep, sedated by his mom's Italian sausage. Once, at 4:15, he hears possible footsteps, but not clear enough to wake me.

They must be off tending to other business.

Over breakfast, before I head back home to Vermont, he reminds me of another of his favorite axioms, what he uses to keep himself humble. "They don't need us."

Snowy December, six months later, and I've come to visit Jerry again. We reach his spot in the woods at four in the afternoon, just dusk. Since I was last here, he's constructed an impressive hut out of trees and branches, leaves, mud, and moss. We start a fire and try to get warm; it's sixteen degrees, and we huddle on a log seat, drink coffee from a thermos.

In a while, we take a short walk up a logging road. The snow is a foot deep and the night is perfectly still. Jerry makes soft whoops, and we listen. The best wood knock I've ever heard greets us, and we slap gloves in celebration. I'd estimate it's a hundred and fifty feet away, but given the prime acoustical conditions, it comes to our ears clean and immediate, THWACK, but without much heft behind it. More like THWACK, then, but definitely all caps, unmistakable. It's like hearing a word in deep space, such an affirmation of our being way out here at all.

"Look how smart these guys are," Jerry says. "They just have to make a little knock here and there and they know where everyone is. That's their radar."

Fifteen minutes later, on a second exploratory foray up the hill, we hear another reassuring wooden smack, even closer.

"How come it's such a dainty knock?" I ask.

"That's what they do. They don't want no one to know they're here. Last winter, that's all I heard, 'cause the one would be here, and one would be over there, and they'd be going back and forth. And a light knock like that here and there. 'Cause these guys are so smart, they know what to do. They're pros at it."

Back in the hut, Jerry whoops, and not thirty seconds later we hear a series of three knocks from the third-of-a-mile range, quieter than the first but only thanks to distance, obviously more powerful at the source: BOOM-BOOM-[pause]-BOOM!

Delighted, Jerry emphasizes, "That's right after I whooped. And that's right in the swamp, and no one goes back in the swamp. See, that's the kind of knocks I'd get last summer. Three in a row...fifteen seconds...three in a row."

After an hour of shivering, banking the fire with twigs, we tap free of snow, and we hear a branch snap not fifty feet behind the hut. We're bowled over. It's not possible that a deer, say, has *stepped* on the branch, because of the muffling layer of snow. It's a branch snapped up in pure air, by something with sure hands, as can be readily discerned from the audio recording.

Even though we return at sunrise (twelve degrees!) and do our best to draw them in again, that snap is our closest pass, and of course it makes perfect sense that they'd keep their distance, not show themselves by daylight or approach any nearer at night, given how radically Jerry's breaking his normal routine, feeding a whole new person, an unknown man, into the mix. Men hunt. And two men are, from a strategic point of view, much more than twice as hard to deal with than one man. It becomes a group-on-group situation and injects a major new level of concern—the possibility of being triangulated or flanked.

Back in August, as he entered the area one day, Jerry found himself trailed by the one he calls "Dude," an adolescent male, six or seven feet tall but still dwarfed by "Buddy." Arriving at the hut, Jerry said, "Hey... there...Dude" as he slowly brought the camera up to his eye and snapped a shot. It's an extremely low-resolution image, but it does show the figure leaning out from behind a tree at approximately two hundred and fifty feet. It's the sort of picture that wouldn't convince anyone who hadn't come to know, and finally trust, the context of these encounters.

All during our mini-expedition, which is entirely satisfying if not Earth-shaking, I am suffused also with the experiences he has conveyed through his emails, this past summer and autumn.

July 8th, 2007: "I had a great time out there today. I whooped in the field on my way in. As soon as I got in the woods I was being followed. It's hard to explain. We were making our ways to our normal spots where we check each other out. When I would stop walking he would too. When I got to my hut I could see someone was playing out there. Well I heard him getting damn close behind me so I looked and there he was concentrating on his next move, ha. I caught him. He looked right at me right away. Shit man it's been about eight or nine months since we gazed into each other's eyes directly since we met. And he was fuckin' close, like three hundred feet away no more than that. And it was Buddy himself crouched down low like when we met. I got a good look at his feet and can see how he leaves twenty-eight-inch tracks. He is *huge*. He has a gorilla head just a lot bigger than one from Africa.

"We stared each other down. I could hear what he was thinking: Oh shit I got too close. With wide eyes and an open mouth he was dumfounded. So I started to talk like a baby real sweet-like ya know. So he wouldn't feel scared to be that close. I turned to take a pee and out of the corner of my eye he took off in a rush so he's still very nervous of me. I can respect that big-time, this will take time like I thought. When he took off he took a few steps and looked to see what I was up to and before ya know it he was in full stride and gone out of sight quick. Man they can blend in good out there."

September 14th, 2007: "Today though there was an honest effort on his behalf to make contact. I was surrounded by like six of them within a half mile, all around me, with caveman talk and a nice three-minute-long set of knocks and some light vocals behind me to mimic my babytalk, that was Moma I think. And running through the woods.

"It happened, they finally made the next step to friendship. Buddy was happy, I could feel it, a feeling of excitement all around me today. Maybe there's a new baby. I knew who I was looking at today right away. One look and it was Buddy. Huge! He's done this to me a lot, follow me in like that. If you recall I've brought this scenario up before. But we've made a good step today. They might want to speed this up a bit before winter for their own reasons, Hey. So I'll know what kind of eats they like, right? I think the quick change in weather has brought this new approach on maybe. Once they figure out what a PBJ is we're set. I'll bring one out next time

"He left a gift today, a walking stick in the trail like he's done for me before. The hut was tampered with but not messed up, like a passing-through inspection. The candle was moved to the other side of the rock and a few other things were moved too. I could tell it was him, Bud, because it was like he flipped it around with his fingers.

"I also thought I heard a baby Squatch out there today with Mama. It didn't cry just a whimper once in a while, I was right about my hunch of the baby. That's probably why they were happy today they probably just started bringing out the baby. That's why they were on that secluded hill a mile away. They need food. I'll bring a food gift next time. For Mama. I'll have to make a separate area instead of my hut but in view of it for the food to be offered at. Soon enough the leaves will be gone.

October 25th, 2008: "I've been getting little whaah's from the new addition, my friend, and Mama's been trying to shush up this one I can hear. I believe I did as good as I did today because I didn't have my camera, it wasn't charged in time before I left. I played some METALLICA for them. They liked it a lot. I guess that's what I'll name the baby, METALLICA. They really can do good human vocals. It was like a celebration in the woods."

See YouTube: "Visiting Jerry: Upstate New York Habituation Site."

5. Texas #1

This is a family of six. The parents are in their forties, with two grown children and, still living at home, a thirteen-year-old son and their daughter Rachel, who is fifteen. The first speaker is the mother.

Since 1982

Things have been happening here for twenty-six years. I think the first episode I remember is being out late one night (about 10:30), feeding some dogs I had in a pen out behind the house. I was by myself and it was dark. I believe the weather was a little on the cool side so maybe it was in the fall. Anyway, as I started to open the gate to give the dogs food, I heard a really low growl and then teeth clicking together. I've always lived in the country, so really I'm not afraid of being outside after dark by myself. In fact we grew up playing outside all the time till the early hours of the morning.

But these teeth sounds were close and very loud. It scared me. It scared me a lot! I didn't recognize the sounds and had never heard them before, so I just dropped the food and walked very quickly to the house.

Over the years we've had some things disappear as well as heard strange sounds in the woods. We never really thought much about it, though. Until Rachel came in one day saying she had seen a bear. As she described what she saw, I was thinking it sounded like a Bigfoot but was a little skeptical. I'd never really believed one way or another. Then when I talked to my oldest son, he mentioned he had just seen one walk in front of his truck on his way home late one night.

That's when we started searching out sightings on the internet and found the BFRO. It's hard to say how frequently things have happened, since we weren't really looking or paying attention to such things. Since we've been watching for signs, we notice things almost daily.

Mostly it's just calls in the woods, but sometimes there are close encounters. They usually show themselves to the younger kids, more than to us grownups. Our daughter is the main one to see them. She's actually seen the mom and twin babies!

If our chronology is accurate, we saw the mom pregnant outside our backdoor early last December. She was huge and we think her giving birth was imminent. Then Rachel saw two babies in our pasture that ran for their momma and they were about the size of a mid-size dog. They ran on all fours, like a chimp runs.

In terms of "gifts," yes we do leave things out for them sometimes. I wouldn't say we do it regularly. Sometimes when Roy [local BFRO Investigator] is here, he brings food for them. We especially leave food for Christmas. They seem to like it. Usually fruit, pancakes and hot dogs.

Rachel shows rabbits. One time, one went missing and a big rock was found in its cage. So, yes they have left things. What's really funny though is Rachel had several rabbits die pretty close together (they die pretty easily), and she got tired of burying them (because the dogs kept digging them back up). So, she left several right in the edge of the woods behind the house. The next morning we found them on our front porch. I think that was a hint, they didn't want them on their front porch.

Roy leaves a bag hanging in the tree over a little ways from our house. The other day they started calling to us and put the bag in the tree right behind our house...like they wanted us to fill it up again.

Rachel said the mom she saw was beautiful. She had very pretty features. Fine features and very feminine.

But she was "zapped" that one day when she was getting close to the babies. The whole time she felt paralyzed, the mom was cooing to her. She said she wanted to respond and talk to her, but was unable to move or say anything. Then when the babies got out of sight the mom turned to walk away. Rachel followed and called to her asking her to please not go. She turned to my daughter, looked at her, and then walked into the corn. (The corn field was full grown at that point in time.)

I sometimes feel like they are better off than we are because it's so simple. They just live to be together. They don't get caught up in the day-to-day struggle of materialistic things we get hung up on.

Are there stick structures around here? Oh yes. In fact, there's basically a village created out of brush and twigs. It's amazing. It has several huts that are very clean. It is our impression that they travel around from place to place within their territory, never staying too long at any one location. From the calls we know that they are all around us.

I hate the groups that want to kill one to prove their existence. What if that was a member of their own family? How would they feel then. They obviously care about one another. They also live in family groups with a mom and dad.

Rachel is the main one to talk to. They seem to actually interact with her. Usually when she's alone out there with the horses. They really like her. I'll let you talk to her. As long as you don't reveal our specifics, it's fine. It's really not so much a matter of our personal privacy as it is *their* privacy. I would feel horrible if something happened to them because I started this whole thing with the BFRO. We just didn't know much about them in the beginning and now we feel like they are neighbors that are friendly, but like their privacy. They seem to be so protective of one another and truthfully, that includes Rachel. They seem to watch over her. In the beginning we kind of feared they might take her as a pet, but now we know they would never hurt her.

It's not strange to any of us, to me, my husband, my daughter or my son. All of us have seen them now. We just wish we could get some good video. We've got three cameras up, but honestly, haven't gotten much. Roy got some good thermal views last year of three watching me and Rachel. It was on a Sunday about two in the afternoon! They are here all times of the day and night with no rhyme or reason for the timing. I mean you can't say, "Well, every Sunday they'll be here," etc. They just show up when they show up. It's just that it's pretty often. I think they feel safe with us because we interact with them through calls and talking. Then we go and leave them alone.

Even a couple of our neighbors know of them and it's common conversation about the big hairy naked people. But they don't seek out encounters and are not outside that much so don't really interact with them. However, the Feet walk across their roof as well. They are always walking on the roof here. Pretty funny. Last night someone was banging on the outside of my bedroom. I didn't get up. But it was pretty loud.

They knock on the wall, they walk on the roof, I think they may have even jumped on our trampoline before. One night I heard them walking on the roof and then a stumble and bang bang bang (like they fell off the roof) and I went running out to check on them and they were already gone.

We live in a junkyard basically and I think it makes the Feet feel safe. They come around all the time. In fact Roy brought someone here about a week ago and they went walking in the woods about this time of day and walked up on a napping adult. It ran off, startled the humans. Pretty funny. Of course, he didn't take his camera, 'cause he didn't think they'd be out. I keep saying we need to hook up Rachel with a hidden camera and microphone all the time.

From Rachel

I show rabbits. One day I had a show, so I had to get up about 4:30 AM or so and had to go outside to get the rabbits. I had a headlight type thing on my head when I walked outside, the dogs were going crazy and when I looked into the pasture there were four eyes looking back at me, big eyes. I couldn't figure out what it was so I got closer and closer then my dog barked and they both got up and zipped off into the pasture. I shined the light over there, and there were two things laying there. I thought it was maybe a big cat, I couldn't tell, they had BIG eyes. They were looking all around and looking right at me. I was shining the light on them and they were reflecting back. So I started to walk towards them, and when I did, Zeke nipped one of them, and they both tore off running really fast, so fast I don't even remember much of what happened. They went straight up under our neighbor's fence and stood upright and went into the woods, I was like, Oh, that's what those are. It was two baby Bigfoots. I was shocked!

And I shined the light back on the cornfield, and I could see them running through the corn, and I was like, I'm going to go get a closer look, so I ran up to the fence, and I get within about six or eight feet of the fence, and Mama walks out, puts her hands on the fence and just looks at me. I'd seen her a couple times before. She starts making this humming noise? And I couldn't move, I was just like stuck there. I was so scared, couldn't make a noise, couldn't do anything. I was getting really scared, and then she started making like this cooing noise, and then I wasn't so scared anymore. I just kind of stared at her for a little bit. And then, she looked at me and turned around and went back in. I said to her, "Wait." She looked back at me briefly but kept going. I still went ahead and got my rabbits ready and left.

She had a very human face, very pretty. She didn't have hair on her face either. Black skin, chocolate black. More like charcoal.

But way before that, I was the first in my family to say, "Hey, there are Foots in the woods," and of course no one believed it until my big brother saw one. They have been there all my life, I just didn't know it.

I was walking over to my grandmother's house the first time I saw one, and it was probably about dusk. It came out of the woods from behind the little house and walked upright towards our house. And then it got on all fours and ran back in. And I got all freaked out and went and told my mom, "There's a red bear," and she wouldn't believe anything about it. That was when I was nine or ten.

So, I got really upset because she wouldn't believe me. Then the next time, me and my cousin were outside playing in the dirt, because that's what we do, and something came stomping through the woods, breaking branches, making all kinds of racket, and we saw something big and reddish brown-black, running through over by the little house. We got really freaked out and ran inside, and were like, "The bear's back." And she still wouldn't believe us.

And so then, like a week later, my big brother was coming down [route name] right over there, and something ran out in front of the car, and he told my mom, "It looked like a bear but I think it was Bigfoot." And then she put two and two together...and *then* she believed it.

My brother feels as close to them as I do.

I feel like they are part of my family. They are always there.

In the beginning, it probably took six or eight months, and then I started messing with them. I used to feed them almost every day. I made this...I just put some flour, eggs, and milk and sugar and syrup, and put some sprinkles on it and cooked it, and would put it out there and come back a couple hours later and it would be gone. And I'd have it up so high that nothing else could possibly have gotten to it. Sometimes off the eaves of the little house. Or sometimes I had this huge table that was taller than me, I had to get a ladder and put it up there. It would be gone every time.

I stopped putting food out there, I got too lazy.

Sometimes I'd just look at them and they'd run away, but after a while, I'd look at them and they'd just kind of duck down and stay there. If I talked to them, they wouldn't really say anything back, they'd just kind of go lower. If I got closer they'd run away. But if it was after dark you could see their eyes.

They leave me stones sometimes, and they whistle at me all the time. And they imitate my mom and say "Rachel" all the time. They will act like they are my dogs crying far away and as soon I get far far away looking for the dog they say "Rachel" back at the house, my mom's voice. Then when I get to the house my mom's not home, then they make the dog noise again, making me run back over and over till I give up.

Just the other night, someone was mimicking my little brother calling for the dog. We hear that a lot.

Or they take stuff and hide it and when I go to get it they try to scare me but it doesn't work.

The big male isn't friendly but he is only around sometimes and yes he does do the [infrasound] noise thing to me. He does not like me anywhere off the yard. He sometimes throws rocks beside me but not hitting me though.

Back to the Mother

Lots of activity recently. The other night one actually waved to us. It was midnight, but bright moon. It was probably one hundred yards away. We've watched each other from that close before and even whistled or called to each other, but that's the first time they actually waved back. We were pretty excited. We try not to push any situation to a point where they feel uncomfortable. So after we called to them and waved a couple of times, we went in. We're trying to show them that we know they're there and we aren't trying to hurt them. We're non-confrontational. I think that's why they came to our house when the helicopters were pursuing them in the woods that night.

We've been having helicopters flying low over the woods at night, usually late, and sometimes people flushing them towards our house from the back of the woods. We've found lots of evidence that someone has been trying to find them.

As soon as we can cough up some extra money, we're going to put up more cameras and get another DVR. We have one now with three cameras up. But, frankly, I haven't had time to watch it lately. I need to try to get that done.

As I mentioned, Roy got three on thermal camera last year. It was really clear. There were two big ones and one baby crawling through the woods towards our horse barn. It was 2:00 pm and Rachel and I were out there taking care of the horses. You can see two larger figures crawling on their hands and knees and then you see a little one crawl along behind. You can make out their lower legs and feet. Rachel and I didn't even see or hear them. It just reiterates how much they watch us.

Just last night, I was watching Rachel run to Grandma's, when I saw one at the "little house." It was sort of pacing and watching me. They often hang around the little house and watch us go back and forth to Grandma's.

My husband's grandmother lives next door. We live in the country so next door is about a hundred and fifty yards from us. The little house is also about one hundred and fifty yards southeast of us.   It's pretty much just a separate bedroom set away from Grandma's house. She got mad at Grandpa about something one time and made him build it for her as a retreat. Anyway, after Grandpa died, Grandma has been too scared to stay alone. Rachel and/or her brother have been spending the night there most every night since that time. The kids wait until as late as possible to go. We pretty much have a timeline of 10-12 pm when one of them runs across. I usually either walk them or watch them from the fence that runs in between our two properties.

The Feet usually hang out around the little house for the nightly "show" of us running across and playing in the pasture. We often see one run around the little house when we walk out to the fence. Sometimes they call, but most of the time they just watch.

Grandma has heard things and thinks people knock on her house and walk on her roof. She does not believe it is a Foot. We actually spoke of it to her once, but she didn't believe it. Her memory is not that great, so she doesn't remember any of us talking about it. We don't bring it up.

I get excited any time I see them; however, we do see them a lot. My younger son really likes to see them. He comes running in to get me. For me, it's always at night.   During daylight hours, they only show themselves to the kids.

6. Texas #2

This site is one hundred and three miles from Texas #1, but the two families have never met, or communicated, as of the time of these testimonials. The speaker is fifty-four. She was chemically poisoned at work in 1993, and has since been on disability. She currently lives alone in a "flimsy lap-siding house," though in the 1990s she shared the small house with a husband and four teenage daughters. Before she moved back here in late 2007, the structure had stood vacant for five years. Her property and the few properties nearby are surrounded by thousands of acres of uninterrupted forest. Less than twenty miles away is the Sabine River Basin, source of hundreds of Sasquatch sightings since the 1950s.

The Late 1990s

When Bill had the rock fight, we never could figure out who he'd had the rock fight *with,* so we just kind of dismissed it, and after a period of time it just goes into the non-thinking part of the brain. This was in 1998. It was dark out there, there was really no moon, and that area is covered by trees. What he saw was built much like my little spindly daughter. I think it started out as he thought maybe she just chunked a rock at him and inadvertently hit him, but it pissed him off. And so he just reached down and grabbed up a rock and flung one back at her, and hit her, what he thought was her. It made a sound like someone getting their wind knocked out.

Well then they got into this rock fight, and he said it was quick, very agile, in the dark, which he didn't really understand how she could see where she was going because it was so damn dark. And being on the run and side-arming rocks and just beaning him time after time. I was able to look at him later and there were like nine spots on him, because when he'd see the arm move then he'd turn his back to it and it'd get him right in the middle of his back. He must've had eight or nine big ole knots in his back, and a couple on the back of his head, and one on his forehead.

Well, he came inside and he was loaded for bear. He was waiting for her to come in and I said, "What's going on?" and he said, "I'm waiting...just never mind." Then I said, "Well, what's going on?" "I'm waiting on Allison," he said. I called, "Allison," and she comes in from the bedroom, and no of course she wasn't dressed all in black like Ninja Child.

At first he started shaking and then he turned white as a sheet, and I thought it was from getting beaned in the head, like he was going into shock. I thought he'd run into a tree, because he didn't tell me he'd gotten in a rock fight right away, all I knew was he had a big ole knot on his head. But then when I started looking at him, you know, you could see a knot on the back of his head, too. It wasn't till after the kids settled down for the night and we were laying in bed, and I said, "You wanna talk about it?" And he said, "Not really." And I said, "Bill, *what's* going on?" And he said, "Allison never left the bedroom?" And I said, "Bill, she's been working on that school paper all evening." And he said, "I got in a rock fight." And I said, "With who?" And he said, "Well, I thought it was with Allison." I said, "Well, who was it?" And he said, "I don't know, and I don't wanna talk about it anymore. I finally got tired of the rock-throwing, I was just gonna chase her down and whoop her butt." And he chased her down into the ravine and he couldn't figure out how she got down there so dang fast. And where she went.

I think they've been here all along. You know, with four teenage girls, and two of them crawling in and out windows and smoking marijuana, and sleeping with boys (those were *his* two), I was trying to hold down the fort with that, and I was still recovering from being chemical poisoned, and then we had forty heads of milk goat and sixty chickens and thirteen hogs that we were raising from babies and, you know, there was plenty to keep my mind going and my body tired.

So there were a lot of things I would dismiss. Things being moved outside. I'd leave a hoe right there leaning against a tree near the garden. I'd go out there the next day to finish up and it's not there. And I'd find it out by the goat house hanging in a tree. And I'd think, Haven't y'all got something else to do besides mess with my tools? I wish you girls would just leave shit alone, and so, you know, there was ongoing confusion here. All the time. I would get my flower pots and stuff...you know, when you have gardens you've always got *stuff.* And I put all my flower pots in one area and I'd go back and half of them were gone or moved. Mostly I'd notice it overnight.

Then there was the voice trick. The girls would be at school and I would hear, "Mom!" from the woods. And I'd think, That couldn't be the girls because they're at school. But often, you know, it would be so real I would go and check just to see if maybe they got a ride home from school because they were sick? But we had to sign them out…

Or they'd be at home and come inside: "What do you want?" And I'd say, "What are you talking about?" So you know, these Forest People were imitating me and imitating them. I think they'd just sit up in the trees or whatever and that was their entertainment. *Watch this one, watch this one.* Like a prank.

Back in 1999, my daughter had a teenage girlfriend from Arizona visiting. Allison and Michelle (the guest) played in the woods for hours on end, making dams in the creek, exploring, climbing trees, etc. One evening, just before sunset, they came busting out of the woods running as fast as they could go. I could tell they'd been frightened, but they ran right on past those of us sitting on lawn chairs and hid in the bedroom in the closet. I went in and asked what had happened. Allison told me they got scared and came home…but told me no more about *what* had scared them. I believe it took them a couple of hours to finally open up and tell us that they saw a large bear-type creature come down feet-first out of a tree, land behind a bush, stand up on two feet, then side-step behind a large tree trunk and peek out at them. Allison said that the creature didn't move like a bear, nor did it have any "ears" like one. She said she and Michelle had run out of the woods following the well-used path, and the creature followed them, keeping pace—but through the woods to the side of the path. Once they reached the mowed yard area, the creature stayed behind. The girls refused to go into the woods after that, and wouldn't remain outdoors when the sun started setting. After that time, we teased my daughter about her "big, hairy friend" in the woods. Since none of the rest of us had experienced anything remotely similar, she became the butt of some pretty mean jokes.

From Fall 2007

The house had stood vacant for five years when I decided to move back by myself. During this past summer, I came up more and more often and it must have been about the beginning of October I came up and somebody'd taken a big *crap* in the middle of the living room floor. It was just disgusting. I'm thinking, What has this person been eating? I cleaned it up, scrubbed it with Lysol, scrubbed it with bleach, you know, and the smell still was in here for four days. That's how pungent it was.

Then I went into the bedroom and it looked like somebody had brought in a big section of rolled hay. You know how when they bail rolled hay it's in layers? This was one layer. It was about a foot thick by five foot wide and about eight foot long, and it stank hideously, and I thought people around here are using this as a flop house. But this is what I thought was really bizarre, there was a pile of red surveyors' ribbons and orange surveyors' ribbons and different-colored Christmas ribbons and strings and little pieces of wrapping paper.

When I moved back here, there were twelve windows broken out of the house. Two of them looked like somebody had jumped through them from the inside. The back windows looked like they'd been Kung Fu kicked *out*. And I thought, You know what, that's a lot of wasted energy, you kids just have too much energy. Prior to October, some of the windowpanes were broken but the glass was inside the house. But this glass was broken from the inside and pushed out. In hindsight, it kind of scares me: They know the lay-out of the house, too.

One of the ladies on the habituators' forum said, "You know what, I bet you they decided this was a good place for them to get out of the weather, and they are rather warm-natured...they probably kicked it out for air circulation."

Because the house sat empty for so long they may have thought that I'd left it for them. So there was like a failure to communicate.

I had my first sighting on March 2nd, 2008, about 9:00 am when the dogs started pitching a fit. It pretty well changed my world as I knew it. It's one thing to *hear* about the Bigfoot, it's a whole new world when you actually see one. I got probably a twenty-second viewing of my hairy friend, which was quite enough for a first encounter. I was still shaking two days later when the researchers showed up to take my statement. And, when they found the knuckle print, I had to sit down. It was sort of unrealistic until that point. Once they got the eight-foot-long two-by-four board out and I saw *exactly* how big this guy was, that cinched it—I was ready to put out the "For Sale" sign in the yard. But, I started thinking back about all the times they *could* have harmed us, and obviously didn't— and thought also about some backwoods rednecks moving in here and causing them harm. Well, I just couldn't do it. Both my daughters think I'm absolutely out of my mind to live here by myself, but I don't see either one of them volunteering to stay here with me!

So here's how it went that day. I normally get up rather early, put on coffee and let my small dogs and one coonhound out to relieve their bladders. This morning, being rather cool, I didn't stay out with the dogs, but went back into the house. My other daughter, Hannah, was visiting and was still asleep. The dogs began barking. In an effort to quiet them, I stepped out onto the porch. The Chihuahua and sheltie/rat terrier were in a small pen, the coonhound on a tether. The coonhound, instead of going to the end of her tether, was only about 1/4 of the way extended. The small dogs were penned, but were all looking southward, toward the woods. The dogs had a strange bark, not like seeing a person on the road, or a deer— those barks are familiar. The only way I can describe the barking is that it was rather whiney. I looked in the direction the dogs were watching and was shocked to see a large form. The young growth of pine trees was about three to four foot tall. This form appeared to be twice the height of the pine trees. It was really bulky, with no neck, and blended in with the dappling of the larger trees. It was covered in hair, and the length of the hair on its body was maybe six to eight inches. The hair on its head was slightly shorter, roughly four to six inches. You could call the hair color calico: a mixture of charcoal, gray and brown. Overall, the hair was really messy-looking. I think the shoulders were probably between three and three-and-a-half feet wide.

So I kept looking and questioning myself, and realized I truly was seeing something unusual. I pounded on the side of the house, awakening my daughter to also witness this incident. The large form did not turn right or left, but seemed to be moving slowly but steadily backwards into the cover of the woods. By the time my daughter got outside, the creature had blended into the woods.

Then five days later, she had her own sighting. At 8:00 pm, she decided to drive into town. The house has a long driveway that runs right in front of the pine saplings where I saw the figure. Hannah got into her car and drove down the driveway. At the end of the driveway, her headlight beams lit up what she first thought to be a large tree, or stump, in the middle of the saplings. But then this stump started gently swaying back and forth. She turned on her high beams and saw what she could only describe looking "like the lion's head from the Wizard of Oz."

She called me on her cell phone and backed up her car, trying to get the headlights into position so she could see the thing better. Doing this, she took her eyes off it while shifting into reverse, and lost sight of it. Hannah figures the incident lasted about five seconds. She couldn't see the torso or shoulders, just a head. She said the face was like "earthy colors," marbled black and dark brown. There appeared to be a tuft of hair on the nose, but no hair on the cheeks.

She was too scared to get out of her car or drive away, she was basically frozen. After I and my other daughter came out and calmed her down, she finally left.

The researchers arrived the next morning, and here's what they wrote about what they did and found.

"With the witness standing on her front porch, and with an investigator standing at the sighting location with a pre-marked pole, we were able to determine, based on the witness's recollection, that the subject was approximately eight feet tall.

"As is typical of the ground surrounding a growth of young pine trees in East Texas, the sighting area was covered with a thick and heavy layer of dead grass; and the surrounding floor of the mature pines had a thick layer of pine straw and leaves. We performed a detailed search for trace evidence and after quite some time found a fresh impression on a small gopher mound within the pine saplings that exhibited clear digital impressions. Upon examination, it appeared that the impressions represented a knuckle imprint of a large hand, approximately six and one-half inches in width. A cast was made which verified that there were five digits in the print. The print appeared to have been made within the last twenty-four hours as the area had received rain and snow two days earlier. It is possible that the print correlates with the younger daughter's visual incident."

That was seven weeks ago. Since then, all kinds of other stuff has been going on. I had the house bumped. I have a twelve-year-old coonhound, and something was bothering her because she woke me up out of a sound sleep. She was in the living room, just doing this nasal whistling, and I thought, What in the world is bothering that dog? And about that time something hit the southwest corner of my house so hard the windows vibrated. The only thing I could think of is some sort of livestock got loose, or the house fell off the foundation block, or something's trying to get in. So I got my gun, got my flashlight…because it made me *mad*, you know? So I put the flashlight under my arm, got the pistol, and the dog and I went outside. Nothing was there when I shined my flashlight around, but there's this little wiry flowerbed border that was like six foot and it was all torn up where something looked like it had tripped in it.

Often, right outside my window at night I'll have this loud "AAAA!" sound, like the "a" in cat. It was like they were trying to see how far they could push me. So, of course the ladies on the habituators' forum said, "Just start talking to 'em, when you go outside working in your yard." So I had some tomato plants and I was out there and talking to them, saying, you know, "I'm putting my tomatoes in here…It's been a long time since I've been here and had this garden going…" Just jabbering, you know. When I got done doing that I went and sat down on a glider rocker I had put down right at the end of the driveway with the back of it towards the house. And I sat out there for about fifteen, twenty minutes and then said, "Well, if y'all aren't going to talk to me, I'm just gonna go in the house." I got on the second step of the porch and it sounded like I was transported to the Dallas Zoo, in the primate section. It started out with two "Woo Hoo Hoo Hoo!"—two of them doing that. And then it went to that screeching monkeys do when something's been taken away from them.

I started looking around, and north of my house there were five large shapes moving in the trees. They were from about four-and-a-half foot up to I think eight, judging from the trees they were standing behind. There was a row of four-foot trees in front of them and much taller cedars behind them. That's when they started bird-whistling. And then they were frogs. I was getting these calls from just this one little section of the woods. And it blew my mind. So I just stood out there talking to them and all of a sudden...I'm still in the process of mowing down because the house was vacant for five years. There was some grass that was probably two foot high, and through this grass I can see something about three foot wide coming commando-style towards me in the grass, belly-crawling. All I could think of to say was what I said: "Oh for Heaven sakes, I *see* you." And then it froze. And then it crawled backwards. *Backwards.* And I thought, Oh, that is too creepy.

Meanwhile, they were still whistling and pitching a fit out there across the street in the trees north of my house. And then from *south* of my house there came a bird-whistling so loud it made your eardrums vibrate, so you knew it was no bird on the face of the Earth.

A *piercing* whistle, and I looked up and there was one pine tree, about forty foot tall, that was like flapping back and forth, swaying back and forth and the swing was getting bigger and bigger. And about ten foot from the top of it was this wadded-up furry creature. It did not look like a raccoon, and I didn't see a tail. But I cannot honestly say it was a baby Sasquatch. But I'm looking at the tree and thinking, How in the world is that tree getting more and more momentum when the object at the top of it wasn't moving a muscle? Something was moving it from the ground, and the only thing I can figure is it was a baby that had gotten out there where it was too visible, and they wanted to get it back in. It was surreal, and you think, Did I really see that? And I thought, I'm losing my marbles, I am becoming delusional.

. When I saw that one up in the tree, it looked like one of those (I think they're called) "burls," a big ole knot that comes out the side of a tree. That's what I thought I was looking at. I didn't know they could climb trees, see that's how ignorant I am of what they're capable of doing. So I went back there later, and where the big knot on the tree had been there was nothing but sky.

May 14, 2008

Recently, my cat DeeDee that I raised from newborn got feline distemper and I ended up having to put her down. Brought her home, wrapped in a towel, put her in a box, carried her out and buried her. The next day, I was in the backyard mowing and I hear my cat call from behind the goat house. DeeDee had a distinct meow, I knew that cat anywhere. And I thought, You sorry bastard, you don't know she's dead. Then I thought, Okay, I'll play along with this, and I went, "DeeDee? DeeDee Kitty," and it did it twice more. Later on, I started thinking that maybe it was making this sound to comfort me, you know like when you see a photograph of someone who's gone?

The other day, I was walking out behind the goat house, in the middle of the afternoon, and I heard from the woods what I thought was a frog at first, except it said very clearly, "No bite. No bite." Really it was like a cross between a frog voice and a person's voice.

Then I suddenly realized, and it made me laugh. See, I'm still trying to follow the advice of the ladies on the habituators' forum, so I've been going out to the edge of the yard and talking to the woods, saying like, "I'm just an old woman living here by myself, I'm not gonna hurt you. I won't bite. See, I don't even have my teeth in." When I was chemical poisoned all the minerals got leached out and my teeth started breaking off below the gum line. So I just went ahead and had them all pulled and got dentures. Now, with all this stress here at the house recently, I've been clamping my jaws so much my gums've gotten bruised. So I don't wear my teeth as much.

Now I've heard this a few other times, too: "No bite. No bite," and I almost feel like they've *named* me it.

June 11th, 2008

Last night, I had to let the coonhound LuLu out to go to the bathroom. She's on a forty-foot rope. And I'm getting ready to go to bed and went out and called to her and she wouldn't come in. And I called her again and she wouldn't come in. So I went off my porch to the south, fifteen foot, and just as I came around the edge of the house I hear this "HUH!" And it was so loud I nearly wet myself. And I said, "Look, I'm just going to get my coonhound and I'm going right back in the house." And I could hear it breathing. It was standing in the shadows. See, the only light I've got here right now is the front porch light, which does not shine on the south side of the house, where it's completely, pitch-black dark. I could hear it breathing as I was shaking, grabbing the rope and bringing Lu in, but Lu was almost like she was frozen. And I don't know if I drug, carried, or how I got her in the house.

It traumatized me. They are bound to know that this type of action instills fear. I go out there and I'm telling them, you know, "I live here by myself, now when you make the loud noises close to my house it scares me. I feel like I'm being *threatened*. When I heard that breathing, all the hair on my body stood up, and my heart was beating so loud in my ears. Had it approached me any closer I think I would have had a coronary. I said, "I think I'm going to go in the house now." And of course I know my voice was just shaking.

June 16th, 2008

Today when I was mowing, mowed the front yard, didn't have a bit of problem till I got on the north side, where I'm trying to push back the growth from the woods and reclaim my yard. And where that one was commando-style coming up through the grass? When I started mowing through there, my heart started pounding. It wasn't because I was thinking about the Ninja guy, no I'm thinking about are there any rocks in here.... All of a sudden I had this unexplainable fear, and I yelled out, "You bastards, you are *not* taking over my property!"   And my heart's still pounding, and so I tilted the lawnmower up and ran it into that grass, and whatever it was just *left*.   So then I'm going in the back, and I haven't mowed way back by the goat house yet, I'm getting there, but the whole time I am mowing I get hit with like "Essence of Gym Locker #3," and "Ode to Skunk," and the third time smelled like dead body.   And after the third time I said, "Look, I know you've got all these acres of woods, all I'm asking for is my *yard*."   And I said, "Whether you like it or not, I'm mowing." And the smells quit.

These things…they are agile, they can be vicious…you know, any primate pushed can be vicious.   I wish I could get you down here and put you over on the other side of the house and let you experience this. I feel like I'm under siege at night.   While I was mowing I was getting assaulted with these odors and my heart's pounding because I know they're close, and I started thinking, What is the *purpose* of them making themselves known. There's bound to be some sort of reason.   There's nothing I have that they could want, except knowledge.   It's not like they want to live in my house.   It's not like they want to borrow my *truck*.   If they ever got to know human beings and what we are capable of….   I feel like a guinea pig. *Okay, this makes her anxious, and this makes her feel good, watch her relax.*   What would happen if they decided, *You know what, we want to take back this area*?   There's really no way to explain it except I almost feel like I'm in a war zone.   At night, every single window is covered.

July 11th, 2008, a Phone Conversation between No-Bite and Me (after midnight)

— I can just barely make him out.

—You mean hearing him or seeing him?

—I'm seeing him.   He's hiding his face behind a tree, but he's about two foot on each side of this one-foot tree.

—Is he moving at all, or stock still?

—He's just swaying, with his head right behind the tree. Oh, that is so   strange.   He's   just   standing   out   there   behind   that   tree.

—How far away?

—Forty foot?

[She goes back indoors]

—I'm still shaking. Had you not been on the phone, I would not have gone out there.

—Can you peek out any windows, or are they all just completely blacked out?

—Let me go into the bedroom. I got sheers on there that I can hide behind. I don't see him behind that tree, but that doesn't mean he hasn't moved to another one. Hold on just a second... Okay, I have a half-moon-shaped driveway, and he has moved to the other side of the driveway...

—What's he doing right now?

—They just stand and *look*.

—Behind anything or—

—Behind another tree, but he's not really all that behind it now, it's like half of him is behind it and half of him is not, because I can see where his head is...

—What's the light source? Is it moon or stars?

—The only light I got right now is from the front porch and I can just barely make him out, only because he's swaying. I don't understand why they sway. If they'd hold their asses still they wouldn't be seen so easily.

—I know, but often people say they sway, like gorillas. As though they need to be more intimidating than they already are.

—I'm wondering if it helps their binocular vision.

—That's an idea, yeah.

—He's walking off, he's going toward the south, he's going back over to the pine grove.

—You can see him walking?

—Yeah. It just looks like a leisurely walk, just woop-de-doop, ,you know.

— Aren't you just amazed that they even exist?

—It's sort of like looking at a gruesome car wreck. You can't take your eyes off of it, but you can't dare look away. I feel intimidated more than anything else. I'm amazed at how graceful they are. When they move out of view it's a glide. You don't see them *step*. It's like they're on tracks, and it blows me away because you can't hear the bastards. They are big, they are hairy, they're everything that nightmares are made of, but they're not imagination any—eye-glow, hold on. This one's shorter. All I saw was the eye-glow, in the same area across my driveway. I'm shaking so bad. If I drop the phone I'll grab ya as quick as I can. I don't understand why they're so damn curious. From watching me the months I was here, without anybody here, from Halloween until January 10th, until my daughter moved here. So for all those days, I was here by myself. So what is so damn *fascinating*? I got an epiphany today where it was like, We're losing our spot on the food chain, folks.

—We're probably like a car wreck to them, too. If they have an opportunity, where they don't feel threatened, like in this case, and they can just feast their eyes on a human being in its—

—In its own little habitat, too?

—You're like a zoo to them. If they'd wanted to hurt you, they'd have done it a long time ago.

—Unless they were sizing me up.

—They're probably just playing around with you.

—Well, I *don't like the way they play*. Oh there goes another one. That one was little, though.

—What's he doing?

—He just turbo-charged across the driveway on all fours, and disappeared into the trees. Man, he was *quick*. It's like watching a movie and using the fast-forward button X2.

July 19th, 2008

I've made an all-out effort to repel them.

First, I did a big hunt through the house and scrounged up four cameras, which don't work anymore. I mounted them on all four sides of my house.

Second, I spread chemical crystals, flea and tick repellent, on lots of fire ant mounds and by the edge of my lawn. The ladies on the forum suggested this, because it's worked for them.

And then third, I went around my property line and told them *again* that this is *my place* and that they could have all the miles of woods around here but to leave me my house and yard.

Late yesterday evening I was able to sit on the front porch (porch light on) without heightened anxiety. The coonhound, although alert, was more relaxed. She did not bark or whine even during the period of time she was alone outside, which has not happened for many weeks. Lu was so relaxed while I was outdoors she laid down on her side and even closed her eyes.

Whether the result of walking the property and establishing "boundaries," chemically treating the mounds of fireants in the yard, mounting dummy cameras on the house, or even the beneficial psychological effects of me actually doing something constructive—I slept like a baby last night! Nothing hit the window screens, no vocalizations in the yard, even the dogs and cats appear to be much more relaxed.

Right now, I get the feeling the Ancient Ones (as I like to call them) are a *bit* upset with me. When I talk to the woods, it almost feels I am talking to myself. No longer do they give me a responding wood knock. I feel a bit guilty, but I certainly did enjoy that full night of sleep last night. And I definitely enjoy being able to sit on my front porch without being intimidated.

July 20th, 2008

I think I'm busted. I heard a racket on the south side of the house during the night, and I now have a pile of eight sticks lying right under one of the dummy cameras. The whacking on the side of the house was probably a Foot systematically lobbing sticks at the camera trying to activate it. Most likely they have now either figured out it doesn't work or they're wondering how it works without flashing. Dang! These rascals are smart! I figured with the dummy cameras AND chemically treating the yard so they can't approach the cameras would solve the problem for at least a week or so. It took them EXACTLY TWO DAYS. Guess it's back to the drawing board. I know who the dummy is now!

The Jacobs Creature
Clear Photos of a Juvenile Sasquatch, NE Pennsylvania, 2007

One of the remarkable features of Sasquatch behavior is their uncanny ability to avoid trail cameras. Researchers have found their machines: 1) violently destroyed; 2) still strapped to the same trees but pulled around 180 degrees, now facing thick brush instead of the trail; 3) turned off; 4) filled with pictures of sticks or branches being waved in front of the lens, apparently in order to trip the mechanism.

Sasquatch are endowed with a brain at least twice the size of our own, much of which is probably devoted to memorizing their territory in exquisite detail. A camera suddenly appearing, even if "cleverly" camouflaged, would stand out like a fresh pile of doo-doo on our living-room carpet.

As researchers have come to know, this creature goes to great lengths not to be filmed or photographed, even at habituation sites. Linguist Scott Nelson, who studies Sasquatch spoken language (see Chapter Six), has offered a parallel: "American Indians felt that a photograph captured a part of their spirit, their soul. We modern, species-centric humans think, 'How can Sasquatch *possibly* understand what photographs even are?' But who are we to say? Why do we hardly ever catch Sasquatch on trail cameras? I believe that we take two steps into the forest and they know exactly what's going on."

However, the young of any species are far less savvy, less cautious than the adults, and thus, in late September 2007, among various images of wildlife on his trail camera, hunter Rick Jacobs found two that he couldn't explain.

Images Captured by Rick Jacobs; the first shows a black bear cub

Such is the strange level of resistance even among Sasquatch researchers themselves, and cryptozoologists generally, that many have dismissed "The Jacobs Creature" as a sickly black bear, and a raging controversy has ensued, even though the arms and legs, in relation to the torso, are obviously much longer than those of any bear on the face of the Earth.

Based on measurements taken by researcher Paul Mateja, who visited the site, this juvenile Sasquatch would stand less than three feet tall.

With the help of limb-to-torso-ratio calculations by several colleagues, I have been able to conclusively demonstrate the provenance of the little figure shown in these images; see YouTube: "The Jacobs Creature: Photo Analysis."

****

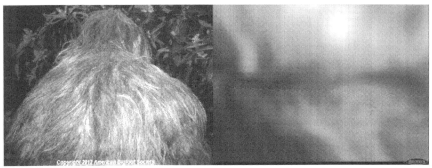

Trail camera photo submitted anonymously to researcher Melissa Hovey; it's not 100% authenticated, but thanks to M.K. Davis's analysis, I'm inclined to take it as genuine.

Close-up image of a mouth up against the lens of an Olympic Project camera; saliva recovered was found by the Ketchum Study to contain Sasquatch DNA (see Chapter Seven).

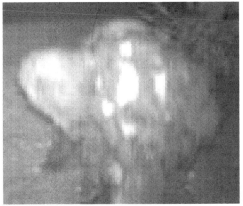

Figure photographed beneath Frank Siecienski's apple tree, southwestern Vermont, dwarfs any man pictured in the same spot (see Steve Kulls: Squatch Detective Radio Archive).

Chapter Four

TIMBER!
(The Vermont Project 2009-2010)

The bogeyman finds its genesis in the old central European gods. The Slavic for god is "bog." After Christianity came to central Europe and made its way to the British Isles, many of the deities from previous beliefs became evil spirits. It is natural to assume that the gods of pre-Christian Britain became known as these nasty, horrible, frightening or mischievous beings—ancient pagan gods, demons and devils, bogs, bogeys, or boggles. There was a time when a saucer of milk or a slice of bread left outside the door at night became an offering to the old gods.

—The BBC Homepage

Werewolf legends appear to have originated in the German countryside around Cologne and Bedburg in the year 1591. Many claimed to have found torn limbs on their properties and scores feared to travel in the surrounding wooded areas.

—Maryann Paige

Spring 2009—Sounds of a Sasquatch Stakeout

Late April, I duly report to the ravine, ready for a fresh and dramatic season of research, now equipped with a just-purchased FLIR PathfindIR thermal imaging camera, prepared for Thumper's next visit; I'll be able to "see" him through his heat signature, passively, without recourse to any harsh, visible light.

But I find the area badly compromised by clear-cut logging, great swathes of forest leveled and, up along the ridgeline, human structures springing up, driveways pushing through woods, leading to cement foundations and orderly stacks of lumber.

Undeterred, I camp in my old haunt, where Thumper visited and circled me for six hours the year before. This time around, though, night after night after night...simply zero luck. Maybe my breaking out the spotlight ruined our game after all; perhaps Thumper himself was not alienated (witness the three gifts) but those in *charge* of him were. Also, I find no new stick or tree structures, just the decaying remains of those from the past.

Okay, *improvise*, I think. *Diversify, be like them.* I think, *No wonder they've vacated this scene, people messing it up*, and then I remember a spot twelve miles due west of here, a small, secluded lake, and a certain BFRO report I once investigated. On May 28, 2006, a young man wrote to tell us,

> I was going four-wheeling and right when I got to the middle of the woods on the trail, I saw a log blocking the trail so I decided to turn around to go back the way I came. Right when I started to turn around I saw this thing that was about 7 feet tall running on 2 feet through the woods. It jumped over a log and went down a hill. So I bolted back to my camp and told everyone my experience. Almost all of them believed me so I had my uncle come back to where I saw it and we found a huge track about 16 inches long with 5 toes just like a human.

When I interviewed the witness, I found him to be articulate and credible. I also visited his grandparents at their seasonal "camp" (little house) and they vividly conveyed how freaked out the poor guy had been when he returned from his abortive trail ride: "White as a sheet." I'd found his account especially interesting because the Sasquatch of the area would definitely know the human routines by heart, including the sound and usual trajectories of ATV travel, so it made sense that when this one vehicle uncharacteristically halted and turned about, *that's* when the male, having assumed the coast was clear, found himself suddenly caught out.

I spoke with the uncle, too, who told me the following story. Nineteen years earlier, he'd been partying with a group of friends on the shore of this same small lake—just half a mile from his nephew's future sighting—and there began a frightening barrage of large rocks sailing over their heads, launched from somewhere above on the wooded hillside. "They must have been at least the size of soccer balls, because they made this gigantic splash in the water," he said, "and no *person* could heave rocks that big anywhere near that far. I think there were probably eight or ten rocks thrown over us. We didn't really hang around after that."

And here's the kicker: This incident also took place during the last week of May.

I leave the ravine and begin exploring this new area, finding indeed many suggestive tree and stick structures, as well as trees whose bark has been removed in patches, possibly to expose a solid knocking surface.

May 18th, at dusk, near the little lake and alongside the same trail our ATV rider used, I set up my audio recorder as well as my thermal camera.   When I retrieve the equipment the next morning and then review, first, the audio file, I am treated to the best array of wood knocks I've ever heard on any recording—numerous firm thwacks, some distant but some extremely near the microphone, perhaps less than thirty feet.

Between 7:59 PM and 2:09 AM (when the audio recorder's battery quit), I count twenty-seven separate knocks, several of which are clustered into apparent communication *episodes*. In one instance, at 8:41 PM, three distinct impacts come from three distances (middle, then far, then very close) within just seven seconds. In another, at 10:33 PM, this very close knocker delivers two impacts, three seconds apart. And in a third instance, at 12:06 AM, eighteen seconds elapse between a nearby knock and an answer from middle distance.

Of course, the survival genius of this species includes their relationship to time, their enormous patience, how beneficially out of phase they are with our own temporal scale, so that what sounds to us like two unrelated knocks, twenty-five or fifty-five minutes apart, or more, may indeed be a paired call and response. They are playing the long game, while our meager attention span disables us from readily interpreting these signals as communication.

(You can eavesdrop with me upon this evasive language world at YouTube: "Sounds of a Sasquatch Stakeout.")

At first, I figure that a group must have been conducting a deer hunt, the knocks used as check-ins, to keep tabs on others' locations, and perhaps also to spook the deer in a certain direction. Sasquatch hunters coordinate their movements, gradually and deliberately driving the deer to where the killer hides, ready to pounce. Many "deer stashes" have been found continent-wide in which the carcasses' front legs are snapped—a rough and ready means of disabling nimble prey.

But another explanation is probably more accurate—that they became aware of the presence of my equipment in their territory, or that at least one did, initially. You'll notice that the knocker we hear most remains stationed for the duration not far from the microphone/thermal camera (which I failed to hide very well), perhaps a sentinel warning others away—or else keeping them away *in effect*, given that the knocks likely serve not only to inform group members of all their respective positions, but also to maintain tactical distance *between* these positions; thus, staying parked by the camera (once you recognize it as a threat) and then periodically knocking would keep your fellow group members safely clear of the compromised location. The single signals could mean, "I'm over here, where are you?   Hold your position until further notice," whereas doubles, triples, and various other patterns convey different messages.

Or indeed, both explanations could be true, because why even set up a system to establish a security zone around a camera if you are not also committed to hunting here tonight, beside this lake that's a magnet for deer and other game? Otherwise, why not simply vacate the area till the coast is clear?

Maybe there are even *three* sentinels deployed, one near, one far, and one at middle-distance, in order to cover the whole area with this strategic alert.   But we can't take *seeming* to the bank here, because how can we be sure the middle-distance and far percussions come from the same direction and quite the same distance each time?

But listening to the entire six-plus hours in real time does reveal that between knock events, there is nothing but silence from this nearest member—not only no vocals or stick-breaks or footsteps, but not even the slightest rustle in the leaves—which suggests that he is not, in fact, relocating at all but rather performing patient, solemn, ancient duty while the heat is on, and inadvertently providing us with an object lesson in how Sasquatch avoids Man.

I'm not sure, but this audio session may be the first documented case of their communicating in a forest setting over such an extended period of time, though long-term recording has been done at habituation sites.

Well, to put it mildly, I'm eager, after absorbing the audio, to view the video footage, which seems sure to contain pure gold. I inch through all nine hours scrupulously, second by second, but alas, the authors of the knocking do not once appear on-screen. (At 3:35 AM, the first and only creature cameo is a bobcat streaking across the trail.)

In other words: Camera-shunning mission accomplished.

I remember Jerry telling me, as we stood in the mid-winter night in Upstate New York, "Look how smart these guys are. They just have to make a little knock here and there and they know where everyone is. That's their radar."

And as linguist Scott Nelson observes (see Chapter Six), "American Indians felt that a photograph captured part of their spirit, their soul. If Sasquatch have anything in common with American Indians, that would explain one thing right there. We modern, species-centric humans think, How can they possibly understand what photographs even *are*? But who are we to say? Why do we hardly ever catch them on trail cameras? I believe that we take two steps into the forest and they know exactly what's going on."

And yet, I start camping here as often as possible.

My daughter, now three years old, likes to accompany me on reconnaissance missions in the area. One afternoon, we're exploring along a snowmobile trail little used in the off-season. We're about two miles from where I recorded the wood knocks, and we find a likely print, clear and distinct, seventeen inches long by eight inches wide, and impressed an inch into firm mud. She kneels with me to examine the find, and though toes are not evident, the imprint does lack any footwear tread. Also, we can make out a slight rise and fall, peaking in the middle, apparently reflecting the well-known "mid-tarsal break"; Sasquatch feet flex like that, as do those of the great apes, whereas ours feature the relatively rigid instep arch.

A little way down the trail, we come upon more tracks, this time a startling *series* of them, made by someone different, the imprints slimmer and just thirteen inches long, but just as smoothly free of tread marks. These steps form a nearly straight line, rather than the staggered pattern human trackways tend to exhibit. I measure the distance from toe of one print to heal of the next at thirty-two inches, about twice my own natural stride. The line proceeds eighty-five feet before veering into the thick ferns of the forest.

We return here periodically over the ensuing months but don't discover any new tracks—not through lack of application on my daughter's part, however. She'll squat down, considering, and say, "Nope, that one's not pushed down enough." Or: "Okay, let's pick the leaves outa there and see what we got…"

Half a dozen nights, I set up audio and video surveillance, aiming down this path, but succeed only in documenting the existence of a female moose.

Camping solo, I lie still while twilight thickens, receptively taking in the theater of life around me, trying to emanate good will, occasionally whooping or making wood knocks. I sleep behind a mossy boulder just a couple hundred feet down the trail from the wood-knocking extravaganza. It's the perfect spot because I am well hidden but can stand quickly, elbows on rock, and train my thermal camera on them as they pass on the trail.

They don't. I attach the camera to a tree to keep watch while I sleep. The video and audio files reveal nothing—no knocks, no vocalizations, no footsteps, no subtle stick-breaks.

One thing you learn: Beware "the perfect spot."

Leaflets Campaign

Memorial Day Weekend, I'm making small talk in my local country store and the owner mentions where she lives. I realize this is just half a mile from the young ATV driver's encounter. I tell her a little about my research (thankfully, she's open-minded) and then imitate a wood knock by making a hollow cluck with my tongue.

She looks at me in disbelief. "We hear that all the time by our place. I've always wondered what the heck it *was*. My husband says it's just a woodpecker, but I know it's not, because it's always just two knocks, and they sound exactly like the one you just did."

She goes on to explain that for years, her routine has been to get up and leave the house between 5:10 and 5:20 AM, in order to go open the store. "As soon as my screen door slaps shut behind me, that's when I'll hear it—a double knock coming through the woods from somewhere down near the base of the driveway, maybe a hundred and fifty feet away. This happens," she explains, "maybe four days a week."

I'm happy to hear this. "Are you usually the first person out on the road in the morning, in your area?"

"Yup, that's right. I never see another car on my road that early."

"Well, maybe this is a sentry, and he's signaling to the others: *They're up now, time to go.*"

"Wow."

Nor is this local meeting place finished offering me fruit. One morning soon after, I stop in for coffee and conversation. While I'm trying to poke holes in the skepticism of the clerk on duty, a man standing beside me at the counter asks, "You talking about Bigfoot?" "That's right." "Buddy of mine was hunting in the woods near here last November and saw what he thought was a bear scratching its back against a tree. But when it got done scratching, it walked away on two legs. He hasn't told anyone except me and his wife."

(I later learn that this sighting occurred less than two miles from the ravine.)

I start thinking: *If just in this one shop, serving a village of eight hundred, I've gotten two compelling leads, how many more resources might live in our several-town cluster?* So on a lark, I make up a leaflet summarizing my research and seeking information. I then spend two long afternoons sneaking two hundred and fifty copies into mailboxes. Eighty-seven are immediately returned to me by an angry rural mail carrier. One hundred and sixty-two go unanswered. Only one elicits a response, but one is plenty, and sets the course for the rest of my research season.

When I get home from my second round of deliveries, a voicemail awaits me. "Hi, it's amazing you dropped this sheet off. We need to talk." She expands when I call back. For the past five years, she's been hearing distinct wood knocks directly behind her house during the summer and fall, from the round mountain and the valley beside it. "They've been driving me kind of crazy, actually. I've never known what they could be."

"Have you heard knocks going back and forth, seeming to answer from different parts of the woods?"

"Sometimes, yes. They are kind of high-pitched and hollow, like bamboo. I've sat by the open window for hours at night, trying to figure this out. It mostly happens in the summertime."

Aha. This woman's property is located just three miles from the small lake where I recorded the knocks. It abuts an undeveloped wilderness area featuring two mountains, a ridge, and an extended valley. The lake is no longer quiet now; the summer people began returning to their camps back on Memorial Day Weekend, as they do every year. This explains a lot. Both of the reported events that prompted me to relocate here—the ATV encounter and the rock-throwing incident—occurred just before this human reflux, before the end of May, the last chance for Sasquatch to operate freely near the body of water, with its associated concentration of game. Then they simply relocate to this private nearby valley, where my new witness hears the knocks.

The woman takes my daughter and me up into the forest behind her house, at the base of her mountain, where we follow an overgrown logging road. Right away, I begin noticing broken branches on both sides, which range from very obvious, inch-and-a-half-thick limbs snapped and still hanging by a thread, to pencil-thin twigs, also hanging, or twisted off entirely, leaving a frayed nub. Some of these breaks are low, others nine feet high. In one case, a major limb halfway up a sapling has been yanked down, so that a remaining band of flesh is exposed and, on the opposite side of the tree, a lesser branch is treated the exact same way.

What we're finding amazes the leaflet responder; she's lived here for years and never noticed. I tell her nobody tends to notice such signs if they aren't clued in already, adding that there may be a connection to the behavior of great apes. Jane Goodall and Sue Savage-Rumbaugh, in their respective research projects, have found that male chimpanzees and bonobos, when foraging, will often scout on ahead, marking their trails so that the females and the young can follow along later. Then again, of course, in the case of Sasquatch, this behavior may have a very different purpose; perhaps each family employs its own style of marking—a territorial alert to outsiders.

Another day, exploring nearby, my daughter and I come across two trees framing a trailhead that exhibit no fewer than eleven such branch-breaks, two of which are more than eight feet high. Interestingly, this tree is located just at the head of a narrow valley, likely a prime hunting area. Also noted are several fresh pine boughs placed across the entrance to the trail.

See YouTube: "Entrance Breaks"

Just fifty feet past this tree, beside the trail, we find this simple RSS or T-pee made of trees brought from elsewhere and leaned here. This would still be interesting, but less so, if it weren't for its close proximity to the breaks and boughs.

No Trespassing!

As I poke around myself in this same valley, later, a striking thing occurs: I get chest pains. However, hypochondriac though I am, I do not seriously suspect angina. After all, I've been romping through woods, playing basketball, several times a week, and have never experienced the same. Also, the onset of pressure and discomfort coincides precisely with my entry into a particular portion of the forest, rife with stick and tree structures, and definitely charged with that "sizzle" of Sasquatch proximity, of brainy, musky power, of pure hominin craftiness.

Trees thicker than saplings are arched around me, higher than my head, each tied down by a weaving of branches into low bushes, or pinned to the ground by dead trees that have obviously been transported here from their source—no root system or stump appearing anywhere near. Limbs have been snapped and twisted; branches and other lengths of wood or bark have been leaned against one side of trees, and also against their opposite side, in a roughly symmetrical manner.

These chest pains interest, even *flatter* me, as I assume I'm being mildly "zapped." I squint up the incline, but can't see far through full summer foliage, so I experiment a little, finding that the sensations fluctuate with every slight shift in my posture, intensifying when I turn uphill and try even a single ascending step, tightening my respiration so as to actually *prevent* me from advancing. If this is due to small exertion alone, my heart is in terrible shape indeed, but no, I get the distinct impression, as many have reported, that I am not supposed to trespass any further, and in fact, I say aloud, "Okay, I understand. I'm going back down." The instant I turn around, all symptoms vanish.

Too Close for Comfort?

Over the rest of the summer, my camping nights are empty and quiet, until one night in the middle of September. I've been leaving food and gifts, in presumably propitious spots, since early spring, each time first taking a bite of the food myself, to show it's not dangerous, and devoutly sending out benign energy. Yet, these offerings are never taken, much less *exchanged*. I even build a gracious, sincere stick structure at one of my gifting stations. If the problem is not, somehow, *me*, then I think perhaps the forest primates in this neighborhood are just a lot more self-possessed than others, more scrupulous in the mandate not to consort with the hairless ones. I know that they are here, thanks to the witnesses, the tracks, the knocks I've recorded, and the structures, yet they will not accept anything from me. I tell myself that it all depends upon the tactical disposition of the adults (or just the Alpha male?) in any given clan, the boundaries and degree of order and control instilled in the group—how well the leaders are able to rein in the more venturesome juveniles—and that so-called "hot spots" simply represent family systems where such discipline is lax.

One murky August pre-dawn, after yet another fruitless night, I'm driven from my fern nest by a downpour. Drenched and crestfallen, dragging all my gear, slipping in mud, unable to find the trail, I'm suddenly cheered by the memory of an anecdote: Glenn Miller's orchestra was en route to a gig one winter night when their bus broke down a mile from the venue, forcing them to slog across a slushy cornfield, dressed in their tuxedoes, carrying their instruments, shoes getting stuck in the mud. On the other side of the field, they came upon a charming little farmhouse, and through the window they saw a family sitting by a fire, cozy and laughing. One musician turns to another and says, "I can't believe people actually *live* like that."

All told, during this research season of 2009, I plant my night media kit twenty-three times, sleep in the woods myself nineteen times, and of these forty-two field tests, exactly *two* come back positive; thus, my pet estimate of five percent "action" has held firm. The first is the hi-fidelity wood knocks recorded at the lake in May; the second is what befalls me on September 15th.

Desperate, by this point, for some contact, one late afternoon I assault a mountain I've only eyed with trepidation, from many angles, these past months. It's connected by a saddleback to the mountain rising from behind my leaflet responder's property, but is more secluded, has always seemed remote, somehow off-limits, *theirs*.

With twenty-five pounds of gear in my backpack (the thermal camera's 12v battery comprising most of that) and pulling behind me an unwieldy black plastic bagful of bedding, I make my way through dense forest to the base, then climb. There are no human pathways up here, scarcely any game trails, so I keep simply pushing through brambles and thick deadfall as the grade increases, slipping occasionally onto my butt, needing to stop to rest more and more often, sweating heavily.

Though I keep reminding myself not to be surprised if it should recur, this time no cardiothoracic warning puts me in my place, so I take the liberty of continuing to rise gradually into the sky, till, at sunset, chilly, I can see the entire valley, the ridges and swells that form it, all covered with autumn colors now, spread out below me in every direction.

Checking the clock, I'm startled to learn I've been at this ascent for more than two hours. Still a healthy distance from the summit, I fall to in a hollow and break out the food, water, and blankets.

By 10:17, I've already been snoring for two hours (as the audio recording attests). It's a perfectly still night until the first crack—a quick, sharp split of heartwood—but this does not wake me. At 10:17:29, two clear thumps hit the ground, very reminiscent of my visitor in the ravine fifteen months earlier. This sound, too, fails to wake me, and the scene falls quiet for four minutes, except for the human's breathing. At 10:22, the tree cracks again, much louder this time. I wake up and say, "Hello?" Propping myself on an elbow, I try to look around, but on this moonless night, under a thick canopy of leaves, can't see two feet in front of me.

And then, the tree undergoes a stretched-out process, for thirteen long seconds, of creaking, snapping, resisting, being downed by force. Bewildered, I say, "Whoa!" I'm not afraid because, when I look straight up I can make out the top of the tree tilting slowly against a backdrop of stars, awfully close by, yes, but tipping in an arc *next* to me rather than on top of me. After it crashes, massively yet invisibly, I take stock of the situation. I'm okay, something has happened, and now it's time to lift the thermal camera and pan the area.

This is a good model, but just one-quarter the price of those used on BFRO expeditions; and it lacks a very useful feature, an eye-piece, and connects by cable directly to my video camera. The upshot is that, until the next day when I review the footage, I can't see what the thermal imager is seeing. Of course, I could have flipped open the camcorder's LCD screen, but it would have glowed brightly, and ever since Thumper, I've drilled myself on staying, no matter what, in *dark mode*.

I scan the camera back and forth, slowly, blindly. Here I am, in a situation similar to that of the East Texas night ten months earlier, but the trouble is, just like back then, *I do not allow myself to realize it.* How strange that even someone who is devoting himself to this quest can still be afflicted by what Jerry in Upstate New York identified as the most common stumbling blocks: disbelief and impatience. Hearing nothing, I wield the camera for only two minutes, and then simply lie back down and return to sleep. *Return to sleep!?* It's as if some drug of thoughtlessness or apathy was administered to me.

The video file shows my panning across bland gray forest and then—what's this? Sitting in my office back home, peering at the tiny screen on my video camera, I actually do a double-take. The faint outline of a figure, person-like, stock still on its hands and knees. I remember numerous reports of Sasquatch "hitting the deck" and freezing when trying to elude perception, not moving a muscle, not making a sound, applying an ancient gift for patience against *Homo sapiens*' meager attention span.

What I now conclude is that this slow, deliberate daredevil first gave the tree a little push—CRACK!—and then, when that didn't get a rise out of me, he thumped the turf, waited a while longer, and then went ahead with the main event, though even then, he drew the process out. And I rewarded his tactics—"Hello?" "Whoa!"—like a puppet on strings.

I switch from camera screen to computer monitor, playing and replaying the relevant sequence of footage, adjusting the contrast.   The crouching figure doesn't appear as bright as a living organism, in clear view, normally would on thermal, but Sasquatch do not tend to permit any clear view, and this one appears to be hiding behind a bush or other screen of leaves, accounting for the hazy quality of the image.

I should have said that *most* of the figure appears dim in the footage. Its left foot is a much starker white, which would only make sense: The sole is pointed toward the camera lens, skin that, presumably bare, would emanate more heat. Considering hair-cover, then, it also strikes me that at this time of year in Vermont, mammals' thick winter coats would be mostly grown in, making them appear much dimmer on thermal than in spring or summer.

That dawn, I open my eyes to see that the felled tree lies perfectly parallel to my body, and I can hardly believe how close; I get up and measure it at six and a half feet from my sleeping pad. Of all the hundreds of trees within earshot on every side of me, it was just this one that came down. Examining it, I find that it's not, indeed, a very healthy specimen, but a) it sounded plenty stout enough to resist the steady force being applied, and b) a hardier tree would not have represented such an attractive target for a prankster, especially if, as is my guess, this prankster was a juvenile, like Thumper, probably; adults tend not to take such playful chances.

(You can follow the whole incident on YouTube: "The Vermont Project 2009" and "Field Audio from my Two Close Encounters in Vermont.")

But what if he wasn't *playing*? Over time, I do start to wonder, and about the ethics of "invading their territory" to begin with. It all hinges, of course, on the underlying attitude, which is a tall order to interpret, on the definition of *Timber!*—good-natured joust or grievous warning? I suppose the latter would be easier to lean toward, if it weren't for the thumps beforehand; if you're trying to rouse someone from gentle sleep, and then wait patiently for four minutes before escalating the gambit, do you likely *hate* his presence on the mountain?   Why not just drop the bomb immediately? Was this enforcer or imp?

(The same questions apply to an incident two years later. Listen at YouTube: "New Hampshire Tree-Push: September 25th, 2011, 5:31 AM.")

And don't forget, they come freely to *our* properties, ready for a rousing game of wits, slapping our homes, swiping or relocating our yard things, peeking in our windows, pestering us with pebbles tossed on roofs,

Mimicking our voices, spying on our young—and no doubt taking great pleasure in all of our comical reactions. I'm just turning the tables, and much less mischievously, to say nothing of any weapon or ill intent. I'm lying here on a pad, trying to get some sleep. We are two species who have co-existed alongside one another for millennia, mostly segregated. We do occasionally tangle, tease and harass each other; is this not, too, in our core nature?

Or is my effort at documentation a deadly weapon in its own right, a form of would-be capture, a violation of the fundamental spirit of the game, given that their very survival depends upon never becoming widely known?

The 2010 Season

Signs of Mind

After another unbearable winter stuck inside—I don't ski or snowshoe—I get an early start on the forest again. As though scatter-shot from a cannon, unable or unwilling to settle down, I camp in every conceivable kind of location within my ten-square-mile grid—from lakeshore to mountain summits to rocky grottoes to a flat boulder-top nine feet off the ground—still "armed" with my thermal camera, avid for footage, but during the next seven months, the Sasquatch clan keeps its distance.

Signs of their presence abound, however. In April, I discover another "pinwheel" formation, ten miles from the one I found three years ago in the ravine. It's at the base of a feature I chose to explore because on old maps it is called "Satan's Point." It's often fruitful to key in on such spooky place names; these may reflect earlier generations' healthy respect for areas not fit for human trespass, especially after dark.

Sasquatch probably return year after year, century after century, to land offering private havens, valuable dietary resources, and good hunting; moreover—who can say?—certain spots may exercise an emotional or spiritual pull, due, for instance, to ancient burial grounds.

Like the other wheel, this one too has eight spokes, but whereas the structure back in the ravine formed its total with four trees traveling clean through the center and out the other side, this one uses five, two of which do not go through; both wheels, though, intersect tightly at their hubs.

Found at the new site (2010), ten miles from the ravine; see YouTube: "The Vermont Project 2010"

Compare to the one found in the ravine (2007)

I also find an excellent arch that, unlike most others, exhibits a dramatic rupture at the top, demonstrating great force applied in the formation.

Photographed much later, in January 2012;
see YouTube: "'Squatchiest Place in Vermont?"

And really, is it any wonder? What if, having never heard of Sasquatch, we were asked to consider the notion of a primate operating in our forests, endowed with an enormous brain, brimming with creative spirit and manual skill but blocked for security reasons from fully expressing itself, exercising these faculties, in any blatant, unguarded manner—would we not be obliged to *predict* something very like the deep-woods manifestations, made from available materials, that North Americans have been coming across for centuries, puzzling over or, more often dismissing with a shrug? A few of these constructions may be ambitious symbols or artworks, others mere directional signs, trail or territorial markers… the rest simply idle doodling born of nervous energy, boredom, or the need for the young to practice their craft.

A young gorilla at play

An orangutan building a nest

Serendipities

In June, I present an informal public lecture about Sasquatch, after which an old high school friend comes up to me. It's great to see her again, and even better once she shares some information. Mind you, during my talk I did not share with the audience where my research area is, only that it's in our general vicinity. So my old friend says, "I've been interested in this topic for a long time, and over the last few years two different people have told me they've seen a Bigfoot crossing the road in front of them, on Route 'X.'" When she mentions the route number, it's another of those delicious moments, because this is the same state highway that runs between the small lake (where I recorded the knocks) and, three miles away, the mountain where the tree crashed beside me, behind the leaflet responder's house. Of all the hundreds of area roads this woman could have specified, this is the one most affirming match; not that I don't already know they are here, or here at *times*, but in this business, doubt can always sneak in again after numerous lonesome overnights.

Now more thoroughly than ever, I scrutinize Route X, trying out every measly side-road. The least traveled of these, muddy and narrow and strewn with undercarriage-damaging rocks, leads eventually to the base of the very mountain where *Timber!* occurred, putting me in position to ascend from a new angle. Halfway up, I find a trail lined by young trees and leading to a large open field of ferns. Along this trail, looking carefully, I find a snapped branch, then two, then quickly more and more, until they total sixteen, all within just seventy feet of progress. This all looks very much the same as the marked trail up behind the witness's house, last summer, just a quarter mile away on a different face of the mountain. Here, too, some breaks are at my height, some far above my head, too high for deer. And do deer, anyway, snap thick branches and leave them hanging? Also, in light of what happens next, signs point to primate.

(See YouTube: "The Vermont Project 2010.")

Independence Day, this year, turns out to be one of those pivotal moments in a person's life. I am slated to attend a softball game and barbeque in the afternoon—a gathering put on by the writing program I've been teaching in for the past twenty years, since 1989. Before that, I got my MFA degree through this same program, starting at age twenty-two; in six months I will be fifty. In other words, basically my entire adult life has been spent here at this institution, in the field of writing and literature. Yet, for the past couple of years, since I released the first edition of this book, *Impossible Visits*, the atmosphere around my involvement has shifted. Although many students are fascinated by my research, pumping me for further information, none of my faculty colleagues seems to place even an ounce of value on this avenue of inquiry; nor do they esteem my choice to produce the book "off the grid," independent of the traditional system of publishing houses; in fact, I have been placed on unpaid leave-of-absence, so that I can "correct" my publishing picture. So we're dealing with stigma on top of stigma here. The faculty chairperson has recommended to me that I "diversify" my writing output, which I take as code for, "You better get out of this Bigfoot rut"; this increasing chill in the air has made me feel distinctly unwanted.

Before driving to campus for the softball game, though, I visit the mountainside, and this newly discovered high fern field, to retrieve the gear I've left overnight—audio recorder and thermal camera, strapped to a birch, aimed back toward that "trail of interest" with all those snapped branches. No sooner have I removed camera from tree than I hear, not far upslope through thick trees, maybe fifty yards away, a double wood knock, so resonant and rich and real that it brings tears to my eyes. It is by far the finest I have ever been graced with in person, and second only to the all-night series of knocks I recorded last year, down by the lake. Furthermore, this one has occurred at 3:10, smack dab in the middle of a bright afternoon.

(Overnight, the audio recorder picks up numerous similar examples, though of course nothing appears on the thermal video footage.)

I say, "Hello hello?" but, lacking my knocking club today, I cannot respond in kind, can only whoop nervously several times, which is met with silence. No matter; I take what I just heard as a robust overture. Even if the signal was meant for another Sasquatch, warning him or her of this human intruder, I was nonetheless *allowed* to hear it—and so I let myself feel, if momentarily, lifted from the modern world and gathered up into the fold, ancient and embracing.

At the softball game, then, true to form, the students are sweet and appreciative, the faculty, cordial yet cool. All the while, replaying through my head is the woody welcome from the forest.

The next day, I hand in my resignation and decide to devote myself now, full-time, unapologetically and for the rest of my life, to the study of this kindred species. Oddly, our government seems to back me; I qualify for unemployment insurance because Sasquatch research, and publishing its outcomes within a new-media venue, does not yet constitute "egregious misconduct on the job."

Once upon a time, I valued the aesthetics of language and storytelling above subject matter. Indeed, fiction writing offered the freedom my imagination craved. But ever since my first BFRO expedition in 2005, I've been undergoing an internal shift away from story for story's sake, toward content and calling—a shift that culminated the moment a dense tree trunk was struck twice, above me.

Sometimes, I used to ask my father, while he hunkered year after year over piles of student manuscripts, whether he'd be doing so, rather than writing his own books, if he knew he only had a short while left to live. Showing no signs of illness, still youthful in his early-to-mid-sixties, he'd always brush off my macabre and cheeky question.

And then, he died of a heart attack at sixty-six. Suddenly now, he's been gone for eight and a half years already. Before very long, I'll have been gone for eight and a half years already, too. I've enjoyed working with students, helping their literary projects to evolve, but at my own death, will I wish I'd spent more time on their work, diluting the main chance, while intelligent giants waited out there, with so much to teach me?

Halloween Night

Peanut M&Ms and pitch dark are a constant, but while I huddle beneath several thick blankets here on my last camp-out till next spring, I reflect on how much has changed since my first BFRO expeditions, six years ago. *That* guy was so fresh and naïve, expecting Earth-shaking encounters each night; by the same token, he didn't understand how to believe in Sasquatch. Now I am way past belief, planted in certain knowledge, yet this progress also brings disappointment, because I can't fool myself anymore: They vastly prefer their own company.

It's been an awfully long and unrequited season out here, though October has finally brought more daylight wood knocks, including a strong series of four across a valley, in immediate response to my own. (Again, see YouTube: "The Vermont Project 2010.")   But why have they immaculately avoided me after sunset, not even deigning to *threaten* me like last year? Maybe they are saying, *During daylight, if we feel like it, we might play, but at night you're in a whole different game, Fella—The world belongs to us, you should not be out here, and we won't give you the satisfaction of sharing it.*

Stubbornly, however, I keep on coming out, even now that fourteen hours stretch between dusk and dawn. But why? Frustration, a sense of personal insult, some chip on my shoulder...*What?!*

As clouds swallow the last few stars, I try to dig to the root emotion. It's as though I feel abandoned by someone, someone who has never been *with* me to begin with.

"But they don't need us." Jerry's voice echoes in my head.

I guess I simply want them to *know* me. Whenever I envision myself coming face to face with a Sasquatch, I see a puny man breaking down in sobs of gratitude and relief. Yet, how can their apathy have *anything* whatsoever to do with a person, making him sulk up in the sky? I could just as well complain of being neglected by the outer planets, or by zinc.

Unless...some ancient rupture occurred between our two races, some persistent wound that needs mending. If so, then my solo camping campaign (or anyone's) can be seen as positively heroic. Here I am, single-handedly bucking the entire trend of human culture over these past ten thousand years, ever since we began growing crops and staying put in villages, fortified against the night, ever since the die was cast, the grand roles established, *Homo sapiens* proceeding to make over the Earth in our image, Sasquatch operating in what's left over, in the negative spaces, a strategic lifestyle of family and clan, appropriating the land only modestly with sapling bends, tree twists, the occasional incautious set of prints for a human girl in Vermont to step in, comparing feet.

My thermometer now reads thirty-one. I wish I had a campfire, but I'm sticking with my chosen method, passive receptivity in pitch dark. Not sleepy, I've got plenty of time to assess these past four research seasons, from 2007 to the present. 112 times I have camped out or planted my stealth media kit, about half of each. These gambits have yielded precisely *five* unmistakable "hits":

1) The tree crash on my first overnight in the ravine, September 2007;
2) The extended visit from Thumper, June 2008, followed by three successive gifts left at my home;
3) The excellent wood knocks recorded in May of 2009;
4) September 2010's *Timber!*; and
5) The knocks recorded on the night of July 3rd-4th, 2010.

And these past two seasons have found me constantly switching sites, using no fewer than *thirty-seven*, falling into the weak-minded notion, after each new dud night, that the grass must be greener "over there," past the crest of that next hill. At the time, my forays seemed valiant; in retrospect, juvenile—a breathless, jittery array of lunges. Yes, it all flies in the face of the wise counsel of veteran habituators, the patience counseled by Robert W. Morgan in his *Field Manual,* a consistent and repetitive routine, rooted to a single special spot, for as long as it takes.

Occasionally, I project a plaintive whoop into the void and then listen, hungry yet hopeless. Meanwhile, away off in the human settlements below—and I imagine I can even hear their high-pitched calls, floating on the breeze—kids dressed as monsters are going door to door, ogres, trolls, goblins, zombies, vampires, and werewolves, all manner of spirits at home in the night, who ordinarily respect the threshold between worlds. Once a year, though, our childlike yearning for concourse with the Other Side can be indulged, as we   catch a glimpse of whatever may chance to show out—"monster" comes from the Latin "monstrare," *to show*—but only in the form of safe and miniature renditions of these primordial bogeymen, parading briefly before our hearth.

Our approach to transcendence is to *schedule* it, to take a glimpse into another world, and then to slam the door tight again. But Sasquatch, I think, occupies one world, with no opaque structures to block the view. As Molly Gloss writes in *Wild Life,* "Perhaps they are not lower animals after all, but an evolutionary advance—have grown beyond poor *Homo sapiens* and understand the world well enough that they have no need to construct a civilization upon it."

Here's what I think, Sasquatch. I think you arrived already exactly where you need to be weeks before we mastered flint, and you've stayed put ever since. This is your species knack, to live in an expansive present tense, in self-sufficient cells, microcosmic clans. The only "progress" you pay attention to is each new cycle of seasons spinning across the land, each recurring shift in game and vegetation, your circuit of favorite haunts and havens. And any wood knocks I may hear from you tonight are the selfsame heard, this morning, by mastodons.

The Clock of the Long Now
An Impulse toward the Sasquatch Time Scale

"I want to build a clock that ticks once a year," said project designer Danny Hillis. "The century hand advances once every one hundred years, and the cuckoo comes out on the millennium. I want the cuckoo to come out every millennium for the next 10,000 years. In some sense, we've run out our story, which was the story of taking power over nature."

In 1999, The Long Now Foundation purchased part of a mountain in eastern Nevada, at an elevation of 10,000 feet, whose white limestone cliffs make an ideal site for the 10,000-year Clock. Most of the two-mile-long swath of land is covered by a forest of ancient bristlecone pine trees. Bristlecones are considered the world's oldest living thing. One tree in the Snake Range was determined to be over 4,900 years old.

Ideally, it will do for our thinking about time what the photographs of Earth from space have done for our thinking about the environment. The clock will be like a telescope through time. The world's slowest computer. It serves no useful purpose, unless you think that taking a long view is the responsible thing to do for us as a civilization. We are in the middle of the long now—a span of 20,000 years. We don't know how to think of ourselves as a civilization. 10,000 years is about as long as the history of human technology. We have fragments of pots that old.

You arrive at a flat knoll where you see a cave ahead. Peering into the cave, you gradually make out a giant pendulum swinging back and forth, one pass every ten seconds. You proceed into the cave and realize you are actually within the clock mechanism itself. Climbing up a spiral staircase, you come to the fastest of the mechanical calculation devices, which chimes once per day. You climb up flight after flight through slower and slower mechanisms until you arrive at the last one, which records the procession of the equinoxes. When you reach the top of the stairs you are in a room several stories high that, at midday, is brightly lit by the sun coming directly in line with a slit in the wall.

In a world of hurry, the clock is a *patience machine*. (LongNow.org)

Chapter Five

"A Radical Society that is Very Well Disciplined"— Habituation Sites Revisited

> The only thing I can compare it to is being mentally reborn. Nearly everything I thought I knew has been given a different slant. Once I dropped what I expected of these people, an entire culture was opened up to me. Because I was so fearful, these beings spoonfed me a little at a time. What I am able to tell you so far is this: These are a people who do not want to be "found." They fit in with humans like "gears." What humans lack, these people possess. What these people lack, humans possess.
>
> —No-Bite (Texas #2)

In early November, 2008, I travel south to spend time with the families of Texas #1 and Texas #2. I also meet up with Ammi from North Carolina, who has been forced to flee her home due to physical abuse by her husband. She was helped to relocate by Texas #2, whom she came to know through the habituators' private online forum.

Since 2008, I've been able to visit Texas #2 on three further occasions, making for a total of eighteen days (and nights) on-site; see Epilogue.

North Carolina

May 14ᵗʰ

We got some bad tornadoes through this area a few days back—eleven in this part of the state alone that night. We were in bed, and just before a storm hit here, someone outside our window said very loud, "Wah-Coh'-Too!" Just that one word, but it woke up my husband. I hadn't fallen asleep yet, and heard it clearly. It was like it was yelled at the window. It then sounded like someone tried to lift the back window. Frank jumped up, and headed toward the window, and about then, the storm winds hit hard. We both dove into a closet, until it passed. It didn't touch down right here, but just down the road.

It got really scary for a while, but all we lost was some large limbs here. Frank was getting mad, because I was excited that I finally heard one of their words clearly. I was saying, "Do you think it means, 'Wake up!' or that it is their word for 'tornado'?"

He says, "Who gives a shit, I'm in a friggin' storm, and you are worried about *them*?"

I said, "Yep, they worried about us, and they are still outside."

That just pissed his puppet more, so I shut up about it.

I still wonder what that word means.

May 18ᵗʰ

Had a bit more fun today....a poor soul broke down on the road in front of my house, with a cycle. I have to admit, I took some zoom shots first, from the porch, before I saw how scared he was getting. He actually got off the bike, and tried to hide behind it. Said my dogs were creeping him out, barking at him. He said the barks were coming from the dogs, and echoing behind him...poor guy was really scared. Never saw anyone load a bike so quick.

I didn't explain the wooks or the infrasound to him...just let him think it was the dogs. Actually, one dog *was* barking, but the rest were just laying there watching him. The one kept barking when I came out. He commented how she seemed to "look right thru him." She was barking at the wooks behind him.

They backed up out of the wheat when I came out to the road, and I fussed at them about scaring him, when he left. I'm sure they got a kick out of it. I got a "fear wave" of infrasound when I fussed at them, and told them, "Nice try, it don't work on me anymore, I know what it is." It stopped.

It is going to be a strange summer, knowing about them this year.

I searched some online for Indian words. The closest I could find is Apache. "ya-kos'" = "clouds," and "tu'" = "water." Together it would sound very close to what I heard.

[To me:] Best of luck in that ravine tonight, Chris. I still won't camp with them. I'm not that bold here yet at night.

May 22nd

I found two ripe mulberries on my art easel today....Wow...I went straight to the tree, didn't know they had dropped. The ground was clean under the tree, except for one small pile left there. Guess I'm on rations for those.

Can't blame them, I love them too. That explains why they have left my strawberries alone for a few days. Well, at least they are sharing this year. They didn't do anything else at the easel yet....just swiping a bottle of paint every couple days, and leaving me "gifts".... mostly rocks, and a few pinecones.

Even now, I still feel some days that I am no closer to knowing them than when I started. And really I'm not. Nights can still get crazy on a whim, but those have gotten to be more rare than normal here now. There are a few of them who interact, and respond to me here, when they want to, but it is never on demand, anytime I want. They still won't just come out and show themselves, without it being accidental, or as a threat, a brief move. And I still piss them off when I cut the grass, or go into my woods for any reason. They let me know, by disrespecting my house, and hitting on it, climbing up on the roof or porch just to make noise, or irritating the dogs to keep them barking all night.

I can also draw a whizzed-by pinecone, stick, or dirt clod, if I am mowing. So I let hubby mow now.   I have pics of him yelling at the woods here, and just staring them down.   He has given up on the total unbelief in them existing, and has settled into just not wanting to discuss them at all.

I think I have established that the house is ours. But they still claim the outside, including the outbuildings here.   And we have a day/night sharing of the yard. But they want it left alone.

The garden I planted is mine, but they feel free to "trade me" my crops for rocks, sticks, pinecones, feathers, and bits of trash they find, of any kind.   Occasionally, I get a dead bird, turtle, frog, or rodent. "Mmmm...wookie stew" is all I can say when I find it raided, and those in the place of it. "Wookie stew" is a running joke between me and my hubby, when he asks on the phone from work, "What's for dinner tonight?"   Hubby really hates that joke.   They still consider all of the old fruit trees and berries here as theirs, and have let me know that.

They do make me smile and laugh at times.   Sometimes one will abandon the usual bird and animal calls, for a funky sound, to get my attention. Taking all of my garden tools and stacking them all up together. Lining pinecones in a circle, around my flower beds.   I find pinecones in the strangest places here.... and that always makes me smile.   I guess I like that they care to make me smile and laugh.   It makes me feel as if I am gaining some trust with them.   Sometimes I wonder if there are just one or two that "get a kick" out of watching the old woman happy, while the rest just still hate me being here at all.   One of those things I want to know, but may be better off not knowing.

I have learned to be vocal here with them.   I tell them if I like something they have done, and if I don't.   It's the mom in me...I have to "train everyone" to get along together, like I did when my kids where young. Or like a new relationship and the "control games" to establish the boundaries.   Only now, it's me and some people I can't usually see, sometimes can't hear, and whose language I don't know.   I think they do understand English.   I just don't know the other language they speak.   I think it is a very old native language, and like ours, has probably developed its own slang thru time.

Sometimes I enjoy them being here, and other times I wish my life was normal, and I didn't know about them. Normal as in, not discussing or arguing about what the people in our woods are doing, or have done. Normal as in Frank not yelling at me, "STOP INTERACTING WITH THEM!"

There are days when I try to interact with them, and days when I just ignore them. They do the same with me...days of interaction, and days you wonder where they are, as they are so quiet. I worry about them in stormy, very cold, and very hot weather.

I wonder how they deal with the bugs, as the biting flies and mosquitoes get bad here. Then I remind myself that they have never done it different, and are probably fine.

The hardest thing is pretending not to hear or notice them, when people who don't know stop in, and they decide to give a mid-day owl/dog chatter/bark and whistle number, from the nearby brush. When it stops your guests in their tracks, and they are staring at the spot it came from, and looking at you, or asking questions you don't want to answer, well it can be funny to me at times. I have a bad habit of laughing at that, and offering no explanation except "Yeah, that was weird." I have lost a few friends over that. But I would rather they think it is this place that is haunted, or strange, than tell them, and them think me crazy. I have done both, so I opt for the "strange place" and just meet them elsewhere, for company.

Finding out that my closest neighbor also knows about them helped a lot. It was a very awkward conversation start for us both, to learn it. "What do you hear?" "Have you ever heard...seen...?" Once we both realized we both knew, it was great. Plus we are both relieved that we have the places on both sides of their sleeping area, so we know they won't be bothered there. We agree that our nights are better spent in our houses. Seems they also have that night ownership in his yard too. It took us five years to have that conversation. Mainly, because he thought my dogs were stealing his chickens. Once I was able to tell him they have been known to "trade" for chickens too, we have gotten along better, though he wasn't aware of the "gift/trade value" of the local pinecones and rocks! He had never actually seen one of my dogs over there, but he had found some strange stuff in his chicken house. It also explained how the "dogs" were getting the coop unlatched. I had lost rabbits from cages here the same way.

May 28th

I did my easel thing here. Set it up right at the very edge of the woods, and with my back to them. I painted a pic of one peeking thru leaves, and left it and blank paper out. The first night they swiped (er *traded* for) a bottle of bright metallic blue, for two dead baby snapping turtles, and left paint splattered all over my chair, the ground, and the surrounding leaves.

When I found it the next day, I painted a picture of one of the turtles, and left it there, with some blank paper on the side. That night, they "painted" all over my easel, my pic, the paper next to it, the chair, leaves. Looked like a three-year-old got ahold of it. They gained a bottle of pink, and a sky blue that night. They also scattered my brushes all over the ground, around and under my chair.

The ground around the easel looked like I had eighty people stomping around it for a week, completely mashed and compacted down hard. A new very stomped trail appeared from the woods, leading directly to that spot.

Rain had me bring it up on the porch, where it has been since. I have heard them play around there late at night, and find a bottle or brush moved now and then, but no more painting, nor have they taken anything. They have left a few gifts, like a ripe mulberry on my easel. My kids are grown, so now I have some new "art" to hang on my fridge!

May 31st

I went out to water the garden today, and took my camera. I was home alone, and when I got to one side of the house, I decided to "make a rainbow" with the spray, into the sunlight there, partly to amuse myself.

So I was spraying away, and snapping pics, and I started thinking about when my granddaughter stayed with me last year, and how she loved to see me make rainbows, and she would play in the spray, running in and out, and singing "Somewhere Over the Rainbow" with me. I started singing it out loud, and was doing a silly little dance we used to do together, and didn't notice or hear hubby pull in the driveway from work. He walked up behind me, to see what I was doing, and here I was, just spraying the hose in the air, and singing, and dancing away.

He laughed really loud, and it made me jump and stop. He said something about how I had finally just lost it, and started back to get his stuff from the car.

After dinner, I sat down to check the pics. Wow, seems our friends liked the rainbows too!

And the hose. I have woken up many mornings to find the hose on, and have the water bills to prove it. Hubby always blames me for forgetting and leaving it on. Like even when it was spraying all over the porch, towards the front door...like I just walked thru the spray, inside, and didn't notice it was on?

The last time, I fussed and yelled at them about not turning it off, and it has been on two times since, but the nozzle has been shut to close the spray.

They also empty my dog tub at night. It holds fifteen gallons, and they will empty it, on hot days, when I have just refreshed it. This winter, I got pics of a five-gallon bucket that went missing here, and showed up in the woods near the pump house, sitting upright, full to the brim with fresh water. I think I busted them trying to carry it off, and they just sat it down and hid. It was on the start of one of the trails that leads to the nest area. I left it there, and it disappeared that night, and the empty bucket showed back up in the pumphouse the next night. So I have set up another tub, near that woods area, and kept it with fresh water. Nope, they never touched it, but they still hit the dog's tub. I figured they trust more what they know I leave for my dogs.

I see them dart across that area at lot, out of the corner of my eye. I think that is what Frank is seeing too. He will turn suddenly, and just stare.

That or he got popped with another pine cone, or a stick, for ending the rainbow dance. He usually gets mean when they pop him.

He did go out and take the trimmers to the yard edges, and he really cut up some of the areas they like to hide and watch in. I was kinda mad he did that, but I know they mess with him from those areas, when he mows, so I just figured he is trying to keep them back off him some.

He got ill with me just now when I asked him why such a severe trim job there. Has to be hell at times, being him.

June 5th

Hubby came walking with me around, just going on dusk. He was picking with me, because I found a pile of sticks, next to the back of the barn, and I took pics, and took one piece that looked chipped up, and put it in my pocket.

I was pretty surprised he stayed with me, as I went behind the barn looking...where he usually won't go. Well it didn't last long, next thing I knew, I heard him make a kind of "hmmmptf" sound, and he turned and was walking fast towards the house.

I had just heard some twigs snapping, and rustling, close, and figured it spooked him. Oh well. I turned back around to look where I had heard it and...they just sat there, and let me take two pics. Then I felt strange just taking pics, and I lowered the camera. They turned and left. I stood there a minute, and then went into the house to see if hubby had seen them.

He was sitting on the couch, looking at the TV, and wouldn't even look at me, but he was shook up. I started to ask him if he saw them and he just yelled, "OK...I DON'T WANT TO TALK ABOUT IT!! EVER!" And then he went and got in bed. I went in the bedroom, and he shoved my pillows at me, and said, "Just leave me alone tonight, please."

So I am on the couch tonight I guess.

I guess he saw them...

They were like in a pile. Little furry ones, kind of stacked in a pyramid shape.

Well, that was a definite first here. I'm still trying to process it, and am wondering why they did that, and if they will do it again. I can't even joke about this one. Not feeling scared, just don't really know what to think about it.

I haven't heard them at all tonight, and the dogs are not up and barking like they usually do. Come to think of it, the dogs usually follow us all over the yard, but today, none of them came behind the barn with us. They followed us up until I found those sticks, and I didn't notice them leave, but none were around when I turned to go back to the house. They were all up on the porch.

Do you think I should leave them a gift there in the morning?

Or should I just ignore it?

I think it did kind of scare me. Not then, but now it kind of does...not knowing why they did that.

From a Phone Conversation between Ammi and Me

—I was talking to [another member of the habituators' forum] and you know what I realized?

—What?

—The other day Frank had gone and trimmed up those bushes just there, where the little ones showed out yesterday evening, severely clipped those things. I was really torqued with him that he did that. And he got ill with me, talking about, "Oh, you just trying to give them things a place to—" And I said, "Yeah, because that's the way they are, y'know, you gotta give 'em respect." And I said, "That's why you're getting napped with pinecones." And then he says, "I don't believe in that crap!" And I'm like, "Yeah okay, it's the dogs and the deers and the owls throwing that shit..."

So when I went outside, I apologized to them. I was talking to the woods, y'know, and I was telling them, "You know I would *never*—'cause I'm the one that usually does the trimming—I would never, ever trim this so severe." And I said, "He's just an idiot. He refuses to believe in you. I know you guys are throwing stuff at him." I said, "I wish you would just step out in front of him."

—Oh, and this was just a few days before the episode?

—Two days before.

—When I was talking to [fellow habituator], I was saying, "Why did they do that?"

And I said, "Well you know he trimmed up that hedge over there, that bush." And as I said that I said, "Oh my God!" Have you ever got that feeling, like when someone hits a certain note in a song, where you get that tingle all the way through your body? Well, that's what it was like, I knew that was it. I got that tingle from my head to my toes.

—So they were in the same place that would've been hidden if he had not trimmed the bushes back in there?

—Yes sir. They sure were. They were crouched down like they were hiding behind the same bush but it wasn't there. And they were in a pyramid, a pile of them.

—What size were they?

—Different. Different sizes.

—Were there two?

—Two? No, there was a pyramid of them. I felt stupid. I still felt stupid this morning, because here all this time I've been feeding these things, trying to interact with them, thinking what you want is an interaction with them, y'know. And what did I do when they finally showed themselves? I took pictures of them like they were some kind of freak show. I didn't say a word to them. I just took two pictures and then stood there realizing how stupid it was, so I just lowered the camera and stood there staring at them. Still didn't know what to say. And when they left, they didn't stand up and turn around or nothing. They just faded backward into shadow, and the foliage. It was pretty deep dusk. You can't make out details in the pictures, just general shapes. It was maybe a minute or less between when I put the camera down and they faded.

—But before that, you got the chance to really feast your eyes on these folks.

—Yeah, and they looked just as confusing as...I figured out why so many of the pictures are so confusing. I'm going to be able to pick them out better from now on. They stack up on each other. You got arms and legs and faces all tangled together from a whole bunch of them. That's why it's looking so weird.

—And like the little ones are gripping onto the fur and…

—I mean, some of them are laying down, some got their heads stuck in sideways. Some are over from the top. They got their arms over top of their head.

—Ah, just to mess with your eyes?

—Yeah, it's all an eye-screw. And I was like, *that*'s why you can't make out a clear face. One will have his hand cupped over his face, or one of them next to them's got their hand cupped over the other one's face. It's wild, and smart.

June 13*th*

I have always left the blinds open parts of the day, and some of the night, before bed, so they can look in here also. That is probably why if I get up and move around in here for over an hour, and don't raise those blinds, they will start to "tap tap tap" lightly on the windows. They know my reaction is to simply raise the blinds, and go about my business. They know I won't run or jump to try to see them. I may ease a camera around the corner but my face won't be with it. They are getting me trained pretty well here. They almost have me tamed, habituated.

I also know, if I don't walk around for a few days, and just ignore them, take no pics, etc., they come in closer, and get more vocal, to try to get my attention. They are like children like that. I haven't had them show out again, but I notice in the pics, they are right at the edge.

June 28*th*

Frank was loaded up to take his daughter back to Georgia. She and her boyfriend have been here a week, and besides one tour around our place, have stayed at his mom's house. Frank was in the car, and the boyfriend also....Robyn decided she wanted some apples from my tree, about the same time I came out to say my good-byes.

Boyfriend got out to hug me bye, Robyn was walking back from the apple tree next to the barn, and we all heard a very loud, "Frank!" yelled from behind the barn.

I had to just laugh, it was a very good imitation of my voice.

Robyn *ran* to the car, Frank jumped out glaring at the barn area, Boyfriend and Robyn looked at me confused.

I just kept laughing, and told Frank, "You explain it on the ride." I looked at Robyn and Boyfriend and told them, "They are harmless, and your dad still doesn't believe in them. Ya'll have a nice safe trip home."

And I went inside...

I finally get to spend a couple hours with Ammi in Texas, November 13th. After No-Bite, at Texas #2 helped her to relocate, to escape a dire situation back home, and put her up for several weeks, Ammi has found a steady living situation just seventeen miles away. Her current place abuts the same type of undeveloped woodland as at Texas #2. And both houses sit near the Sabine River Basin, a major river system rich with sightings over hundreds of years.

Not surprisingly, then, this new spot is "active," as well, especially to the trained eye and ear. She points, first, to the roof, where two bricks sit, too far from their source (brick chimneys) to have simply fallen like that.

"The couple that stays here sometimes told me they heard footsteps on the roof, really freaked them out. And they also keep seeing movement in the woods out of the corner of their eyes. They don't stay here much anymore."

We go outside and enter the forest just there, fifty yards behind her house. She has been back here only once before, and where she crossed the barbed-wire fence, a tree has now been laid, along with lots of branches, sagging the wires.

"They'll do this. A human comes in their area, they'll do what they can to discourage you from coming back. And make it look as natural as they can. Well, to most people."

Proceeding deeper into the woods, we find many characteristic structures—little sapling bows, larger tree arches, and cases of branches being woven together to form rudimentary enclosures, the ground beneath often swept smooth, free of brambles and other undergrowth.

I'm impressed by Ammi's capacity to distinguish between natural and constructed formations, agree with her assessments, and generally find her level-headed and just as perceptive and articulate as her many months of emails, and her telephone presence, have conveyed.

Independent photographer Jon D. Patton visited Ammi and set up his high-resolution camera on her front porch, aimed and focused just inside the thick screen of leaves at the edge of her yard. From inside the house, he then remotely snapped a shot every ninety seconds for two hours. Patton shared the resulting images with me, which I was able to render into a time-lapse animation sequence; near the end, a face and fingers briefly come to view. See this animation, another striking picture taken by Ammi herself inside a suspected "nest" area, and a brief tour of her property, on YouTube: "Faces in the Foliage: North Carolina Habituation Site."

Oklahoma

June 28ᵗʰ

Last night one of the Locals nearly made an appearance. I was sitting on the swing facing my son-in-law who was dropping off my grandchildren. The yard was set up with the wading pool beside the large pool. The kids had already bailed into the pool. Roger was saying good-bye. Sprout [grandson] was in the wading pool and facing towards the house. It was just before dark. I saw movement at the corner of the house. It was a black shadowy figure that darted around from the back towards the front door. The figure moved further out than necessary before diverting back towards the front door.

This was behind Roger's back. Sprout started pointing and yelling, "Granmaa ook ook!" He took a couple of steps forward watching the area where the shadow had moved through. He got out of the pool, walked a few more steps in that direction, then turned around and came over, crawled up and sat down by me on the swing. Son-in-law was fat dumb and happy and missed the whole thing.

This Local was so dark/black that it even stood out against dusk. I am not sure how to describe it other than it was about the size of a medium-sized adult. Broad shoulders. I am not sure if he was hunched. I got the impression he was ducking as he went under the limb of the pine tree.

Later, Dragon Hunter and Fuzzy Wuzzy took some sandwiches out to put in the snack buckets and both were quite unsettled when they came back in. This was about 10:30 pm. Bobbie said that the yard was scary, he saw one of the monkey people out there. He didn't know this one. That for some reason scared him.

Around 11 pm I stepped out for a smoke and on the west side of the house I heard something moving around. It sounded large. It also sounded as if it was picking up a sheet of plywood and dropping it repeatedly. It was not exactly inviting vibes. The geese and dogs were very noticeably quiet.

After the face painting and the hair spray, Dragon Hunter announced that one of the monkey people had been standing off to the north in the bushes watching us. He had seen him. He showed me about where he had been. Same area as last year.

Sprout tried to bolt for the brush a couple of times, pointing and saying, "Dah." He never gets loud when he says, "Dah." It's always said quietly. I don't know what's up with that. He can be quite loud when he is playing.

June 29th

Today, Sunday, we cooked out. While hubby and my son were talking at the patio, Sprout was on the trampoline playing. He stood up, pointed towards the playhouse, and said, "Dah." He looked at me and pointed, saying, "Dah" over and over. He walked to the edge of the trampoline as if to get a better look.

Fuzzy Wuzzy asked him where was Addy [another name he uses] and he pointed towards the north. He looked back towards where he had been looking and seemed disappointed. He went back to playing.

Later, around 7 pm, just before it was time for the kids to leave, Sprout and I walked out into the play yard. I had walked away from him, leaving him sitting on the swing. Fuzzy Wuzzy was talking to me and when I turned around Sprout said, "Ook ook!" pointing towards the gifting stump and habitat pile. I couldn't see anything from where I was standing. I watched his expressions as he looked towards the stump. The best way to describe it is recognition, like when you run into an old friend and you just feel happy to see them. Sprout's eyes light up and he smiles and laughs. When he pointed to Dah earlier and now when sitting on the swing looking towards the stump, he shows happiness from the inside out.

I was going through some of my pictures. Sprout and Prissy Princess was looking at them with me. Both Prissy and Sprout were quick to point out the blobs. Sprout pointed to several, clearly saying Dah. Others he just pointed to and looked at me like who is that.

July 1st

While I was on the phone with Furbaby [fellow habituator], Sprout came into the kitchen. Furbaby suggested I ask him if Addy and Dah were outside. He climbed up on his bench and began looking out the window. He stared off towards the habitat pile while looking. That look of recognition in his eyes. I didn't see anything out there. Then it was as if he shut down. He has done this for months. When I begin trying to see what he sees he stops looking.

Today while he was in the play yard Magilla and I asked him, "Where is Addy and Dah?" He stopped playing and looked all around. He walked around the yard looking. He was quiet, then he pointed to the front of the property. He stared hard at the cedars and said, "There." Very plainly said, "There." I had my back to the cedars and was making an effort not to look where he was looking.

I can't prove it but I think a lot of the sapling bows are just children at play. I know what the researchers say. They try to make it so complicated that there are these big mysteries. I think that the little ones play like children do and at times they ride the trees that are bent while they are playing. There are lots of signs that indicate communication, I won't deny that. I just think that little ones use the trees to play in also.

I have several trees that are bowing and up top in adjacent trees the leaves are missing. These are the same type of leaves that Dragon Hunter and Fuzzy Wuzzy have said they see them eating. They hide well in the trees also. They like to watch us from these places. I have also noticed when one tree is bowed to the point I start paying attention to that area then another tree somewhere else starts bowing.

July 3rd

This is the second time this summer this has happened. Someone short knocks on the front door. Or maybe it is someone taller with a long reach. Twice within the last month someone has knocked on the front door. No one has been there. The first time hubby and Magilla were here and heard it. The first time it happened we thought that Sprout and Fuzzy Wuzzy had arrived. The knock was three then three. Today was a steady knocking on the bottom half of the door. As if someone was trying to get our attention. Magilla and I immediately went out to see what was going on. Nothing absolutely nothing.

August 16th

I believe they may have those that are from the wilderness and those that are closer to our back doors. That makes the differences in population, evolution habits, and even the way they look. The ones closer to us are on warp drive adapting to us, continually changing. Those in the wilderness are on a much slower pace.

August 28th

This happened Sunday late afternoon/evening. I was out in the yard. I think better when I am outside. Less distractions in the flowerbeds. Anyway I looked up and across the yard a large male (probably around 7.5 ft) was standing just outside of the tree line. He was watching me. It was as if he was waiting to get my attention. When I noticed him I watched for a couple of seconds and could even see the white teeth. It was not actually a shock, more of a surprise. I blinked and was wiping sweat from my face. He disappeared.

It only lasted a few seconds.

My impression was he wanted me to know that he had come for his family. They have now gone. I don't know where. I feel better knowing that the female didn't leave alone with little ones. Nothing I can put my finger on. It was as if he was letting me know he had come for his female. He was very black in color. His hair around his head was shoulder length. The body was covered in black hair. His hair appeared short and uniform. Well groomed. His head was round not like a gorilla. Not a huge bulky male more tall and slender. I checked the area where he had been. He had actually stepped from the woods into the yard, there were impressions in the grass.

About three weeks ago, I sent Fuzzy Wuzzy out to turn on the lights around the patio. He came back in and indicated that it was very creepy out. I finally pinned him down. He said he saw a new guy in the yard. Around 9 ft tall. He looked funny because his head was a different color than his body. Fuzzy used the trees this one was near to measure the height. He says it's too weird to explain, it was like meeting a stranger in the yard. He said when it's the ones that stay around more it's just like "Oh hi."

September 21st

I have some odd things and (as hubby says) "new hillbillies" around. They are just different. They are more tense when they come through here. I believe that Addy left with that male. She may be back in the area but not like she was.... I can't put my finger on things to say for certain, but there is some kind of change or disturbance in patterns. My locals that were comfortable around here seem to be less noticeable. It could be just me also. Addy, Dah, and the other little guys were around a lot. I would see flashes. Sprout was quick to point them out. Now he isn't pointing them out. He looks for them. He has pointed to a couple of shadows. When asked about them, he don't seem to know them. Not like Addy and Dah. Kinzi says she has seen several that look more monkey than monkey kid. She don't seem to know them either.

On September 24th, while crossing the street, Sprout and his mother were struck by a car, and the boy suffered several injuries, including a skull fracture.

October 28th

Since Sprout's accident he has not rested very well. He often dreams of the accident. Or I believe he is dreaming about it. He screams in his sleep Help me Help me. Stop it Stop it. During these dreams he is restless. I have to physically restrain him at times. Often it is hard to wake him up.

Once he is awake he don't want to sleep again.

On Thursday Oct. 23, he had finally gone to sleep around 11 pm. Around midnight the dreams began. Not able to settle him down I woke him up. After a few minutes I changed the tv to a public tv children's channel and he half watched it, while complaining about his tummy. Then he became excited looking out the front window into the dark (not unusual). He started saying Henry. Henry's here. He pointed out the window and jabbered to the dark and Henry. After doing this. Sprout hopped down and went to the door. He tried to open the door. During this time he was saying, Henry come in the house. Come on in, Henry. He invited Henry to come in several times. I sat watching this, thinking I hope Henry isn't heavy and breaks the porch. A minute or two later Sprout climbed back up to the window looking out. He didn't mention Henry again.

The next night Sprout was again restless and having bad dreams. Around 11 pm I began to hear a humming/singing outside. Really. It was a low sound. As odd as this sounds Sprout settled down and seemed to sleep peacefully. I don't know how long the humming went on. In the wee hours of the morning Sprout became restless again. I barely recall holding him and the humming beginning again. This was the third time I have heard the humming now. There has not been any wind when I hear the humming. Or that is to say I don't observe the trees swaying in the wind. I have investigated around the house looking for some sort of device that the wind could blow through to make the sound, should somehow I have missed noticing the wind. I have not found anything. I can say if it's a hairless person humming they are either bundled up or freezing their butts off. I have not attempted to record anything in a while. I have debated each time I hear the humming on trying to sneak the recorder out. I have decided against this each time. I somehow suspect the humming will come to an end.

October 30th

This evening Sprout came out on the porch. He flipped on the porch light and called to Dah. He called several times softly. Then he yelled it very loudly a half a dozen more times or so. He acted very excited while calling for him. Then he went back into the house. A couple of minutes later he came busting out the door a second time and said, KeeKee! KeeKee's here! He looked around as if expecting her to step up to the porch. He went and got a sack of cat food and proceeded to pour a pile on the porch. After making a mess of the cat food he picked it up and put it into a bowl and proceeded to tell the cats they couldn't have it.

Texas #1

November 10th and 11th, I am taken in warmly by this family, the parents and their two children, fifteen-year-old Rachel and her thirteen-year-old brother, whom we'll call Mowgli, because he tends not to wear shoes outside, running through pastures and woods. These are bright, handsome teenagers, only too eager to share their experiences with me.

In fact, both kids go barefoot this afternoon, and so do I, as we cross a vast cornfield. The stalks have been cut and ploughed under, so what's left is a wet mudflat probably two-thirds of a mile from tree line to tree line. Shoes or boots would be sucked off immediately; our feet sink six inches each slimy step.

Rachel's leading us to "the village," a site famous within the family, a sylvan spot where "the Foots" have sculpted huts out of bushes and low trees, bending and weaving them together into a fine mesh, half a dozen green domes with small entrances down by the ground. I've seen pictures.

"I used to come here in the summer, sit in the huts with my friends. It's so peaceful inside there. I went maybe twenty times."

It takes her a while to pinpoint the location, though, because things here have been changed around dramatically; the village is largely destroyed, leaving just a few tattered remnants of the former structures. Rachel is saddened, thinks maybe she visited too much, making the outpost no longer so desirable.

In case they've rebuilt somewhere nearby, we poke around. And sure enough, after fifteen minutes, Mowgli finds a large structure, a sort of "blind" that one can walk into, sit inside on a matted floor that he pronounces "really comfy." This place is formed, up top, by a thick tree that's been obviously broken and bent back downward at a forty-five-degree angle to the Earth. The resulting screen of leaves and branches has been augmented by many vines and further branches, stuck and twisted in.

And it makes for a peculiar phenomenon, just like the "one-way mirror" effect Ammi noted in North Carolina, where she could see nothing past the wall of foliage at the edge of her backyard, whereas when she'd enter the brush, her own home and grounds are very plainly visible.

Mowgli and I stand inside and watch Rachel's red shirt, moving. "Can you see us?"

"Not at all!"

We exit, she enters, and promptly vanishes, confirming, "I can see you *both*!" Back at the house, thoroughly mud-covered, we survey the two dozen cages, stacked in rows, now standing empty, many of them badly busted.

"They took some rabbits," Rachel tells me, "and they broke some rabbits' backs."

"Didn't that piss you off!?"

"Oh, I knew they didn't mean anything *by* it. Sometimes, they'd just move them around. And the rabbits are really sensitive. Like even if I were to hold them and make a loud noise, they'd have a heart attack and die. So something that big coming through and opening the cages and moving them around...they'd either have a heart attack and die or they'd be put in too roughly and get broken backs and die."

"Why'd they do it?"

"They did it because they watched *me* moving the rabbits around. I knew they were watching me. I could see them sometimes watching me. I'd go out and take care of the rabbits every day. And I'd move them around or whatnot, make sure everybody was where they were supposed to be. And then eventually *they* started moving them around, or trying to. The cages would be all smashed up. One time, I found a live cardinal in a cage. When I opened it, he flew away."

That night, over coffee in the kitchen, she fills me in on some background I haven't heard.

"I was out taking care of my rabbits, one evening, and I glanced back at the wood pile. There was one sitting with his back up against the wood pile, and he had his leg crossed over. I watched him and he watched me. I just stared at him for a long time. He just sat there. He had a gorilla-looking face, definitely. I ran in to go get a flashlight and by the time I got back he was gone."

Her mother joins us. "Remember," she asks her daughter, "that one night we were sitting out in the yard, and having a cookout, and they were hollering and whooping, from the north of us, the south, east and west?"

"Mmmm hmmmm."

"That was early on in us discovering things about them. We were having a lot of cookouts, and they'd be talking to us. We'd whistle and they'd talk back, whistling and whooping."

"We were sitting there on the yard that night and we could see their eyes shining in the trees."

"Green and yellow eyes..."

"And blue..."

"And one night," her mother recalls, "we were sitting watching TV, and we heard somebody running across the *roof*, Boom Boom Boom, and then it sounded like they fell—CRASH! And then you could hear them roll down the roof and hit the ground. But by the time we got outside, they were gone. They ran around up there more than once, but we've only heard them fall that once."

"Was it funny?" I ask.

"Yeah, we were laughing! Somebody *fell*!"

She goes on to tell me about a spy-structure that appeared, over a few weeks, at the back of their property. "They watch the kids on the trampoline, they sit back there. They made a bench, where there's wood in front so they can see through it, and it's tall, and they sit on it, and they can watch the kids at the house. They made an actual *bench*. They moved the wood around, piled it up. An observation post!"

Also, the next morning, before I have to leave, to visit Texas #2, Rachel shows me where, in her room, they used to come and pop the plastic cover off the doggie door, and tap on her window, in the lower right-hand corner. She imitates with her fingernails...tap tap tap tap.

"Trying to wake me up, trying to get some reaction out of me. And they'd smack the wall, too, right here. Late at night."

"Would it make you feel good, like, Oh, my friends are back?"

"No! I'm like, I'm *sleeping*, leave me alone!"

Since my last visit, researcher Bob Truskowski has spent hundreds of hours at this location, and has obtained high-quality audio, including Sasquatch calls and "chatter." You can hear many excellent clips at SasquatchSounds.com. He has also documented two other phenomena occurring here, the braiding and knotting of the family horses' manes (his photographs are included earlier, in "Horse Mane Braiding") and many familiar types of stick and tree structure (also shown elsewhere), such as these.

Compare to the tree structure I saw in Ohio, below...

...and to two barkless leaning trees at Texas #2, below

...to a structure found in Vermont, below left...

...and to the one photographed by researcher Mike Paterson in
Ontario, above right

Texas #2

June 17th

I came inside from mowing, cooled down, took a bath, and relaxed a bit. Just as the sun was beginning to set, I was talking to [a friend] on the phone and looked back by the goat house–OMG! There was a young BF! It was about 5-5 ½ feet tall, medium build, and even had a *neck*! I don't know if it realized I spotted it, or if it was in a hurry. It made the distance from the goat house to the road in about two seconds. I was *stunned* at how fast this creature ran! Now I know how my husband could have mistaken a young BF for Allison during that rock fight. With the exception of how fast and agile the creature was, it was remarkably like Allison in proportion.

June 19th

This evening, about 6:30, I let the dogs out to run a bit and go to the bathroom. I'd been outside about ten minutes when I heard a squalling baby animal coming from near the back fence. The shortest and easiest route to where the racket was coming from was to head west on [road name]. Initially, I thought a coyote had gotten one of my cats. I ran down the asphalt and got about thirty feet from the back fence when a doe busted out of the woods from behind my property, whirled around to her right and stood staring at the woods where she'd just left. I could still hear the animal squalling in panic/pain, and got within about fifteen feet of the doe before she realized I was there. That *should* have been a warning to me that it wasn't a coyote, but I was more focused on the cry from the woods.

In hindsight, it sounded much like one of the baby goats we used to have, that's probably why I was intent on rescuing the baby from the jaws of the coyote. The doe spotted me, then spun and headed away from the squalling young one. I guess the predator and then the addition of a human being was too much for her to deal with. One of the chihuahuas ran ahead of me into the woods, then came running back and stood on the road.

I ran into the woods, across the rocky ground covered by dry leaves, making quite a racket as I went. As I got within about twenty feet (still at a dead run) I hollered out as loudly as I could, "HEY!" Well, instead of a coyote scurrying off into the woods, I was met with a very loud, very intimidating AAAAAAAAUUUGGG GGGG GGHHHHHH!" I froze. I was too petrified to move. I was located on ground about three or four feet higher than the creature in the woods. Even at that elevation, the hairy creature was nearly at eye level with me. I could see the top of the head, the left shoulder and a very large muscular left arm. The rest was behind brush. Thankfully, the being in the woods took the still squalling young deer and headed into the ravine. At about twenty feet from where the confrontation occurred, the fawn quit making any noise.

By this time, I realized I had been within just a very few feet of one of the Ancient Ones, and a very large, mature one at that. I was shaking all over, scared half to death, my heart was racing and my most urgent thought was to get my stupid butt away from there before the deer killer changed his mind and came back to thump me.

I got back to the house and had a difficult time climbing the four steps to the front porch I was shaking so badly. I immediately went to the bathroom and threw up, then sat on the porcelain throne and found some relief. It was nearly an hour and a half before I was able to compose myself enough to call [friends on the phone]. The Ancient One in the woods beat a hasty retreat when he/she realized I was *not* the doe coming back for her fawn, most likely a bit embarrassed that a human had gotten so close. Had it chosen to attack, I would not have been able to even move. [My friend] said that the poor, scared critter was probably still sitting off in the woods shaking and trying to regain composure from such a scary incident. I should be ashamed of myself! [He] didn't seem to think I should worry much about any retaliation. He said just behave as normally as you have in the past, and don't let the big critter get the idea it had scared me. It's possible that if it thought I had gotten intimidated, then it could try it again on me, or even someone else. If I go through the motions of things being usual, then the critter will just be more careful next time it goes hunting and the prey makes a fuss. And, since I didn't keep him from catching and keeping his meal, there was no harm/no foul (so to speak).

I had suspected the ravine area was used for catching prey, but never realized it was used during daylight hours, too. It *was* getting toward evening, but the sun was still definitely up in the sky, it was basically broad daylight even in the woods. Several weeks ago I recorded the "Whistler" back in the ravine well after dark. The Whistler came steadily up the ravine, accompanied by random wood knocks.

I estimate tonight's hunter to be about eight foot tall. He was dark, kind of a chocolate color, with a semi-peaked head. Not a huge crown like a large gorilla has, about half as large. The hair was between three and four inches long, but longer on the forearm, probably nearly six inches. I couldn't tell due to the amount of brush between us (thank GOD) whether it was male or female. To be honest, it didn't matter! I was just very thankful to still be alive. I didn't notice any odor, either.

Now it's almost 11:30 pm, nearly five hours since the encounter. I'm still a bit shaken, but thanks to the calm conversation with friends, I'm doing much better. I have learned another valuable lesson, and survived to tell others. Or, I dodged another bullet, depending on how you look at it.

June 29th

The only "retaliation" I have received was finding all my lawn chairs in the far backyard. I laughed, brought the five chairs back to the front. The next night, the chairs in addition to some of my flower pots and all four of my antique milk cans were moved to the far backyard. Again I laughed, but said, "Okay, that should make us even now because it is harder for me to move all this stuff back to where it belongs than it was for you to bring it here." I haven't had anything else relocated.

I have to admit, this new reality I'm living is an entirely new world, much like *Alice in Wonderland* where nothing is what it seems. Could the Ancient One world be similar to our world where there are "civilized" AOs and some AOs a bit wild and opportunistic? My thinking is: There are many more AOs than ever estimated by humans. These beings don't exactly put out mailboxes or construct houses. *If* women were being attacked by these beings, I truly believe it would be on the Internet. I believe in my heart these are a society and culture that is very well disciplined. It would not surprise me at all to find out these beings are much more civilized than we hairless human beings are. I have no fear at all of being raped or pillaged when I'm out alone. Even when I first "discovered" them, my fear was more of being the main course of their dinner...definitely not sexual entertainment. For some reason, it is the *men* who seem fixated on this aspect of the AO interaction. I think these men are missing the whole point. I believe with all my heart that the interaction has much deeper spiritual implications.

The government does not want to admit these creatures/beings exist. They'd have to admit they have absolutely no control over their behavior. If forced to "protect" the Bigfoot, then the government would have all sorts of lawsuits requesting restitution for lost livestock, property damage, etc. If it is found this creature is a human-type being, then that poses a whole different hornet's nest. Then they've got this radical society to deal with. These creatures don't wear clothing, don't pay taxes, don't get their children vaccinated, or put them in school. They have not bowed down to the authority of the U.S. government, and I doubt they ever will or could be forced to do so. You know what the government and the settlers did to the Native American Indian. God knows, it was a great effort to wipe them out. And it nearly succeeded. That is what could happen to these beings. By "outing" them [to research organizations that can't be trusted to keep one's location secret], you could be forcing the government to deal with a very delicate problem.

I almost feel I am a "Nazi sympathizer" turning in information on the location and behavior of the Jews. That is how seriously I feel about the information I pass on. The more familiar I become with the Ancient Ones' behavior, vocalizations, social structure and annual "celebrations," the more I feel I am being entrusted with what should be *private knowledge*. It may be that *everyone* is not supposed to know they exist. I think those who are drawn to investigate these beings should ask themselves *why*. Some folks always like a good mystery. Some folks have had a sighting and just want to get all the information possible. And some folks like me are *thrust* into the center of this whole thing. I don't believe it was an accident.

July 6*th*

The Ancient Ones have helped me discover a part of me that was missing. This new reality is quite a bit like going back to childhood and discovering the wonders of the world again. I get to re-look at everything with different eyes. If it weren't for the ladies on the forum, I would never be as far along as I am now, and I am eternally thankful. They helped me to see that the great surge of activity I was experiencing here last spring was not a siege but a celebration, connected in some way with the ancient spring ritual called Beltane, Spring Equinox.

What fun it is to go outside and find yard ornaments rearranged during the night! When I misplace some tool, I can now blame the hairy neighbors rather than my own mind! I am finally discovering joy in my life again, and it's been gone a long, long time. It's satisfying to know about the existence of these beings—and no one else in the area has a clue. It's almost like having a secret life: On the surface I look like your typical old woman, living a meager life, eking out an existence in the middle of nowhere, but if the truth be known, I have a very spiritually fulfilling, adventure-strewn, busy, by no means boring life. Pretty cool!

I don't have a clue why these Ancient Ones have revealed themselves to me, but life would truly be lonesome here otherwise. Yes, I have the four dogs and the three cats to keep me company, but nothing compares to a good mystery needing solved. This alter-reality keeps my mind working overtime. I find myself more alert while driving. I tackle plumbing problems myself rather than invite someone over who also might discover my forest secret. And even if they didn't, I don't want the interruption! At night while I'm at the computer, I hear bumping on the rear wall of the house. It's rather comforting to know they are around.

And that is another change I have discovered in myself—I am more observant of the activities and sounds around me. Instead of slogging through my daily projects, when I rest, I look and listen. I watch what the dogs are doing, where they are looking. I look for the cats to see if they are dozing, or if they are on guard and alert, or if they are chasing each other and energetic. I listen to the sounds of the night. I used to be so closed up to these simple pleasures, now they are mine in abundance. Ancient Ones are amazing mimics. I've heard a brook in my back window—a brook!! I could just imagine a bubbling brook feet outside my kitchen window…what a pleasant thought! Not long ago I heard a cow in my backyard about midnight. There are cows in the area, but close examination the next morning revealed no hoofed creatures back there.

July 19th

I ran into one of the lady neighbors as I was walking up the road. She asked what I was doing out in the heat, then said, "OHHH! I know— you were looking for Bigfoot signs, weren't you?" I confessed, then she asked where it was I had my initial sighting, and I told her. Okay, she lives about a half mile northeast of me. I asked her if she had looked around her pond and she said, "Oh, we don't have those things around our place. The dogs keep them run off." I just smiled, said I sure hoped so, then went on walking to the house. Folks certainly have funny ideas about where these hairy woods folks stay and where they go.

July 21st

Well, I just got zapped with infrasound *again*. I was trying to put a recorder outside the house, on the north steps. Thinking I'd be kind of slick, I acted like I was moving the bowl of cat food away from ants and relocating a window screen (I'm scraping paint off windows). I moved the bowls of cat food successfully, but when I went back to move the window screen it had gotten darker. I turned on the flashlight and a glint of light caught my eye. I was on the north side of the house, facing the west. The glint was to the northwest about forty feet. I used the flashlight and walked toward the light and realized it was a pane of broken glass leaning against the base of a big tree. The pane of glass was about an inch thick, and I was seeing the reflection on the edge of the glass. At this point, I heard the "white-tailed deer bark" about twelve to fifteen feet *up the tree* I had just illuminated with the flashlight. Knowing this was no deer, but also knowing the AOs rarely attack, I backtracked and picked up the window screen, but for some reason I decided I wanted to peek around to the house. While holding the window screen I used the flashlight to light up a portion of the backyard which is enclosed with fencing. When I did that, I immediately got hit with infrasound.

As I've said, I was familiar with the heart pounding, feeling of fear, heightened anxiety. I heard no accompanying growl or bark, I just felt the pulse of the infrasound. This "pulse" was also picked up on the window screen; I was able to feel it with my fingertips. I decided I had pushed my luck as far as I dared, placed the screen on the steps, and left the area, going back inside the house.

The effects of this session of infrasound so far have lasted about forty-five minutes. I am experiencing nausea, rapid heartbeat, anxiety, fear, tremors and a dull headache. I am still having difficulty typing and collecting my thoughts in a rational, coherent order. The side effects do appear to be subsiding.

August 1st

I went into the backyard to cut down some fencing. The atmosphere was a bit anxious. I started cutting the wires holding up the gate and got a rock thrown near me. I had come prepared. I said in the most authoritative voice I could muster, "Okay! I just want you to be aware that I have a camera *and* a digital recorder with me, and I know how to use them!"

I hear this very hesitant voice from across the ravine. "Ummm, lady? Are you okay over there? Do you need some help?" Oh man, I felt like a dingbat... Feeling rather sheepish, I hollered back, "No, I think I've got things under control now, but thanks for the concern!" If the folks in white coats ever question him, I'm sure he'll testify against me.

While I was out there later putting out food for them, [a seventeen-year-old neighbor boy] came by on the road and began with small talk. Then he got to the point of asking what I was putting out the fruit for. I told them, "Well, just about whatever *wants* it, I guess." I could tell this boy was a bit uncomfortable, so I said, "Young'un, what's eating you?" He said that he'd *heard* I had Bigfoot on my property, to which I responded, "Kid, they're all over [this part of] Texas. I don't have a corner on the market here." He asked me what he needed to look for to see if they were near his house, so I told him about the tree bends, the X's and the wood knocks. I told him they are not aggressive, but that if you happen to get close to one of their little ones, they use something like a real low growl that we can't hear to make us feel spooked. His eyes lit up and he said, "Oh man! That's what happened that night." And he went on to tell about getting scared when walking home. I told him never to shoot one unless his life absolutely depended on it, because they never travel alone, and getting shot they take *real* personal.

August 12ᵗʰ

While I was scraping the overspray off the outside windows, I was able to catch one of the AOs observing me from the brushy area between the house and the county road. I was able to view the being without spooking it off. The reflection in the window wasn't all that good, though, because I had to keep working and vibrating the glass, otherwise I was concerned the AO would catch on to what I was doing. From what I could observe, it was crouched down in a squatting position, the head almost even with the back of the lawn furniture. Even the face had short hair on it. How they can sit there so very still for such a long time is remarkable. If I squatted like that and then had to move quickly, I couldn't do it.

Visiting No-Bite

I arrive on a mild, sunny late afternoon, Texas autumn, and, accepting my gift of genuine Vermont maple syrup, she introduces me around to her two adult cats, two kittens, three Chihuahuas, a sheltie/rat terrier mix, and of course LuLu, the coonhound whom I'm especially glad to wrestle on the grass—famous, to me, from her role in this woman's arresting accounts.

I'll call her No-Bite, the name her Ancient Ones gave her last spring, after she assured them, "I'm not going to bite you."

We sit out on her lawn, chatting, getting acquainted in person after so much long-distance communication. She's a sweet, kind-faced soul who has been cooking a beef brisket for me all day. As evening descends, one of her neighbors can be heard above us, taking his paraglider up for a spin at several hundred feet.

"Oh, there he goes again. I don't even know who it is, but he's been flying the last couple weeks. Always at dusk."

As the single-person craft approaches, we can hear, from down in the ravine behind her house, five distinct wood knocks, separated by intervals of distance and time. No-Bite's ravine is a lot shallower than mine but still, at two hundred feet deep and a quarter mile long, and filled with brambles, downed trees, bowed saplings, it proves formidable to traverse. Also, the whole affair proceeds slightly uphill, and it's in this direction that the coyote and Sasquatch drive their game—hogs and deer—through. At its outlet, by the road, is where the hunt was interrupted several months ago.

"Hear those knocks?" she says. "They're warning each other to hide, to hunker down. The first time that man flew over, they made a terrible commotion, now it's gotten more subtle." I'm delighted.

After dinner, we sit out in the chill, wrapped in blankets. Indeed, I'm able to spend a total of five nights and days here, and not, for the most part, seeking to gather evidence (like the avid researchers who have visited before, alienating No-Bite with their domineering ways) but rather simply getting a feel for the place, communing with it, exploring the forest and sitting attentive in the yard. Occasionally, at night, we make wood-knock overtures and, I'd say a quarter to a third of the time, either right away or minutes later, receive a crisp response knock from the ravine or from the thick pine forest opposite.

With her permission I do put out my audio recorder, overnights. Once, hung from the goat house roof, it picks up some light slaps against the walls. The next night at 1:25, set beside a bowl of black plums at the tree line, the mic captures an ear-splitting, high-pitched SMACK! (Hear it at YouTube: "Black Plum Reprimand.") The plums were not taken.

On one of our treks together, No-Bite leads me to a pond within the pine forest that has often seemed the source of middle-of-the-night vocals. The best thing we find here strikes me as a work of art: four separate tree arches all in the same spot, curving elegantly, the ends fed into a thicket of branches and vines. Unlike my own far-northern arches, these cannot be explained away as a by-product of snow and ice build-up; indeed, the farthest tree travels fifteen feet from home to join the others within the thicket. Sorry, skeptics, this just ain't happening without intention, without hands. (See YouTube: "East Texas Tree Bends.")

Two of four arches are visible here

Another time, she shows me where two long, straight trees have been transported from where they grew, de-limbed, de-barked, and leaned at a steep angle to cross one another twenty feet up in the crook of an ordinary tree. Reminiscent of telephone poles, they're much *more* reminiscent of the elaborate structure we found on the BFRO expedition in Ohio, 2006, the only difference being that, there, *seven* trees were thus stripped, raised, and top-crossed.

And then comes the night of the bonfire in the backyard. No-Bite's twenty-year-old daughter and the daughter's best friend are here with us, and we're roasting the hot dogs and marshmallows, having a good time, the two young women acting like kids, giggling and roughhousing.

I leave the firelight and scan the woods with the thermal imager, looking for an upright figure hiding behind a tree, spying on the revelers, its body heat standing out brightly amid the surrounding (cooler) grays. No such luck. But what's that horizontal bar of light, down near the ground, sticking out from behind the debris pile, a perfect vantage point on the bonfire? Should I approach and investigate, camera rolling? Nah, it's probably nothing...

By day, it's clear how close the bonfire was to the woodpile, about thirty-five feet (picture taken by No-Bite)

The Sasquatch spied on us through an opening
(as indicated) just eight inches off the ground

Written by No-Bite to a Member of a Regional Sasquatch Research Group

As I said before, I don't have anything to hide. Right now the trail camera you installed is just sitting out there, I don't know if it has photos or not. Bob, what bothers me about your organization is the mindset that you feel compelled to collect "evidence." If the Ancient Ones want to *offer* evidence, well that's a whole different ballgame. Right now, I am quite content just to be along for the show.

I've already given you the resources to take this same journey. I've told you how, I've explained what to expect, and that there are no guarantees. I have absolutely *no idea* why some are accepted, some seem to be chosen, and some folks just sit there and get a numb rear end. It's a strange world out there! And the funny part about it? I laugh now! I haven't laughed like this, this deep belly laughing, in years. I had forgotten what it is like to just cut loose, turn my cares over to a Higher Power and relax. How can you forget how to laugh, a basic human response?

Bob, you know what these people in the woods require of us? *Nothing.* Not a single thing, they just are reaching out because they desire friendship. The reason I was in awe of [two recent human guests] was they were unafraid of these woolyboogers in the dark. I now know this is because these are people, not woolyboogers. I'm cautious, because I'm still new and also I'm alone here, but I know there is no need to be afraid of the hairy folks here. I just feel so very blessed to have had my eyes opened so I could feel how *full* my life really is.

I don't care whether science is ever able to prove these people exist. At this point, I have even given up trying to prove to you that I have them here. I don't need proof anymore. Whether or not they are here is so very insignificant when the big picture is considered. I so wanted you to put down your damned game cams, digital cameras, digital recorders, infrared cameras, motion detecting equipment and all the God-blessed *stuff* you constantly tinker with so that *you* could experience a whole new dimension in "research." What do I know—I'm just someone who happened to be blessed with seeing these reclusive beings. These aren't "chance sightings," they are deliberate. These are an indigenous people. They have their own laws to be obeyed, their own culture, their own beliefs, and social order. Finding these people in my own backyard is akin to finding gold! I don't want them dissected, photographed and ID'd, fingerprinted, probed and grilled. I feel they are now my extended family, and when folks mess with family, I get angry and protective.

How many others are experiencing the same things? I'm not certain. Maybe (and this is a guess) several thousand around the world. What's happening here is also happening elsewhere. If I was the only one experiencing these situations and seeing these occurrences, I truly would have to wonder about my mental well-being.

There are those on the fringe of this knowledge that so want to be included, but for whatever reason they can't or don't see. Many individuals who are still intent on collecting evidence and documenting sightings quickly back off when the deeper, more meaningful experiences begin to happen. That's why many of the folks who report sightings soon drop off the radar.

The research approach presently used is demeaning and insulting, and that approach has been abandoned for a more person-to-person approach. Just like if you were trying to get to know your next door neighbor. Once these reclusive people realize you *know* the bluff charges and vocalizations, etc., are basically a hoax, you end up on a fast track to a whole "other world," is the best words I can come up with. The individual has both feet on the ground, but his/her mind becomes open to something that just defies scientific explanation. If you would like to speak with those taking me on this new course, you'll have to get in line behind me— because so far there has been no spoken word. I do know I have to constantly fight back the fear of the unknown and persevere if I want to go further.

You are wanting blood and guts, rock hard evidence of these people. If I *did* have it, I wouldn't provide it to researchers who want to tag and label. I would absolutely love to think you would drop any preconceived notions and just come and sit and visit, but for whatever reason, God has created you with blinders. Maybe you are not supposed to see what is happening.

Bob, my entire perception of "my world" has changed, and I'm just beginning to understand some of the things going on. The only thing I can compare it to is being mentally reborn. Nearly everything I *thought* I knew has been given a different slant. Once I dropped what I *expected* of these people, an entire culture was opened up to me. Because I was so fearful, these beings spoonfed me a little at a time. What I am able to tell you so far is this: These are a people who do *not* want to be "found." A few open-minded people around the world have been blessed with the opportunity to step through the established wall these people have built. These people fit in with humans like "gears." What humans lack, these people possess. What these people lack, humans possess. Why is it that more and more individuals are having sightings? Because I believe the walls are coming down between the two cultures, but not completely. At this point I feel it is my purpose to plant the seed within you.

If They Are Visiting You...
Guidelines for Interaction with Sasquatch
by BFRO Investigator Ronie Powell

Set up a feeding platform—

- It should not be too close to your home;
- It should be set up where there is enough cover for the Sasquatch to approach without feeling exposed and vulnerable;
- It should be high enough off the ground to prevent small animals or deer standing on their hind legs from taking what you put out;
- Try putting pieces of peel-and-stick Velcro (the hook portion, not the loop side) on the feeding platform as a way to potentially collect hair samples;
- If you live in an area that receives a lot of rain, consider putting a "cover" (roof, tarp, etc.) from 2' to 3' above the platform, as this will help keep your gifts and food items dry.
- Announce your presence every time you go to the feeding platform—
- Think about something that will be unique to you and where the sound will carry, like a whistle, unique call, song, or even a recording of your children singing, etc., that you play on a portable recorder;
- Talk to the woods when you are putting out food or gifting, because these creatures have been observing you for some time and the sound of your voice will be both familiar and soothing;
- Do not announce your presence and/or go to the feeding platform without taking

"something" with you;

- When you are putting out food, say that you are bringing them food, using the word "food" frequently.

Gifting (food); try a variety —

- Apples;
- Pancakes with syrup;
- Peanut butter & jelly or honey sandwiches;
- Granola bars;
- Strawberries, leaving them in the plastic, snap-top containers, and wipe the container down to eradicate your own finger prints, and if the empty container is found retrieve it with forceps or pliers to preserve any potential Sasquatch finger prints;
- Cooked bacon (cook it mostly done, but not crispy) left in a plastic zip-type bag that is not sealed, but will have to be "fumbled with" to be opened. Again, wipe the bag clean of your own prints and retrieve it carefully;
- Chocolate: candy bars, brownies, etc. Chocolate appears to be a favorite treat;
- With all of the above, take at least one bite out of the food yourself, making sure you are not sick as we don't know what could potentially be transmitted to the Sasquatch;
- Dogfood.

Gifting (non-food) —

- Non-food gifting should also be done on the feeding platform. Try leaving a variety of items such as small to mid-sized balls, a hand mirror, colorful ribbons, polished stones, stuffed animals, etc. If you live in an area that receives lots of rain you may want to leave gifts that are impervious to getting wet.

What to Expect—

- Once your food items and other gifts are being routinely taken, watch for "gifts" to be left for you in exchange near your home. You may find something on a pathway that you use frequently, near your vehicle, or near or on outdoor furniture, or even on the feeding station.

To discourage them from bothering your home—

- Make sure that pet food, livestock grain, or anything that could be considered a food source for them is stowed away and that storage buildings and containers are locked;
- Do not restock the feeding platform every single day. You don't want to set up a situation where the Sasquatch are "expecting" to be fed daily; about three times a week is good;
- However, it's a wise idea to put out food or gifting items at the same time on the days that you do put something out. The Sasquatch will come to expect your activity at that time of day or night and will be listening for your call.

Document everything in a notebook—

- Note how and when food and gifts are being taken (and what is being left or not taken);
- Note date, time of day (or night), weather conditions, etc., whenever you have an interaction, whether it is a sound event or a visual encounter. Be detailed;
- Be cognizant of any patterns that develop.

If you are lucky enough to see the Sasquatch that are visiting you—

- Consider naming them and calling them by name;
- Remember, you're building a relationship;
- Study, learn from, and enjoy your interaction with these amazing creatures.

[Author's note: I share some of my own adventures in this arena at YouTube: "Sasquatch on the Home Front: Vermont Habituation Site 2007-2012"]

Boundaries: A Note of Caution

I urge the reader of Powell's tips, above, also to pay close attention to Chapters Three and Five of this book, lest you enter into an habituation experiment at your home with any too-casual attitude, without the proper measure of respect for the enormity of the experiences you will be courting.

The local Sasquatch are extremely unlikely to harm you physically—this seems to be against their ancient rules of engagement—but that does not mean you may not feel "under siege," as did No-Bite for a long period of time at Texas #2. They'll spy on you and yours, with special focus on the youngest, which may even cause them to bond with the visitors and to live, as it were, with one foot in each of two worlds; they'll surround your place sometimes and carry on wild, or maddeningly subtle, percussion; they'll bump, scratch, tap, and knock on your walls at all hours of the night and peep in the windows; they'll steal, hide, or relocate your belongings; they'll hurl objects in your direction; they'll growl, clack their teeth, "pop" their jaws at you; they may "zap" you with infrasound, which is profoundly unsettling; they'll learn your daily routines down to the last wrinkle, then use this knowledge to play little tricks, making you laugh yet also driving you to doubt your sanity.

To enter voluntarily into this category of relationship—unique on the face of the Earth—is to relinquish control, to accept the plain fact that they are much more powerful and that living with them is very serious business. Succeeding in this strange enterprise requires a great degree of faith in the benevolence of your visitors, but never blind faith.

I know a woman, whose account is not included in this book,

who found that her visitors are not all beneficent, but she did not recognize this until nearly falling off the deep end. She is a Christian and came to believe that one male Sasquatch, in particular, was attempting to take over her soul. She was able, finally, to rebuff the aggression, cut off communications, and regain her autonomous identity.

I have chosen not to expand upon this variety of habituation because, from what I can tell, it is highly atypical. I mention it here only to flag the underlying gravity of the situation, and to implore you to remain constantly on guard and vigilant, assessing as best you can whether the interactions are uplifting your family's life or not. If not, look out for number one — tell your visitors in every way possible to back off and leave you alone; most likely they will respect your wishes (e.g., see pages 177-178), because territorial borders are fundamental to their worldview.

On the other hand, please don't lose sight of the potential upside, the breathtaking privilege in this opportunity you've been given. Our Oklahoma habituator puts the matter wisely.

> I see no harm in gifting, but boundaries need to be established in habituation for the peace of mind and comfort of both sides. Never give what you do not want taken. Never set boundaries that you cannot live with, and remember…just because you don't want one at your back door doesn't mean you have not encouraged this behavior: Take it slow and easy, there is no other way.

> I didn't start out to form a relationship with any animal. I certainly never expected to have a tribe visit me in the middle of the night, but I do feel that this is a very special gift from them that they have chosen our home as a respite at times.

Chapter Six

A Scientific Revolution Gains Ground—
Main Milestones Pre-Specimen

During revolutions in science the discovery of anomalies leads to a whole new paradigm that changes the rules of the game and the "map" directing new research, asks new questions of old data, and moves beyond the minor puzzle-solving of normal science.

—from Thomas Kuhn's *The Structure of Scientific Revolutions*

I grew up in the shadow of the Griffith Observatory, in L.A., and was always aware of the old, famous astronomers, especially Copernicus and Galileo, who suffered severe personal hardship for daring to go against the prevailing worldview. So with this whole Sasquatch effort, I don't look to primatologists as precursors so much as those earlier pioneers, who simply observed the available data with a cold, objective eye and concluded that reality is radically different from what everyone had forever assumed.

—Matt Moneymaker

1. *Three Minutes and Twenty-Two Seconds in the Life...*
The Michael Greene Thermal Footage (North Carolina)

At midnight on April 28th, 2009, twenty years of dogged effort finally paid off for researcher Michael Greene. Being thermal, the footage is not nearly so visually compelling as what later came out of the Kentucky and San Antonio situations, but what it lacks in resolution it makes up for in duration and revealed behavioral texture. The treatment of this clip on Animal Planet's "Finding Bigfoot," two years later, badly shortchanged its value, replaying again and again just a four-second segment; you can see brief, enhanced selections from the footage at YouTube: "Clips from the Michael Greene Thermal Footage." The original, real-time footage is available at BushLoper.net.

For nearly three and a half minutes, the viewer is privileged to witness, for the first time in documented history, a Sasquatch "just being itself," so to speak, unaware of being observed. In the three earlier famous sequences--the Patterson/Gimlin Film; the Paul Freeman video; the Memorial Day footage--the subject's behavior is clearly affected by being in the presence of human onlookers, not panicked but displaying a certain fugitive air. Here, on the other hand, the primate seems relaxed, going about its business, only a bit curious about a slight whirring sound fifty feet away.

"I was about to start recording and hit the sack," Michael Greene relates, "when I heard slight movement in the woods down behind the tree stump where for a long time I had been leaving food and other gifts. On an impulse I took the thermal, a Ratheon 250, out of the car and placed it on the ground, still on its tripod. I covered it with a piece of leaf-cut camo cloth. Then I got in my car and drove several hundred yards away to a field where I spent two hours playing my handheld electronic solitaire game. In the morning when I got home I reviewed the tape and there, about thirty minutes into it, came the Squatch. I really wasn't prepared for success after so many years of failure."

Two years earlier, Michael had had his first thermal sighting, less than a mile from the eventual filming, and less than three feet from yours truly. As I related earlier in this book, we were on expedition in North Carolina, sitting together late at night at a picnic table.   "Every few minutes, I would stand up and thermal scan the area, and the last time I did....there it was, walking sideways to me, some eighty feet away: massive shoulders, arms, and back muscles, no neck. I stupidly said, 'Our friend is here,' and of course everyone stopped talking. I lowered the thermal imager to turn on the DVR velcroed to its top (this takes perhaps six seconds), and by the time I completed this small task and got the thermal back up to my eye, it was gone.

"But I had finally seen one for myself. I have met hundreds of people who have recounted their sightings to me and had no reason to doubt them, but there was always this little coal of uncertainty that burned inside. That coal was now extinguished.

"I started returning to this spot over and over, since I had moved to North Carolina and it was within an hour's drive. I left out fruit, peanut butter, pennies, little squeaky bathtub kids' toys. Whenever I had cameras rolling it wouldn't show up, or there would be a loud, angry, screaming yell from the woods. If I didn't have the cameras on, it would sometimes come while I slept and take something, once returning the favor with five small rocks, neatly placed on the stump.

"Frustrated, but determined, I kept trying different ways to disguise the thermal camera. This model, the Ratheon Palm IR250, has what is called a 'chopper' in it, a disk that whirls very fast inside and spreads the pixels around the screen. It makes a faint whirring sound.

"This last time, I left the rear hatch of my Toyota Highlander open, folded down the rear seat and placed the thermal on a small tripod facing to the rear, just behind the driver's seat. My hope was obviously that the animal would perceive it as part of the car, and that the mass of the car would help to muffle the whirring sound. I had forgotten my peanut butter but had earlier bought a Zagnut candy bar for myself (like a Clark Bar rolled in peanut brickle powder). Taking one for the team, I sacrificed the Zagnut bar and put it on the stump. Soon after, I heard the movement in the woods and that's when I decided to radically change tactics, placing the tripod on the ground instead, and very blatantly vacating the area."

First, we the viewer can see the figure arriving, like a bright shadow, up the hill on the far side of the stump from us, coming into full view for eight seconds, taking slow, deliberate steps--during which his long, thick arms are clear to see, as well as his dome-shaped head and lack of neck—before settling down, sitting, kneeling, or squatting on his haunches. In this posture, barely visible anymore, he waits for fifty-five seconds before reaching abruptly to the stump, the Zagnut. After apparently withdrawing the gift, he settles back again and for the next nineteen seconds does *something* with his hands, possibly working the wrapper. At this point, a truly remarkable thing occurs.

The Sasquatch vanishes. Or so it seems. What actually happens, we soon learn, is that he has dipped out of sight and crawled away *along the ground.* We can tell it's along the ground because if it were not he would recede in the same manner that he arrived--that is, gradually and visibly.

Most likely, he's simply snuck off to snack in peace, at a remove from the source, for good measure. It reminds me of how dogs will take their food away to eat by themselves--and that's only about intra-pack competition, not survival in the face of a dominant species whose offerings might be a fatal trap.

This low-slung behavior is an evidential gem because it matches what's been widely reported by witnesses over the years, that this primate routinely makes use of the turf, rapidly hitting the deck, as an integral element in its basic repertoire of stealth. (It may also account for occasional claims that Sasquatch is capable of literally disappearing.) In other words, there's no reason to suppose that such a departure strategy indicates that this individual knows he is being watched, because if he did he'd hardly have come for the treat in the first place. Nor is it even that he's just now figured out he's under surveillance, because, after just twenty-six seconds, back he comes, this time more forthrightly, standing in plain view, at full height, later estimated at between seven and seven and a half feet. During this encore phase, lasting fifty-one further seconds, the Sasquatch sways in place between two trees, looking in "our" direction, probably hearing the whirr of the Raytheon. Here, we get another precious eyeful of his general bulk, the extended arms, and again the skull's sagittal crest. At one point, endearingly, he slaps the tree trunk beside him with the back of his hand.

This swaying, too, is very commonly noted in the annals of observed Sasquatch behavior. No-Bite narrated it to me over the phone last year, in real time, and when I showed the Greene footage to a habituation family in New Hampshire, the mother gasped and said, "That's *exactly* what the one up behind here was doing. He was swaying back and forth, peeking out from behind the tree I showed you."

2. *On the Frontier of Language—*
Ninety Minutes of Sasquatch Vocalizations Analyzed by Crypto-Linguist Scott Nelson
(California: The Sierra Nevada Mountains)

Scott Nelson

"By accident, one night in 2008," Scott Nelson recalls, "I stumbled onto what we think is a pretty big discovery. My eleven-year-old son wanted a subject for a school paper, so we're Googling 'Bigfoot Sounds,' and found the BFRO website, and I clicked on 'Samurai Chatter.' Of course I was curious, since I'm a linguist: What are they talking about with 'chatter'? Almost immediately, I recognized this as having characteristics of language. And you know, I'm sure I would have passed over it just like any average guy if it had not been for the thousands of hours that I spent in the Navy speeding voice communications up, and slowing them down, and analyzing them for every characteristic that we could retrieve. It would have sounded to me just like apes fighting, like it's been described to me a hundred times since. Until you put it on a transcription program and retrieve those sounds off of there, you don't perceive the sounds. They're simply too fast. In fact they're so fast, and the conversational turns that the creatures execute are so quick that they're virtually stepping on each other. So, I listened the first time through, and my son saw the look on my face, and he said, 'What? What is it, Dad?' And I said, 'Hold on.' And I played it over and I played it over, and there were very few, limited samplings of sound on the website. But I recognized language, and I said, 'Stevie, this is language. This is not human, I can tell, 'cause I don't know how many hundreds of humans I've listened to for hours on tape, and these are not humans. Yet, they're speaking a language."

One can hear audio samples at BigfootSounds.com, and much more on "The Sierra Sounds" CD set, available through this site. Also, listen at YouTube: "Sasquatch Vocalizations: Clips from the Berry/Morehead Recordings"; "Sasquatch Language 1: Scott Nelson and Ron Morehead Interviewed August 15th, 2011"; and "Sasquatch Language 2: Scott Nelson Interviewed January 18th, 2012."

Thirty-six years earlier, in 1972, at an isolated deer camp in the High Sierra Mountains of Eastern California, a site that takes eight hours on horseback to reach, newspaper reporter Alan Berry had succeeded in making high-quality cassette tape recordings of bizarre vocalizations coming at night from nearby in the woods. Other than in the form of fleeing shadows through the trees, he and the others at this camp, cowering inside a primitive lean-to, never caught sight of the authors of these sounds, but during the day they did find massive five-toed footprints in the mud, up to eighteen inches long.

Businessman and hunter Ron Morehead joined the project, and was able to collect further clear audio, upping the total take to more than ninety minutes. The sounds include not only the typical wood knocks, howls, and whoop-calls, but also a rich array of other forceful vocalizations—some snarling, bestial, threatening, but many also uncannily speech-like, highly articulated, and all of it strikes the listener as issuing from throats and lungs much more prodigious than their human counterparts. Indeed, in 1978, a year-long study, based at the University of Wyoming, was not only unable to detect any evidence of technical manipulation, but further, Professor R. Lynn Kirlin and Lasse Hertel wrote, "Having analyzed the Berry-Morehead tape recording of purported Bigfoot speech using accepted techniques of signal processing [taking into account pitch, amplitude, etc.], the authors find an average vocal tract length of 20.2 cm. This is significantly longer than for a normal human male. Extrapolation of average estimators, using human proportions, gives height estimates of between 6' 4" and 8' 2"."

"There are some vocalizations on these tapes that sound like juveniles," observes Nelson, "and one that we call 'the big male.' I can say that on Ron's tapes there are at least three distinct individuals. On Al's tape, there are at least two."

Berry and Morehead can be heard, at times, actually calling out to, and receiving responses from, their unseen neighbors across a distance of several hundred feet, the exchange occasionally seeming quite playful and impassioned. The Sasquatch evince a fascinating degree of interest in this tight band of humans, in forging and sustaining contact, a willingness to make their presence plainly known that is extremely rare, but not unheard of, in the history of our two species on the continent.

Not surprisingly, though, the dramatic relationship at that site never escalated into a visual interface or, of course, any sort of closer-range conversation; and it lasted, on and off, only until the late fall of 1974, when one incident put an abrupt halt to all such visitations--the men shot and killed a large black bear who'd been prowling through camp.

Readers can learn a great deal more of the story surrounding these encounters in Morehead's recent release, *Voices in the Wilderness*, and in the 1976 book *Bigfoot*, by B. Ann Slate and Alan Berry.

Most who have followed this field of study will be familiar with "The Sierra Sounds" CDs, but this startling evidence has not been widely disseminated, a state of affairs that will change now thanks to this researcher, who is uniquely positioned to extract its fuller significance.

"Before 2008," recalls Nelson, "I wasn't even interested in Bigfoot." He was just coming off a long career as a crypto-linguist, having joined the Navy as a young man and undergone training to retrieve the elements of language off of tape. "'Cryptology' means the deciphering of codes/secrets, so a 'crypto-linguist' uncovers secrets hidden in language." He had an innate aptitude for learning languages and graduated from the Voice Transcription School, twice, once for Russian, and once for Spanish. For more than thirty years, he worked as an interceptor, a collector, and an analyst of spoken language.

"After the night I first listened to the short clips with my son," Nelson explains in an interview on the "Bigfoot Quest" radio program (blogtalkradio.com), "I realized, 'I've got to get my hands on the original tapes.' So immediately, I set out to do whatever I could to contact Ron Morehead and Alan Berry. I could not believe that no one else had ever heard this on here. Nobody else had noticed this. But even before I did gain access to the full recordings, I copied what was available on the BFRO and played it for one of my colleagues, a math teacher and native Japanese speaker. At one point, he said, 'Oh my God.' And I hadn't told him that the BFRO was calling this 'Samuri Chatter' or claiming it was Bigfoot. Just his immediate response to me was, 'My God, Scott, that sounds like an old form of Japanese.' I said, 'Do you recognize any of the words?' He said, 'It sounds like they're saying the archaic word for "danger" or "to be careful," in old Japanese.' And I said, 'Well, what is it?' And he said, 'It's *kumati* or *kumai.'* And that's when I told him, 'It's believed that these are Bigfoot creatures.' Of course he was astounded, and he said, 'You know, it really does not sound human.'

"They have a much larger range in their vocal abilities, the resonance is much greater, not even counting when you throw in all the whoops and howls. Just the tone and the resonance of the voice alone is enough to tell me that they are not like any human I have ever listened to on tape, and I can tell you I don't know anyone who has listened to more human voice on tape than I have.

"Five seconds of vocalization might take three hours to transcribe. Very painstaking. And this speech is much too fast for me to imitate. I can enunciate much faster than most people, and I can only get up to maybe half the speed on the tapes, once I've broken down the elements and know them. You just can't hear these morphemes at real time. When you slow it down and you retrieve the sounds out of it, phoneme by phoneme, there are a lot of things that could sound like English words or phrases.

But I always have to qualify that statement by saying it's a natural thing for us to recognize or to pick bits and pieces out of any vocalization that we would recognize from our own language. I have sat native Spanish speakers down and had them listen to the tapes and they've heard a lot of Spanish words and phrases. I have had native Japanese people sit down and listen to it. I've played them for a colleague of mine who is a native Farsi—or Persian—speaker. And virtually anyone who listens to it, and at various speeds, can pick out something that they recognize. When we talk about 'cognatic' expressions or words from other languages, we have to be careful to qualify it. At the same time, we can't ignore that. There's one spot on one of the Berry tapes where one creature seems to be responding to the campers and the big male says, 'Be careful now, Prosgut.' And it's very clear to everyone who listens to it, and we've got several spots in the transcripts where it sounds like they're actually calling each other by name, which is incredible, I know.

"Interestingly, on the two tapes, two years apart, we can make out two different dialects. There were some words that were shared, but not many words. I believe we are essentially listening to two different clans, or tribes, or whatever you want to call them. So in general, are there some of the same words in different places in the tapes? Yes. Some of the same morphemes are repeated both in query inflections and on retort. It's horribly difficult, though, to define 'words.' So what we have to refer to is morphemes, which are units of meaning. And yes, they are repeated. We have a good start on a database of morphemes and phonemes, even potential words, and a very short list of possible names, where one creature is calling to another."

Attempting to make sense of a language so foreign that it comes with no known framework, no Rosetta Stone, is called "radical translation." The first order of business, Nelson explains, is to apply "a principal of charity," which assumes that any speaker is not contradicting himself. Another initial assumption is that the language has a grammar. Next, one looks for negation, which is something no other animal is able to execute, except for humans. "You try to establish the units for 'yes' and 'no.' We've done that. In fact, the word for 'no' that I think I've uncovered here is actually 'no.'

It's the most repeated morpheme that we have out of all of the transcripts, as it is in most human languages, and that correlation was too much for me to ignore.

"There's one spot on Ron's tape, where the female comes out with what very much sounds like English, where she says, 'Are you talking with them?' And the male very clearly comes out and says, 'No...I...won't.' And very slow; that one you can almost hear in real time.

"There's another one where one creature seems to be talking about the food—on the Berry tape they're offering food essentially throughout the whole tape—and one of the creatures sounds like it's repeating our name for food several times. There's one spot where it says, 'Me wat food plen food,' which is a very close pigeon—just what these creatures *would* speak if they'd assimilated some English from us—for 'I'm watching the food.' And right after that is when another one says, 'Be carcful now, Prosgut.'"

Thanks to some preliminary fieldwork, Nelson can corroborate what many have noted: the species' remarkable capacity for mimicry. "Yes, I have experienced it first-hand. I was put in touch with a local farmer by the BFRO, just to give me a chance to go out and try some of this language. This farmer had had Sasquatch activity for many years around his place. I heard a 900-pound gobbler turkey. Another time, out there, I heard a 900-pound coyote. Scared the heck out of my son. In all the areas that I've tried this, I can count probably twelve more meaningful responses that I've gotten. Nothing big yet, nothing linguistically complex."

When he looks back at the past year and a half, he has to laugh. "I didn't ask for any of this. It has complicated my life beyond what I can tell you. I'm a single father of two kids, and this has become the focus of our lives. It has consumed all of my time. Of course I'm having fun with it, but it's taken a lot of time away from other things that should have had some priority. So it's nothing that I expected or wanted, but I can tell you that once it's happened, I was probably the right guy to do it. And at least, the only guy that I knew who would be willing to do it. From the very beginning, Al and Ron never had an agenda of any sort. All they wanted, and all they agreed to, really, was to send me the tapes. They just wanted the truth."

Nelson is now working on the project with four other linguists, two of whom are also military-trained crypto-linguists, another, a translator proficient in ten languages, and the fourth, a Japanese linguist.

As the meticulous work finally comes to a head, it is forthcoming in book form, *Voices in the Wilderness, Volume 2,* to include the seventy-five-page transcription and a full, contextual, methodological discussion.

"I've come to the conviction," says Nelson, "that, short of a corpse, what greater evidence can you have for the existence of any creature than to have discovered his language, and to have taped it, and transcribed it, analyzed it, and proven that it is indeed a language?"

Nelson has recently sent an open letter to the research community:

Since our ultimate goal is the recovery of Sasquatch Language, I have found it necessary to establish a phonetic alphabet and transcription standard (based on the transcription of the Berry/Morehead tapes), by which the contrast and comparison of all future suspected language can be facilitated. To this end, as an invaluable tool in the future of Sasquatch Language research, I am requesting that the attached standard be published on research websites and that it be copied and   distributed freely. With this, I am also requesting that local investigators begin using this alphabet as soon as possible to accurately document any perceived Sasquatch Language.

This standard should not be limited to first-hand witness accounts or recordings from North America, but should be used by investigators world-wide, since most languages have many of the same non-phonetic characteristics as English. The work is written in the style of a military SOP (Standard Operating Procedure).

It is my belief that there is nothing more important, at this early stage of Sasquatch Language study, than to standardize the documentation of evidence.

The Sasquatch Phonetic Alphabet (SPA) will alternately be known by the more formal denomination, Unclassified Hominin Phonetic Alphabet (UHPA), until such time as the subject Being is scientifically classified, or documented linguistic contact has been established. "Sasquatch" is used here as a generally accepted term for the subject Being.

A variation of the English Reformed Phonetic Alphabet is used, as transcribed from the Berry/Morehead Tapes (BMT). The existence of the Sasquatch Being is hereby assumed, since any creature must exist before his language.

The purpose of this is to standardize all future transcription of suspected Sasquatch Language and to facilitate comparison of language articulations by future researchers, the ultimate goal being the recovery of Sasquatch Language.

Sasquatch Language is spoken approximately twice as fast as any known language in most analyzed recordings; therefore, it must be slowed down to be transcribed accurately. 50% of real-time will be the standard. Since this is an unknown language, transcribed for the first time, the grammar and syntax of it, likewise, cannot be known. Since words cannot be known, and only suspected in cognates, Sasquatch utterances will be given as individual morphemes (or syllables). Untranscribable vocalizations such as grunts or screams will be noted with capital letters within parentheses, e.g. (G) or (SC). An abbreviation key follows the phonetics key.

This alphabet is expected to grow as additional verified recordings of Sasquatch Language are collected and analyzed, and new extra-human articulations are documented. For example: The well-documented howls, whoops, growls, screams and whistles of Sasquatch may someday be found to have linguistic meaning; wood- and rock-knocking or tooth-popping may be found to be encoded. It should not be discounted that manipulated tree, limb and stick formations could be graphic expressions of Sasquatch Language, much like runic or pictographic human writing systems.

With the recovery of Sasquatch Language being the anticipated outcome, cooperation and consensus among language researchers should be the first rule of this study.

Since he shared this open letter, Nelson has expanded his study on the strength of numerous further audio clips submitted to him by North American researchers, captured at various sites within Alabama, Georgia, Minnesota, Wisconsin, California, The Great Smoky Mountains of Tennessee, etc. Nelson has found in these recordings many of the same phonemes documented in the 1970s. "I have some experience, outside of my Naval career, dealing with populations that have what they would consider a secret language. I'm talking about the Romano Gypsies. From that experience, and knowing the nature of language, and knowing that one of the biggest concerns for Sasquatch, we assume, is the avoidance of people, what I would have to assume is that Sasquatch speaks an assimilated language that includes Spanish, English and Native American, depending on where they are, but that they also have their own basic language, and that they can speak in more than one language.

"Have I heard Spanish words in Sasquatch language? Yes. Have I heard English words? Yes. Language is a living entity that evolves and changes. In Spain, Spanish is not quite the same in different *valleys.* So, would Sasquatch in Georgia speak a different dialect from Sasquatch in Washington State? Yeah, we'd have to assume that. But I would say that they also have a common language that they could both understand at the same time. And the only thing that would preclude that from happening is extreme isolation. And we know that Sasquatch is so migratory, so fast, can travel such great distances, that I don't believe that that type of isolation exists for them.

"To truly discover them as a people we need contact, to *speak* with them. How do we understand a Sasquatch by collecting a body, a specimen? One property of language, for something to qualify as a language, is that it be learnable. I think we will be able to learn how to communicate with them someday. I don't think we will ever learn their language fully, because I think secrecy and self-preservation will always be important to them. Again, I can use the example of the Romano Gypsies: I think they will always keep part of their language to themselves. But if nothing else I think Sasquatch will be able to communicate with us through our own language. So it will be an effort on both our parts. We may end up communicating in what we would call a *pidgin*—half human and half Sasquatch."

A caller to the show adds: "I know from experience how deep the inroads can go with somebody when you can just out a couple words even. It shows them that you're trying."

Nelson: "The first thing that I try to do when I go out, and up there at the Berry/Morehead camp in the High Sierras, is to read from the original transcripts. My first intention is to let them know that I'm trying to communicate to them, in their own language. They have to know I have no clue as to what I'm saying. I have gotten numerous responses, especially what I refer to as an 'acquiescence snarl.' I believe this to be like a gift. They are letting you know that they're there and that they're listening, and that's probably as far as they're going to go with you. I really believe that you don't hear anything from a Sasquatch that he does not want you to hear. I don't think that you trick them into responding to you with call-blasting or anything like that, or certainly not at close range. That's why I call this an 'acquiescence snarl'; they are accepting the fact that they understand you're trying to communicate with them."

Another caller asks why they seem so much less averse to having their audio recorded than to having their picture taken.

Nelson: "American Indians felt that a photograph captured part of their spirit, their soul. If Sasquatch have anything in common with American Indians, that would explain one thing right there. We modern, species-centric humans think, How can they possibly understand what photographs even *are*? But who are we to say? Why do we hardly ever catch them on trail cameras? I believe that we take two steps into the forest and they know exactly what's going on."

Another caller asks whether Sasquatch sing.

"I've had some people tell me they have heard singing coming from parts of the forest where there could not be any humans over there. I can also tell you that part of the Morehead tape contains a female Sasquatch and she is sort of chanting the same word over and over, but in a very sing-song intonation. So yes, I've heard of the idea of them singing, and why would they *not*?

"In the Sierras, we got some reciprocal drumming. The last three years going up into that camp...and this is not easy because I have to carry this huge drum up there with me, an ancient Irish drum that has roots going back to Central Asia...so I take this up there and I play it, always in the evening before we go to bed. Four mornings in a row, when we woke up, we'd start our fire and get some coffee going, start cooking some oatmeal, and we'd start hearing from one direction in the forest a tap-tap...tap-tap-tap, and our ears would kind of perk up and Ron [Morehead] would say, 'Oh, there's a woodpecker.' And then, from the opposite direction, we'd hear the same type of tapping, and more quiet and rhythmic than a woodpecker. And then, from a *third* position. So we were surrounded by 'woodpeckers' that were not pecking a tree but were somehow tapping on trees in a rhythmic pattern and they were trading off. And when you added all three rhythms up together, it was exactly the rhythm of doubling the stick on my drum.

"We made three trips up there this past summer, and Ron was so disappointed, as we all were. But this place is only fifty to a hundred miles from where the [Sierra Kills] murders took place [see Chapter Seven], so they left us entirely alone. After that, Ron took it upon himself, though he promised me he would never do this, to go back up there alone, closer to autumn. He was talking to the woods, as we always did, like, 'I'm going into my tent now, please don't scare me...' No sooner did he get into his tent than between his tent and the old hunting hutch...and we're talking a distance of maybe twenty yards...he hears a classic wood knock, a very loud, sharp wood knock—CRACK! So he's sitting up and he's saying, 'Please don't scare me. Please don't scare me.' Then something walks very heavily, bipedally, right up to the tent and stations himself, kneeling down outside the tent, and Ron can hear his breath, and he is of course scared stiff, he's up there by himself. The thing eventually gets up and walks away, after a couple minutes.

"Ron stays up all night long. And it's several hours later that he hears the toilet lid [heard being banged in the original recordings], way out maybe forty yards away, being picked up and slammed down. And then he hears it walk back up, right next to the tent again, and it lets out a sound that Ron describes as metallic. It didn't sound like it was an organic sound of a living being. He said it sounded machine-like, but it was right next to the tent, and it was ear-piercing—a very high-pitched buzzing that lasted for like thirty seconds. It seemed like an eternity, just blasting into the tent. And then it stopped as abruptly as it began, and everything went silent. As soon as it was light, Ron gathered up as much as he could carry, didn't pack everything up, and hiked the eight hours that it takes to get down off that mountain, got the hell out of there, without any sleep.

"I hear an argument all the time by some of the biologists in this field: 'Well, but they don't have culture.' Of course they have culture, language itself implies culture. Culture is *in* the language. Culture means that you learn something from your parents and you teach it to your children. Language more than anything else implies that. Now, do they have *material* culture? Do they create fire or do they make weapons or tools? We don't know, but they don't build buildings. They don't need to, probably. So they may not have much material culture, but they have culture. They create music...that's culture. They seem to create art in stick and tree structures. Ron and I and [my son] Stevie, in our daily hikes at the Sierra camp, have come upon rock arrangements that look like the Sun Cross or Celtic Cross—an equilateral cross with a circle around it. And that's very much an American Indian symbol as well."

In Autumn Williams' book *Enoch—A Bigfoot Story*, discussed in the next section, the subject of Sasquatch speech plays a central role. At one point, [long-term witness Mike saw that] two of the males "were talking to each other and gesturing. One of them kept looking over at me while they were talking and I could tell that they were *discussing* me."

3. *Genesis of a New Nonfiction Genre— Recent Habituation Books*

Though only a handful of such books exist, their number has doubled in just the past five years, and I expect this trend to continue, quickly gaining momentum. At the time of this writing, I am aware of only eight books, besides the one you're reading, that fall into this category. The five newest I will discuss below. Three precursors are *The Creature— Personal Experiences with Bigfoot*, by Jan Klement (1976); *Fifty Years with Bigfoot: Tennessee Chronicles of Co-Existence*, by Mary Green and Janice Carter Coy (2002); and *Night Shadows—A Journal of Hominid Research*, by Mary Green (2005).

Unfortunately, our cause is hampered right off the bat by the fact that not only are Mary Green's two volumes out of print, but *Fifty Years with Bigfoot* has lost credibility, due to poor writing, inconsistent presentation of "facts," multiple self-contradictions by Carter Coy, and very public infighting between the co-authors. Fairly or not, this ugliness casts Green's other book in a questionable light as well, although if she were to re-issue *Night Shadows*, we could try to judge it on its own merits.

This leaves *The Creature,* which is also out of print, but it can be downloaded as an e-book thanks to a thirtieth-anniversary re-release.

> I had built a cabin in a small wooded area in southwestern Pennsylvania. The land comprises about eleven acres…[with] a south-facing slope and a stream. This was to be my retreat from the world of teaching Earth Science in a small college…. The adventure I am about to relate began on a hot August day. I had been digging a small pond by hand. After I had worked enough and sweated enough my habits called for me to retire to the porch of the cabin and enjoy a beer. I…flipped open the can and sat on the side of the porch with my feet up on a bench in front of me. I heard a slight noise to my right and so I lifted myself and peered around to the side of the cabin and there crouched before me was a large hairy

creature. [Several months later, in the autumn, came the second sighting.] I had made myself comfortable on the porch at dusk was munching an apple when the creature appeared at the railing about eight feet from me. The neck and head of the creature were above the railing and with a hairy arm it reached out, took two apples, stared at me, then turned and bounded into the bushes again….[I later estimated by the height of this railing that the creature] must have stood seven feet tall.

I find Klement's to be an engrossing and persuasive account, containing much specific detail that comports well with the observations of habituators over the ensuing decades. The Sasquatch turns out to be ill—which probably accounts for the highly atypical lack of caution from the beginning—and eventually, after receiving much food and solicitude from his human host, he passes away. The author buries him, having forged a bond that renders any scientific use of the corpse unthinkable.

It's noteworthy that until very recently, there have been no credible, long-term studies of the habituation phenomenon since *The Creature*, written during the Ford Administration and recounting events that occurred ten years earlier still. The five studies featured below begin to remedy this dearth and set the stage for many more to come.

a) *Valley of the Skookum—Four Years of Encounters with Bigfoot,* by Sali Sheppard-Wolford, 2006
(Washington State)

This book, too, is written in retrospect, thirty years after the events reported. The author, her husband and their three daughters move into a rustic cabin near the Carbon River in Orting, Washington. One morning, Sali is walking in the forest with her two-year-old.

My arms were loaded with wood and Autumn trailed

slightly behind, singing happy songs softly to herself.
Then I rounded the bend in the trail and stopped cold.
Back in the shadows…stood the huge shape of a man.
By his side was a smaller, lighter shape. I heard Autumn
come up behind me. None of us moved. From the
shadows they appeared to be watching us just like we
were watching them. The only things I could see
[clearly] were their eyes: enormous round eyes with a
slightly greenish cast…. The larger one cocked his head,
with a questioning look. *I wonder if he's curious about
my fur coat.* His movement brought me back to reality
and I whispered to Autumn, "Turn around, honey, and
walk, don't run."

Thereafter, Sali experiences further brief sightings, smells the typical
odor of decay often associated with Sasquatch encounters, and hears night
screams, "a woman-like cry that echoed off the ridge across the river."
After the family acquires rabbits to raise for food, she is awakened one
night

by the clattering of metal at about 2:00 a.m. I could hear
odd sounds, like a group of people speaking Chinese. I
hesitated to wake my snoring husband and instead
slipped silently from bed. I tiptoed to the window
overlooking the trashcans. The yard light was off but a
full moon lit up the yard. Then the shadow of what
appeared to be a huge man appeared, passed between the
moon and me. When I gasped, I got a whiff of the smell
I knew well. Outside [the next morning,] a scene of
utter destruction met my eyes. Trash cans had been
thrown like toys around the yard. One was flattened.
Their contents had been dumped into a large pile.
[My husband] was cursing and filling new garbage bags.
I came up beside him, putting my hand on his arm.
    "John?"
    He shook himself free. "Leave me alone. I've
got to clean up this mess. Smells like a skunk has been
here too."
    "Don't you notice anything unusual about all

this?"

"All I know is I'm gonna shoot some dogs."

"No. Stop, and look closer. No animal I know unties a bag. They rip it to shreds. All those carefully wrapped rabbit guts have been carefully *un*wrapped." I showed him a stack of papers spread out on a rock.

"What kind of animal unhooks bungee cords, or flattens a trash can?"

"So, what did all this? Oh, I get it, Bigfoot. Is that what you're getting at? Give me a break."

I am reminded here of another cache of rabbits, those kept by Rachel at Texas #1, and of their similar apparent irresistibility. Also, very much in the hostile spirit of Ammi's husband in North Carolina and No-Bite's husband at Texas #2, Sali's remains mockingly dismissive until the day he finally sees the creature for himself—and, at times, even *afterward*. A friend who was with him at the time recounts the incident.

"This gigantic, hairy *thing* that looked like a man stood up from where he'd been crouching next to a root ball. When he saw us watching him, he turned and walked up the bank into the trees on the ridge. Every few steps, he looked back to see if we were still there. That thing must have been close to eight feet tall. We saw it clear as day." After [his friend] left, John walked toward the bedroom. He moved like an old man."

This final detail registers the impact upon certain *Homo sapiens*—most often the adult male of the species—of being habituated against their will to the presence of these locals.

A young neighbor boy tells Autumn that he "has monkeys at his house. They come at night to look in his window and they whistle and talk to him so he can't go to sleep. I wish they'd come to our house," Autumn tells her mother. "I like monkeys." And indeed, this avid child grew up to be one of the leading students of Sasquatch, author of *Enoch—A Bigfoot Story*.

A bit later, this young neighbor's parents are able to watch a family group nonstop for three hours during the night, two young ones playing together near the house, the large one hanging back, observing them.

> "It was kind of like watching a spooky movie at the theater. You pay money to see it because it's exciting. You know the monsters aren't real, so it's a safe kind of fear. I felt I was watching all this on a movie screen because the window framed it. It didn't seem real but I knew it was."
>
> Emily giggled. "Now I understand why [my son] said there were monkeys outside…. [The] young ones loped around like huge monkeys."

One day, Sali noticed that a certain wood-lined path never had

> any spider webs to block our way. Elsewhere, at this time of the morning, I had to carry a stick to clear the way. [Also,] this path wasn't overgrown from disuse; rather it was well worn, as though traveled frequently. Curious, I climbed up [from here]. About ten feet off the ground was a moss-lined alcove that appeared to be the resting-place of something large. When I pulled myself up a bit higher, I felt my stomach clench. The spot afforded a direct view of our living room window.

b) *Backyard Bigfoot*, by Lisa A. Shiel, 2006
(Michigan and Texas)

In this well-researched study, Shiel points us to fascinating material-culture representations of large hairy hominins stretching back through history, as well as some provocative speculation about the possible relationship between Sasquatch and UFO experiences.

But for our purposes, the heart of Shiel's study (aside from the braids found in her horses' manes, presented earlier) is her account of "stick signs" found on her property in Michigan's Upper Peninsula, after her move from Texas.

> In July of 2005, the activity escalated. I discovered 38 stick signs that month. Again, parallel sticks and crosses dominated. The 4th of July ushered in a new episode in the saga, with an intriguing twist. A few days earlier, I'd decided to create my own stick sign in an area where I often found signs. By leaving my own sign, I'd let my visitor know I had caught onto the game. If humans were responsible, they might realize they could get into trouble for trespassing and stop their shenanigans. As my initial foray into sign-making, I positioned four sticks into a square. As of July 3rd, my sign remained intact. By July 4th, however, the visitor had rearranged my sign: Two of the sticks now formed a "V," with a third placed as a crossbar atop the "V." The fourth stick lay parallel to the crossbar, a few inches away. Either I had extremely brazen, foolhardy [people] creeping around my property just about every night, or an intelligent creature on a par with humans had initiated contact.

Habituators I have worked with—in Oklahoma, North Carolina, Texas #1 and #2—also report sticks appearing on the ground, after windless nights, arranged in formations that indicate intelligence; and we recall Sylvester's "games" in his Vermont forest, such as leaving a quarter oriented north-south and later finding it rotated to east-west, or missing altogether: "In place of the quarter [was] a cute little arrangement of feathers. Each a different color. And spread out just like a picture, facing east." None of these researchers, though, has engaged in the level of concerted two-way "communication," within a compressed time frame, that Shiel has. I hope that her example will spur others to attempt the same—as it did me; see "Object Communication: Your Place or Mine"— with clear photographs and meticulous record-keeping, and will encourage those who *have* done so to come forward in great numbers, so that we might perhaps begin to formulate something akin to the Rosetta Stone, which allowed for the translation of ancient Egyptian hieroglyphs. On the other hand, of course, Sasquatch semiotics may well be highly idiomatic, bound by time and place, conditioned by the specific cultural history of a given clan, and the local dialects that have arisen. Will we need a separate Rosetta Stone for each neighborhood? Either way, "Manipulated tree, limb and stick formations," Crypto-Linguist Scott Nelson has observed, "could be graphic expressions of Sasquatch Language, much like runic or pictographic human writing systems."

Photos by Lisa A. Shiel, BackyardPhenomena.com

The Oklahoma habituator has found dozens of stick configurations on her property, such as the above

"I continued to find stick signs nearly every day," Shiel writes.

A relative suggested that I leave a stick sign in the shape of a tic-tac-toe board. "Why not?" I thought, and so I did create a tic-tac-toe sign on July 12th. The next day, my nighttime visitor had rearranged the four sticks that comprised the sign into a series of parallel lines. More and more signs appeared as the days passed. I felt I was communicating with someone, though I had no idea what we were saying to each other. At this point I decided to keep going with the stick-sign exchanges, in hopes of learning more about the intelligence behind the responses.

On July 13th, after seeing the changed sign, I created two more signs for my new friend—a square again, near where I'd placed the first square, along with the word "HI!" spelled out in sticks several feet from the square. About twenty feet east of these two signs, I crafted a third sign. This time I fashioned a triangle with, to amuse my visitor, a glow-in-the-dark dog toy inside it. The following day, I received my reply. The visitor had transformed the square into a complex series of crosses. The sticks from the "HI!" sign had vanished. As usual, no tracks gave away my visitor's presence. Over the next few days, I found more crosses and parallel sticks in the spots my visitor favored. The sign-maker started using one stick, snapped in half, to form the shapes. When I discovered these signs, the wood flesh would still be pale, signifying a recent break.

The pieces always fit together, making it clear both had come from one stick. Unless sticks have a mysterious source of energy I don't know about, no natural force could pick up a broken stick then flop it down again in a "T" shape. My visitor also began to incorporate non-stick materials into the signs—everything from blades of dead grass, reeds, and briars to remnants of fireworks my neighbors had shot off on the Fourth. The grass could've originated on my property, though not in the vicinity of the stick sign. As for the reeds and the fireworks, neither came from my property. The nearest crop of reeds grows a quarter mile down the road.

One week after my visitor stole the sticks from the "HI!" sign I created, a new and complex sign appeared overnight in the same spot. The sign included an arrow alongside a number of sticks set both parallel with and at right angles to the arrow. On that day, my triangle sign had been changed too. The sign-maker had moved the dog toy from inside the triangle to a spot ten feet away. The triangle itself remained intact. To top off that day, I found the first signs ever left in front of my house, within 50 feet of the front porch.

c) *Visits from the Forest People—An Eyewitness Report of Extended Encounters with Bigfoot,* by Julie Scott and the Scott Family, 2010 (Washington State)

Here, we find copious journal entries by four Scott family members, relating events that occurred between September 2008 and March 2009. The writers are Julie Scott, her husband Wayne, and her two adult daughters in their early twenties, Elizabeth and Rachel.

Julie:
> Branches that are broken or twisted high up in trees are sometimes a good indication of Sasquatch activity.

> Barb is over again. She and the girls light a big bonfire in the backyard. They hear some…definite rock knocks. Rachel plays a mixture of Bigfoot vocalizations she's recorded from the Internet. Suddenly they hear a loud scream that turns into monkey-like chatter, and finally into a bit of "Squatch talk" sounding rather like Japanese…

> At 2:00 AM, Wayne and I are standing outside of our bedroom door on the porch, when we hear a couple of clear, distinctive, mournful cries coming from across the street in the woods.

Unlike Sali's, Ammi's and No-Bite's husbands, Julie's finds himself free of prideful resistance, able to open up to the experience.

Wayne:
> My first encounter [occurred] after three days of living there. The time was around 10:00 PM, and I was outside on the patio. Suddenly, in the wooded area in front of me…I heard a heavy-sounding biped stomping on the ground as it walked through the thick bushes and trees.

Next came the sound of something fairly heavy being thrown across the bushes maybe fifteen feet, and it seemed to me like what a fifty-pound bale of hay would sound like if it was being thrown through thick brush. It sounded as if whoever or whatever was throwing something…was frustrated. It seemed they were not pleased by our recent arrival at the residence.

[On a night soon thereafter:] I saw over in the bushes behind the house where the forest begins, about twenty-five feet away, a Bigfoot sitting down with his head turning towards me slowly as I also was turning. He had apparently had his hairy head turned away from me the whole time I had been standing out there to prevent me from seeing him. But what helped to expose him...was when he began to look directly at me with a "not friendly at all" look. He turned fully towards me to watch me go into the house.

The third time I saw the amber eyes, they were fairly close to me by the front office. He was just down the slope…staring straight at me. The gaze from the amber eyes in the darkness was very different from the way the first Bigfoot had looked at me. Best way I can explain it is that there was a playfulness in those eyes, even a kind of goofy look, just someone having a fun time.

Elizabeth:

[I developed] my own daily routine of trials and results…. I explored and began to become intimately familiar with all the details of the surrounding forests with my daughter Lilee in tow. As the joy and excitement of her voice filled the air, I often thought that if there really was something out there watching and listening, it could not help but be drawn to her. [My four-year-old daughter] Lilee and I would whoop, sing, and scream at the tops of our lungs…[and] I took note when things were different from one day to the next. For example, branches broken high up in a specific pattern, small trees that appeared to have been pushed over to an exact angle on a path leading up a sharp slope.

This reminds me of my outings with my own young daughter, and Sali's with two- and three-year-old Autumn.

> I would like to mention how different I found both the activity and the overall feeling in the woods when it was just us, in contrast to when we had cameras and strangers there all the time. I think the trust the Squatches had in us was broken when we allowed the invasive research to take place.

> I went into [a] cave on a small hill and saw how perfect the space was for something large to crouch down completely hidden and still view our house and balcony with no obstructions.

Finally, one night, she and her sister Rachel saw one peeking out from behind a tree.

> I saw the large, hairy outline of a round head. A broad, flat nose started between the amber eyes and continued down to a slightly protruding mouth area. My first impression of the expression on its face was that it showed youthful curiosity. It stared at us three consecutive times from behind the tree in a matter of forty seconds. I knew what I was seeing was real and close and tangible enough to fill in the missing piece in my mind.

> Rachel and I savored every moment….The creature then turned directly around and went up the hill and deeper into the darkness. It either seemed to be bored with playing hide-and-seek with us or satisfied that it had established visual contact and now wanted to rejoin its family or clan.

Rachel:

> I attempted to imitate [their] sounds and behavior, vigorously trying to establish some sort of communication. I felt silly and awkward at first, until I started getting responses. Every day became an adventure…
>
> One night, I took a rock and struck it twice on the wooden railing of the balcony. About thirty seconds later, from somewhere in the vast blackness of the woods, came…what sounded like two rocks larger than mine being struck together. I knocked four times, and then he would knock four times. This continued for a couple of hours…. At one point, all responses ceased for over an hour. We thought the beast had gotten bored and moved on, but then the knocking started again, this time from a completely different direction and distance.
>
> Elizabeth and I went [out one night] to make our presence known. We danced and sang about the field, whooping and hollering and hoping to see or hear something. On one side of the field was a steep, wooded hill where we often heard footsteps and branches cracking….As I walked toward the far end of the field, something happened that I can only describe as "hitting a wall." I cannot explain it, but [I heard] a clear mental message saying, "Just to let you know, I am here. Don't come any closer."

This last is a common experience; recall the "infrasound" events at Ammi's place and at No-Bite's, while she held the screen. Moreover, this phenomenon sometimes seems to bridge over into an articulate form of attitude-projection, even telepathy. Thus far, I have deliberately refrained from broaching the topic, although I do frequently hear reports of this type of communication. For my own recent experiences in this realm, please see the Epilogue.

d) *Communion with Sasquatch,* by J.P. Smith and Freeman Young, 2012 (Oklahoma, Ohio, California)

This book lays out the long-term interactions between the species and three men, Dennis, Jeffery, and Freeman. Differing from the case of habituation sites, these are habituation *experiences* in the sense that certain Sasquatch have become familiar with these human beings, approaching them repeatedly over time but not always at the same place.

Like Jerry from Upstate New York, Dennis first encountered them when he was a small boy, but in his case they were often unfriendly.

> They'd take a rock shaped sort of like a hatchet head, and take some wire or string or rope or something, whatever they could get their hands on I guess, and make little tomahawks and throw at us from the cedar trees. See, right behind our house there's this real thick grove of cedar trees. And then sometimes we messed around in our backyard and were in throwing distance from them.

That's like the "rock fight" at No-Bite's house, in 1998, though in the present instance, one-sided.

> It happened ever since we moved there. We were working on the foundation to move the house, we went out there. We took a break because it was hot. And [when we returned] somebody had taken a big old rock and destroyed our drills and all our tools that we left on the work site from day one of moving into that place. The whole thing was they didn't want us being there.

This is very reminiscent of No-Bite's feeling "under siege" when she re-occupied her house after five years away. Dennis also heard them talking when he was in sixth grade, in Hydro, Oklahoma.

> It sounded like talking through a harmonica. The in and out

of the syllables. Like me and you are talking, the air keeps going *out* of our mouth. But when that thing talked, it was sometimes blowing air out and sometimes sucking air in that gave it that harmonica effect.

One day, he attempted to take control over their aggressive behavior, as when No-Bite decided to verbally set boundaries. But here, the outcome is radically different from hers.

> I'm pretty sure they can understand what we say. 'Cause one day I was really mad at 'em, they'd stolen my hatching eggs. I had a guy coming up to buy 'em from Oklahoma City, so I had them all cleaned and packed in boxes, out there in the barn waiting. And the lock had been yanked off, and I knew what did it. And so me and my brother were walking about in the pasture, and kind of looking for them to see if we could catch 'em carrying the eggs or boxes of eggs away. And then I made the statement, "Think I'm gonna set a fire around all them," you know, "around all of 'em, and trap 'em. Then they can't run away from me. I'll just go around the edge. Just light a fire, and it'll go in and we can capture 'em." And see, those were just words I was saying; I didn't mean I was going to actually do it. And then me and my brother went in the house, and my mom was already in the house. No one was outside at our house. And here in a little bit we looked—Mom said, "Come quick, come quick! Our yard's on fire!" The yard all around the house was on fire.

At times, Dennis felt that he experienced another form of communication as well.

> They would be watching me chop wood. From a distance we'd see 'em watch me chop wood, and then later on my axe was stolen. We would find. . .we would be hearing an axe down in the woods so we'd get my brother's spotting scope out and look. And they would be using an axe. Like I said, they're quick learners.

The times like, we would set there watching them with
the spotting scope, and at times I'd tell my brother all the
things I'd like to do to those things and stuff. Just so,
just . . . we were a long ways away, say maybe a quarter
of a mile away from them, or nearly that. And they'd
start looking at me. They'd turn and quit doing what
they were doing and turn around and start looking. As
soon as I would be thinking all these mean things I'd
like to do to them, they'd all turn around and start staring
at us, which was weird.

The second testimonial is from Jeffery, who began researching
Sasquatch only recently, in southeastern Ohio.

We found quite a few tracks and also a lot of stick structures.
I've found some diagonal ones. I started noticing they were
all the same. You know how you break off a stick and one
end's bigger than the other? The smaller end was always
pointed toward either the lake or one of the runoff streams in
the area. Along that trail, the first one we noticed was like a
little T-pee structure, not far off of this trail. It was probably a
mile or so back that we had walked when I saw the first one.
And up on the side of a hill, off the trail . . . and it was a
pretty steep hill . . . a tree about three inches in diameter that
was broken off, about three foot high. It was broken off, and
then I saw the little T-pee-looking thing, and it was kind of
leaning. And I looked up in that direction, and there was this
horizontal stick lying across two small trees. And the small
end was pointing down toward the end of the hill. And there
was another one down there that was pointed off in the
direction where the lake's at.

Jeffery found these formations in the Salt Fork State Park, and this
is also where he captured an important piece of video, called "the tree-
shaker" footage. Its circumstances are fully discussed in *Communion with
Sasquatch*, and despite recent efforts to discredit the clip, I am confident of
its authenticity and urge you to watch for yourself by Googling
"Facebook/FindBigfoot Breaking down tree, voice." Not only do we see,

by daylight, a Sasquatch yanking on a tree and ultimately snapping it off at root level, we can also hear him briefly and emphatically *speaking*.

This remarkably incautious Sasquatch is probably attempting to distract the two humans from a juvenile up in a nearby tree, seen elsewhere in the video, and to drive them away. If so, the tactic worked well, as you'll see.

Co-author Freeman Young's first encounter occurred during childhood, on a golf course.

> This was like 1978. This thing leapt into the air, let out a scream, and I hear it coming through the air. And it lands right in front of me and drops to all fours, on its fingertips, too. I can see clearly in the full moonlight. It's landed and it's gone down onto its fingertips in a push-up. And its nose goes way down and stops, like a quarter inch from the cement. And it sniffs, and it smells me. And it turns and it screams and it does this scream like five feet away from me. And then he jumped, and in the next minute he was gone. He was gone straight up into the oak tree, through the oak tree. Like about ten feet up and through the oak tree, out the other side and down this Par 5 that's like half a mile long. Straight shot. I can see perfect in the full moon. And he's running in this crazy run where he goes . . . one, two, leap! I don't know how far he leaped. And then . . . one, two, leap! One, two, leap! And each time it leaps, it screams. And it was so cool just watching each time it leaped. I thought it was a baboon, because it was a hairy little monkey person. It was a small

one. It was the same size as me, maybe a little smaller.

In 2000, when he found out more about Sasquatch, he came to realize that this had not been a baboon, and began hiking in the woods with new eyes and ears: "I saw stick signs galore. I saw all kinds of stick signs. I heard knocks, tree crashes."

As described in the book, Freeman has now seen the species on many occasions, even in suburban San Francisco; he contends that Sasquatch come much closer to our residential areas than we imagine, especially between midnight and dawn.

Once, he was treated to an astonishing sight.

> I was hidden behind a rock wall. I heard splashing in the water and I looked over with my night vision, and I can see these two. They were kind of jogging. Like double-timing it. It was getting light out, that's why. It was like 5:30 in the morning, and they were coming up the creek. I was in position. And they're talking as they're jogging [but not talking with their mouths]. Their eyes are flashing . . . flash-flash-flash-flash-flash from the one in the water . . . flash-flash-flash-flash-flash from the one in response. Flash from the bank. Flash response from the one in the water. And they don't know I'm watching them. There are some videos on YouTube that show this. There's one from Impossible Visits ["A Figure by the Bench: Oklahoma Habituation Site"] that shows a really good version of what I saw. The Bigfoot's coming in, and he's kind of looking around. And you only see the flash. It looks like a little flashing butterfly. That's what these guys had.

Freeman has learned much from talking to Native Americans.

> I know of some Indian grandmas up in northern California who go out in the springtime and pick all the herbs and specific plants to keep the traditions alive of the connection to the Bigfoot, because they're sacred to their tribe. So these grandmas make an offering every spring. They gather little

sprouts and little flowers and strawberries, and they save nuts from the fall before, and they make like a little hors d'oeuvres tray, if you will, that they specially make for them. And they sing little songs and make it all with prayers. And very much care goes into it. And then they take it out to a certain place by the river, the Trinity River, and they make an offering there to the Bigfoot.

See, it was the warrior tribe, the European nations. The Europeans came, and they just mowed over all those old agreements. Because they used to have old agreements, like, "Okay, the river's mutual. We'll live on one side of the river, you live on the other side of the river. We'll hunt over here, you hunt over there. Our children will both play in the river, and that'll be the middle ground." And for thousands of years that's how it was. And then the Europeans came and just mowed over all of those agreements. And the Indians and the hominoids, who had been living pretty much harmoniously all those thousands of years, without bothering each other—some of them even had more intimate relationships than that, where their children played together, where they made offerings to each other. Like, the humans would offer salmon and the hominoids would offer wood for fire.

You can listen to YouTube: "COMMUNION WITH SASQUATCH: New Book and Interview," which features both co-authors touching on many compelling facets of the subject, including J.P. Smith's own first sighting at the edge of a thick "jungle" behind his recording studio, in Central Florida.

The day before, I went out where I'd heard the knocks and squatted down, looking into this thick jungle area, and I could see there was light behind the trees. And I could see multiple silhouettes just pacing back and forth behind this set of trees, all different sizes. There was one big, lurking shadow, there's always the big one. They don't show themselves that much but they kind of direct what's to be allowed. They definitely chose to show themselves to me at this particular time.

A misconception is that they're always on the ground, walking around on two legs. That's not been my experience. The day before my sighting, I was looking up into the trees, and where the palm trees meet the great swamp oaks, the palm fronds hang over and make perfect little rooms, like little nests. So I started wondering, Could they be hanging out way up in the treetops? I started paying attention to that spot.

So the next day, I went up there at about 5:30 in the afternoon, just before dusk, and I'm sitting near the fence, watching that same area, about fifty or sixty feet away, and I see this overhanging nest area start to shake. We have a lot of big birds down here, like sandhill cranes, so I'm thinking, Could a bird be getting ready to fly up out of here? But a bird didn't fly out of it....A Sasquatch jumped from the little nest onto another palm tree, and then from that palm tree onto a great oak, right at twelve o'clock in front of me, and when he did he clung to the side of the tree but upside down. His head was facing towards the ground. He moved so unnaturally. The closest thing I can compare it to is seeing Spiderman stick to the side of a building. He was so *fast*, man, I saw him fly from the palm tree over to the oak tree...and when I say fly I mean he *soared* across...I don't know, maybe twenty feet? Which wasn't much for him, you know. He was an adult, seven or eight feet tall, and he was all gray. So he didn't look at me or anything, he just stuck on the tree, like...you ever see a jumping spider? Jump, land, turn itself around real quick? That's how fast he turned himself right-side up. And then he quickly shuffled himself to the back of the tree and then came down. But when he moved to the back I could see his hands and his feet hugging the tree, like a tree-climber would, with spikes? But of course he didn't have any spikes. I could see his hands and feet coming down the tree, and then he just stood there, behind it. At that point, he had his back to me. He just stood there with his back to me.

This is the last thing I expected to happen, I'll tell you that much. I just couldn't believe how he moved—it's fluid, it's *so* fluid. I turned to tell somebody, but there was nobody there.

Normally, here, they don't come into the open, hiding instead in the shadows, behind trees or thick foliage. But one afternoon in August of 2011, J.P. scanned the area and (without even realizing it) captured a few seconds of a young Sasquatch clinging to a treetop, about seventy-five feet off the ground. You can see head, shoulders, spine, butt, and his legs straddling the trunk.

On YouTube ("Tree-Hugger Sasquatch"), through a very shaky camera, you can watch the figure quickly slip around to the right side of the tree, at which point—surprise!—another pops out on the left side.

One head...   ...two heads

In late March, 2012, I get the chance to visit J.P. and together, not far from his other close encounters, we approach within fifteen feet of a Sasquatch.

Arriving at dusk, we soon find an impressive pine tree twist in the middle of an open field, within a nature preserve he's not visited before.

As we're examining this evidence—and you'll need to see the video to understand just how radically twisted around this tree is—J.P. hears pops or snaps coming from the tree line to our east, maybe two hundred feet away. A minute later, we're both startled by an *extremely* distinct vocalization from even closer, in the tree line to our south. At first, it sounds oddly *man*-like. After a few seconds, it transitions into more of a wolf howl, even though there are no wolves in Florida. The call sustains for eight to ten seconds, then J.P. and I wait, in case it was a coyote, for the typical chorus to ensue, but there is only silence. A single call, sounding lower-pitched than a coyote's; and would any wild canine simply stand nearby and announce its presence before humans?

We proceed east across the field, in the direction of the pops or snaps, approaching a stately oak festooned with Spanish moss. It's quite dark by now. J.P. whispers that he's just seen a large shape moving beneath the tree, withdrawing further into the shadows. Carrying no night vision devices, we decide to walk slowly that way and just see what happens. "I felt it a little before Chris did," J..P reports later, "but I didn't say anything. A second later, Chris stopped dead in his tracks." It's a sizzling, sparkly, electrical sensation on my chest, my first definitive taste of being "infra-blasted," so I'm delighted, albeit very successfully intimidated. When you confront such a force, you suddenly have no desire whatsoever to push the envelope.

Before we vacate, I leave my audio recorder close by, where it picks up three more solitary, crystalline howls, spaced every couple of hours from 10:36 PM to 2:15 AM, though none as long-winded as what we heard in person. They seem virtually right upon the recorder, which reminds me of the tactic used by the stationary knocker during the 2009 "Sasquatch Stakeout" in Vermont, as discussed on pages 186-188. Now in this Florida instance, too, the sentry may have been signaling for others to steer clear of live human equipment.

Upon our return the next morning to retrieve the unit, we document many further examples of unnatural tree breakage.

(See YouTube: "Encounter at the Old Oak Tree.")

e) *Enoch—A Bigfoot Story*, by Autumn Williams, 2010 (Florida)

This is the only habituation book in which the human witness travels deep into *their* territory. The account is narrated both by Autumn Williams and by a long-term witness who uses the name "Mike."

Mike:
> I didn't like people much and chose to spend most of my time alone. Even as a child, I never felt like I belonged, and was always on the outside looking in.
>
> This place is fifteen miles from the nearest town and you can only get here by boat. Off the main river, there is a small creek that winds deep into the swamp and the trees don't let in much sunlight, so it's dark even in the daytime. The swamp is thousands of acres surrounded by woods.
>
> At the end of this creek, I have a camp—the only high ground in this part of the swamp.
>
> [In 1998, after I saw large footprints on a sandbar,] I would spend all day and night walking and wading around the swamp looking for him. At night, I could hear him scream. It would make the hair stand up on the back of my neck. It was a lonely scream, almost a cry, and I would call back, my voice echoing through the swamp.

Autumn:
> Eventually, Mike began spending weeks at a time in the swamp—living, as he puts it, "Like a Swamp Ape."

Mike:
> For about four years, I tried to get close to him. I would lie in the mud for hours…but he always

> seemed to know I was there. I would climb trees, sit,
> and wait. I would sit in the creek with only my head
> above water, waiting for [food] bait to attract him.
> and sometimes when I would see him I would run
> toward him thinking I could catch up with him, but
> his walking speed is my running speed. I would see
> him [only] from a distance.

One day, instead of the usual food, Mike tried putting out a bundle of aromatic, wrapped-up incense. The primate came to pick it up; Mike stood from his hiding spot, greeted the creature, and then *walked away,* demonstrating that he knew who was the interloper here, and who was in charge. This proved a turning-point, and let's be sure to appreciate fully, here, the unbeatable degree of persistence—*four years* consistently invested before the rich reward.

Mike:

> That night, I was sitting by the fire, wondering if he would
> leave the area. Did I mess up and scare him off? I looked up,
> and at the edge of the firelight, there he was…standing there
> looking at me. He was big, I mean really big. He stood there,
> not moving. After a while, I said, "You going to come in or
> stand there like a stump?"

> He huffed at me, turned around, and walked into the
> darkness. I could hear him moving around behind me. I
> could smell him now. He was upwind and it was bad—like a
> wet, musky garbage dump.

> I waited to see if he would come closer, my back still to him.
> It seemed like hours, [him] standing no more than twenty feet
> away.

> I stood up and said, "I'm Mike. This is my camp. Please
> come in and sit." He didn't move. "You wanna eat?" I
> reached down, got a bag of apples, and tossed them to him. '
> They landed at his feet. He took the apples, huffed at me, and

walked into the night. I was shaking…not scared, but excited.

[Later, I was sleeping] with my arms across my chest, when I felt something bump my hammock, making it rock….He had me…I had nowhere to run. I just lay there. He reached out and picked up my hand ever so gently and turned it over, looking at it, lifting my arm up and with the other hand stroking it, feeling it. He wasn't rough with me. It was like you would pick up a child's hand. I lay there with my eyes wide open.

He looked, saw that my eyes were open, then put my hand down and walked away.

The next morning, I was getting ready to go fishing and was putting my cooler back in the boat. I turned around and there he was, standing about eight feet away. Scared the hell out of me! I stood there looking at him. I could not get over how big he was, all muscle and hair. His eyes were dark brown, his hair was black with a red tint when the sunlight hit it.

[Elsewhere, Mike goes into more detail.] His nose is kind of broad and flat, but not like a gorilla's with those big nostrils. He's got these little pig bristles that stick out from it. And wrinkles. On the bridge, and down a little farther, too. His mouth is wide and his mustache is real thick, like it grows almost out of his nostrils.

What follows is Mike's sustained and fascinating account of a gradually evolving relationship, one filled with startling twists, with danger, discovery, extensive behavioral observations, as well as intense emotional pain and expansion. Williams enters the narrative now and then as an insightful, companionable guide, asking questions, probing the vast implications of this experience, and proposing new ways to think of this species that ring true to me. My temptation is to continue sharing passages here, but instead, I will simply recommend this book to you, trusting that it will enrich your vision as much as it has mine.

Indeed, while reading *Enoch*, I kept wondering, *Could I have fostered an ongoing relationship with Thumper, whom I "met" in the ravine back in June of 2008, if I had only exercised far more patience?*

But this would entail rethinking my whole stance toward the collection of evidence. Thumper approached me before I owned a thermal camera, and but for the audio recording, our long hours of interaction that night, such as it was, occurred entirely in the undocumented dark. A week later, for three mornings running, I found "gifts" beside my car. And yet, during the subsequent two years, abandoning the ravine for the new area, I've camped forty-four nights in various forests, fully locked and loaded with night-defeating video technology, and the only response has been a violent one—a lethal-sized tree shoved down next to me. An equal number of times, I've planted the thermal camera over night, like a trap, and obtained a massive bucketful of nothing. What's wrong with this picture? As Mike himself says, "How can you reach out one hand in friendship—while holding a camera in the other?"

4. Taking the Measure of Public Fascination– "Finding Bigfoot" Draws Millions on Animal Planet; Facebook/ FindBigfoot Harnesses Social Media

On May 25ᵗʰ of 2011, the premiere episode of "Finding Bigfoot" racked up 1.3 million viewers; subsequent airings in June topped two million. These results, more than any flash metric before, testified to the underlying hunger in the population for a fresh approach to the subject. The cast of researchers—Matt Moneymaker, Cliff Barackman, James "Bobo" Fay, and Ranae Holland—heads into the woods in promising locations, executing the same long-standing tactics for eliciting Sasquatch responses that I was taught starting back in 2005.

"Finding Bigfoot" has dramatically spread awareness of the nature of field research as it's been practiced on this continent since the mid-1990s—and first systematically applied by Moneymaker on BFRO expeditions—and has conveyed some behavioral traits long known to researchers, such as whooping, howling, wood-knocking, and intimidation techniques like rock-throwing, tree-pushing, branch- and limb-breaking. The cast of the show banks on this tendency and attempts to elicit responses and approaches in order to obtain clear audio, and perhaps even thermal footage.

This is all well and good, of course, as far as it goes, and it does make for occasionally compelling TV moments. However, there are three issues to be aware of.

First, audio and video "evidence" that pumps up such moments often turns out to have been "enhanced" in post-production, rather than being legitimate *field* audio and video, which lends an air of docudrama hype to the entire enterprise. For instance, fabricated "wood knock" sounds were piped in during the premiere episode and, a few episodes later, the camera pans across an open field one night, resting upon a "large something" that registers a heat signature on the thermal imager; much suspense builds...what can it be? The show then cuts to commercial and, when it returns, does not revisit the scene at all but leaves the question hanging. Come to find out after broadcast, from angry cast members (and to their credit), that when it turned sideways, the "creature" revealed itself to be a horse, and that this outcome had been explicitly stated on camera—in footage destined for the cutting-room floor. This deceptive practice has apparently lessened over time, though it would be very surprising, given ratings pressure, if still today, in Seasons 3 and 4, editorial sleight-of-hand does not come into play.

Second, even when something significant *is* heard in the woods, a vocalization or a knock, most often it's the cast themselves perceiving it rather than—or vastly better than—the home viewer, either because the recording equipment did not capture the sound in question or else captured it so faintly that we can't be sure we heard what Ranae or Bobo say they heard. And before we can perk up and pay proper attention, it's too late, because instead of slowing down at such moments to offer an amplified replay of the event, the show just races forward, expecting us to take the participants' claims on faith, not allowing *us* to fully participate, while we grasp for a hold, like trying to catch smoke in one's hand.

Third, there are distinct limitations embedded in the BFRO methodology itself, which I didn't yet recognize back when I participated in their expeditions and learned important preliminary lessons. Think about a family group or extended-family clan; though they are certainly curious about human beings, this curiosity is not likely to be stirred by researchers armed to the teeth with technology, coordinating their movements via walky-talky, driven by a capture mentality, not *bodily* capture—though no doubt they would if they could—but capture nonetheless. For example, at one point Moneymaker narrates, "Plotting these three eye-witness encounters on the map allows us to tighten the noose around Bigfoot." And the first episode of season two has the cast stalking in the Catskills of New York State; when apparent Sasquatch calls are heard, Moneymaker exclaims, "We've got to move toward it...take the fight to the enemy."

This same heavy-handed posture is reflected in his January 7th, 2012, appearance on the CBS Early Show. When asked, "Bigfoot—man or animal?" Moneymaker replies conclusively, "Oh, animal. They're a line of apes. They're not *anything* related to humans." Shortly afterward, of course, the Ketchum and Sykes studies would demonstrate that Sasquatch finds its genesis in a cross between an ancient human female and an ancient male...something else. (See Chapter Seven.) But even setting aside this genetic result, what strikes me is that this researcher, like so many before him, falls into the simple black-and-white dichotomy between "man" and "animal," whereas the clear, empirical truth of the matter (as revealed at habituation sites, long before any confirming DNA results) is that we are dealing instead with a *continuum*, but that subtle intelligence and a capacity for spoken language place our subject much closer to the human end of that spectrum.

Even when presented with prime habituation sites, the show's format does not allow for any Goodall-like lingering. In season 2's "Moonshine and Bigfoot," the cast visits a deep-woods cabin whose occupants claim vigorous visitations (including rocks hurled at the walls) "about twice a month"; yet Moneymaker and team hastily sample jars of home brew before departing for further quixotic stakeouts. And season 3's "Bigfoot and Wolverines" only investigates in passing the property of a family who hears clear Sasquatch calls, often several times per week. Ideally, there will be a television series someday in which multiple habituation sites are featured, and the viewer gets to know the families and their experiences on an ongoing basis—probably developed by a network not wedded to torquing up false adrenaline, such as PBS.

In other words, the BFRO approach is not hardwired for success, but rather for a merely, at best, for peripheral access to its quarry. Let's try an analogy. Say a colony of beings lived within a walled city....

Our life-ways have flourished here since time immemorial, but one day, a throng of barbarians becomes aware of our existence and decides to storm the city. Luckily, they find that our walls are too thick to penetrate, too high to scale. Yet, the barbarians are so determined to make inroads against us that they listen carefully to our sounds and then produce pale copies. Occasionally, our sentries decide to reply, which we all think is foolish, but after all they do get bored. They are toying with the barbarians, but the barbarians do not understand this and become enormously excited, as if they are gaining knowledge when in truth they are only learning that sentries need entertainment. No matter what bold nighttime assaults the barbarians plan and launch, our walls do not yield, and nothing of our rich interior culture, our real business, shows through.

But here's the secret—our walls do have doors, the kind that the barbarian "fight the enemy" strategy will never discover.

Meanwhile, there does exist a low-budget media alternative that goes much further, affording frequent and instructive glimpses through these "doors"; and I'm not even talking here about the patient, receptive vigilance that goes on at habituation sites, which is hands down the most productive avenue. In March of 2010, researchers Jeff Andersen and Jack Barnes launched Facebook/FindBigfoot—more than a year before the TV show adopted virtually the same title—which has quickly grown into the most popular social media site for all things Sasquatch. FB/FB has assembled "The Top 90 Bigfoot Videos," and at last count, has tallied more than four million views on YouTube and Facebook.

FIND BIGFOOT

7. White Sasquatch filmed in Pennsylvania backyard
10. Baby Bigfoot in craw of tree
15. Athletic Auburn Bigfoot Brachiates and Clears Gap
40. Ontario Bigfoot chatters in my backyard
48. White Sasquatch walking through Soybeans, Ohio

Andersen and Barnes started from the venturesome premise that "Bigfoot has *already* been discovered on the Internet," and so now Barnes' M.O. is to scour YouTube and other online hosts, much more thoroughly than anyone has before him, for clips purporting to show the creature, many of which have been prematurely dismissed or simply neglected. An inexorably rising tide of crowdsourced postings has resulted from the advent of affordable camcorders, flip and cell phone cameras.

Yes, Barnes does slip into elusive logic at times, can mumble, and "authenticates" a few clips that do not seem definitive, but far more of them pass muster, and what impresses me is his very sharp eye for frame-by-frame analysis of the figures' morphology and movement, a fine-grained intimacy of observation as he points out features that would elude others—such as the "rise, pause, fall" of their "compliant gait"; lighter-colored palms and soles; the odd "swivel" that the lower legs execute with every step, so as to lay the leading foot down more directly in front of the preceding foot than is the case in human trackways. As a result, the viewer's own eye becomes more practiced and educated.

In stark contrast to the slick Animal Planet production values, Barnes' informal voice-over leads us through casual home movies taken during hikes, at campsites or on the people's own property—scenes that turn suddenly dramatic as a mysterious stranger shows up, usually hiding or skulking in the background, in the trees, and often unnoticed by the participants at the time. The "doors" of our metaphorical walled city crack ajar in these clips because the amateur videographers find themselves in the right place at the right time by chance, rather than by any coordinated pursuit and "noose-tightening."

Although primarily shot in daylight, these videos tend to be grainy and brief, sometimes lasting only a few frames or seconds—these are glimpses accidentally captured. This fact alone, however, would tend to argue against their being hoaxes, and the cumulative effect of watching many back to back, witnessing the clear convergence of attributes, is an acclimatization to the presence of this species and its typical behavior when around humans—a sense that indeed the species *was* discovered already on the Internet, even before 2013.

In late September of 2012, Barnes picked up on a grainy, 1.2-second clip when it still had only six views on YouTube. He was the first to analyze and authenticate, dubbing it the "camper" video. In the face of blistering criticism and cries of "hoax" from the research community—Moneymaker tweeted, "The 'camper footage' is fake. Halloween always brings out cheesy costumes"—Barnes continued to study this piece of evidence, eventually obtaining from the filmer the original color, higher-resolution file and posting two further treatments that together soon accrued 100,000 YouTube views—an impressive looped version and a comparative analysis showing anatomical similarities between this figure and numerous others in the FB/FB catalogue. Little did we know, however, that even this clear glimpse of muscular upper back, swiveling head, and startlingly manlike face—the best image since "Patty"—would become trivial in retrospect compared to what was to emerge from this situation early in the new year.

The killer of this male Sasquatch adores attention, positive or negative, and is receiving plenty as a result of the BBC/Minnow Films documentary, "Shooting Bigfoot," so this book will feature him no further. His deed was absolutely unnecessary to the progress of our field, because definite footage, coupled with the complete genome sequence, would have sufficed.

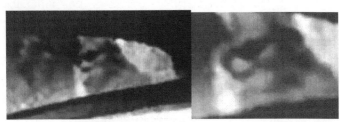

The doomed scavenger

Returning to the issue of the Internet as a surprisingly fertile source of evidence, I would also recommend that you subscribe to the following YouTube channels—and go through their backlogs—where researchers continually post fieldwork updates.

> BFResearcherSE (GA)
> joebblack1963 (TN)
> Greenwave2010fb (for M.K. Davis's videos)
> Redchun (PA)
> robc1219 (WV)
> Sasquatch Ontario (ON)
> SUSANFARNS (AZ)
> Tcsjrbigfoot (OH)
> TheDoc199 (NY, PA, NJ, WA)
> Timbergiantbigfoot (ON)
> Trailriderresearch (BC)
> Treepeekers (FL, CA)

I want to especially commend M.K. Davis's work (available at YouTube channel greenwave2010fb), his precise, field-leading studies of the Patterson/Gimlin figure's anatomy and locomotion, as well as his presentations of numerous other Sasquatch video and audio clips.

My own YouTube channel is impossiblevisits (VT, TX).

The best sites for general information and a vast archive of Sasquatch encounter reports are Autumn Williams' OregonBigfoot.com and BFRO.net; the best site for discussion of various relevant topics is BigfootForums.com; and the richest repositories of audio clips and analysis are at BigfootSounds.com, sasquatchbioacoustic.blogspot.com, sasquatchsounds.com, stancourtney.com, and on YouTube channel BFResearchSE.

As for "Finding Bigfoot," two last observations.

First, aside from the above-mentioned problem of occasionally unreliable evidence, the program risks never surpassing its initial formula—an extended series of near misses, the cast perpetually on the brink of breakthrough, where even "breakthrough" would mean no more than clearer vocals and knocks or, at best, fleeting thermal footage. In other words, the ultimate yield of this popular show will likely be to have whetted our collective appetite for what was soon to emerge, the next-generation daylight footage out of Kentucky and San Antonio and the historic discoveries contained in the Ketchum and Sykes studies.

Second, the most illuminating aspect of the show is, ironically, its very most mundane—the simple raising of hands at town meetings where locals gather to share stories of nearby Sasquatch encounters; this demonstrates the near ubiquity of the species (of its range within heavily forested regions), as well as the eye-opening fact that witnesses are living as neighbors, in communities throughout North America, and they never remotely suspect it.

This startling epiphany parallels what we *all*, as neighbors at large, are experiencing today in light of the extensive, cross-continent sourcing of organic samples used in the Ketchum DNA study. It is time now for us to engage in a spirited "town meeting" that stretches from coast to coast.

If They Are Not Visiting You...
Tips for Conducting Field Research in Your Own Area

Do Extensive Reconnaissance—

- Scour the Internet (starting with the BFRO.net's state-by-state, province-by-province database of encounters) for credible reports from your area, and if possible, make contact with those who submitted the report(s);
- Pore over old maps, looking for spooky place names such as "Devil's Point," "Demon's Run," "Haunted Gorge," even "Ape Valley/Canyon," etc. These may reflect earlier generations' healthy respect for areas not fit for human trespass, especially after dark. Trespass away, though unarmed and with respect. Sasquatch probably return year after year, century after century, to land offering private havens, valuable dietary resources, and good hunting; moreover — who can say? — certain spots may exercise an emotional or spiritual pull, due, for instance, to ancient burial grounds;
- Order topographical maps at mytopo.com, where you can customize maps to cover tracts small and large; these are a valuable orienteering tool that will give you a three-dimensional sense of your selected territory; also, surveil with Google Earth

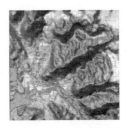

- Explore *any* undeveloped forests near you, especially those possessing variegated topography;
- Look for stick and tree structures as described and displayed in this book, and in the "Sasquatch Structures" video on YouTube;
- Listen for wood knocks;
- Leave your audio recorder out overnight in various spots where humans do no tend to go; review the file carefully after retrieval;
- Ideally, if you have time and energy enough, and multiple audio recorders, set out, retrieve and review frequently, so that many different sites can be auditioned during this recon phase; nor do these recorders need to be very good quality (as opposed to the one you'll take out with you once you select your specific research site), because at this point you're only trying to determine the location of Sasquatch activity; even fuzzy, faint wood knocks (if they can be distinguished from gunshots) are cause for celebration.

Reach Out—

- Don't be shy, make yourself well-known locally as "that Bigfoot person" by talking up the subject in nearby stores and other community hubs;

- Hang posters and widely distribute leaflets (not in PO boxes!) that sincerely lay your cards on the table and convey your interest in connecting with people who may have experienced encounters or come across evidence;
- Start a local "Sasquatch Club" through Front Porch Forum, the wonderful new online network that connects members of neighborhoods; if yours is not yet up and running, you can step forward and sponsor it through frontporchforum.com; within twenty-four hours of posting my invitation to this new club, I heard from a man who saw a Sasquatch not far from Sylvester's research area, and whose daughter saw one in the very field where my daughter and I found the multiple branch breaks, as pictured on page 192; this all supports the notion that *at least* 95% of people who encounter these creatures never go to the lengths of submitting reports to the BFRO or other outlets;
- Call a "town meeting," if possible, as they do on Animal Planet's "Finding Bigfoot"; Sasquatch witnesses are likely to come out of the woodwork;
- Offer to give free talks at any venue that will have you; I use a DVD compilation of compelling video and audio clips from various sources;
- All it takes is one "hit," one solid lead from one person, to initiate a domino effect in your research process;
- You will gradually build up a small cadre of

research assistants who reside in your research area and will be glad to serve as eyes and ears, especially ears, as these listening posts may pick up wood knocks and let you understand the Sasquatch's whereabouts and movement pattern;

- The sole responder to the 249 leaflets that I distributed in the summer of 2009 had heard wood knocks coming from the mountain behind her house; my closest encounter to date, then, took place while I slept on that mountain;

- The first time I gave a public talk on this topic, a woman came up to me afterward and told me that she'd heard from two people, unknown to one another, who'd seen Sasquatch crossing the road, at two different times, and even though I had not mentioned, during my talk, where my research area was, this road is the very one that runs right *through* this area; not only did this anecdotal corroboration delight me and affirm my efforts, it also led me to explore this road more thoroughly and to discover a little-used, narrow dirt road that winds its way to a different side of the same mountain; exploring from there, I came upon a trail, marked by many subtle and obvious branch-breaks, that led to a high field at the edge of which, from higher in the forest, came the best wood knocks I've ever heard in person (excluding those I've only recorded); my fieldwork, from here on, gained new energy and focus;

- The second time I gave a public talk on this topic, before I had gotten to wood knocks, a woman raised her hand and asked doubtfully whether Sasquatch ever make non-verbal sounds, because for many summers she'd gone to a campground twenty miles from my site, and every single time, in the middle of the night, heard a percussion that had mystified her ever since; she'd always thought it must be someone using a hatchet against a tree in the woods, but just once or twice at a time; "I've only mentioned it to a few people over the years, and nobody has any idea what it could have been"; her amazement and relief when I was able to put her experience into context is part of why I feel privileged to be following this path;

- It's been said that "serendipity favors the prepared mind," but in the case of this strange endeavor, it also favors the act of open communication, which prepares the ground for collaborative illumination.

Plan and Employ a Consistent Strategy —

- Choose a campsite that lies in a suspected "active" area, as pinpointed by your witness outreach and your own field reconnaissance;
- If possible, camp halfway up a densely forested incline, ideally a significant hill or mountain, the steeper the better; this puts you closer to where they likely spend most of their time, yet gives them the strategic advantage, above you;
- I recommend that you camp solo as often as possible, making yourself small and vulnerable, because this will tend to promote relaxation and curiosity; even two human beings may feel too much like a *group* to

them, given that they must then worry about being *flanked* by us;

- Follow the same routine every time, such as starting your audio recorder even before you arrive at your site (Sasquatch will often knock to alert others to human arrival in the area), then making your personal "signature" sounds: I recommend a CD of gentle music and/or a young child's or children's voices; the latter choice has the advantage of alleviating fear and loneliness on your part;
- The darker the better; my own closest contacts have come on nights when I couldn't see my hand in front of my face; to Sasquatch, darkness is a cloak of safety; *never* use, or even carry, major hand-held spotlights, as they are second only to guns on the list of tokens of human hostility and danger;
- Tents are for babies! They don't offer increased safety and they reduce your acoustics significantly; you want to be able to hear the slightest twig snap and be ready to experience an approach; if insects are a problem, use Deet and a head net;
- Speaking of acoustics, I don't go out if it's going to rain or is very windy; I want to hear and document any encounters;
- Sleep beside an "escape tree" in case of dangerous animals, but be careful not to sleep within range of any heavy, relatively weak trees. (Remember Chapter Four: *TIMBER!*)

Equip Yourself Well —

- Camp with an excellent audio recorder, such as the Edirol R-09HR ($260); with this brand you will not need external microphones because the unit's own built-in mics are outstanding;
- If possible, get yourself a thermal camera; many are on the market for $4500-$9000, but I recommend a much cheaper option: the FLIR PathfindIR; buy new for $2600 (with video/power cable) or find it pre-owned for less;

- It bears repeating: Do *not* pack either bright flashlights or hand-held spotlights; their use will be interpreted as hostile, "playing dirty," and will alienate your primate visitors, perhaps forever;
- For the same reason, do not use infrared night-vision equipment either (scopes, binoculars, cameras); it sends out a beam visible to Sasquatch, whereas a thermal camera is an entirely *passive* technology, sending out no beam, reading the heat signatures given off by objects;
- If you do acquire the FLIR PathfindIR, you will further need:
  - A power source; the FLIR runs on 12V DC batteries, but car batteries are too heavy; I recommend the Jump-N-Carry

JNC300XL 900 Peak Amp Ultraportable 12V Jump Starter, available on Amazon for $55; at ten pounds, it's much lighter than a car battery, and will power your thermal camera for more than twenty-four hours, allowing you to use the battery for several overnights before having to carry it home for a recharge;

- Something to record the footage onto, such as a DVR or a video camera that has a "video-in" port; I use the SONY DCR-SR100 ($300-$400) with an extended-life battery, such as model # NP-FH100 ($65);

- Do not carry a gun or powerful light, as this will project the very opposite of the open, receptive and benign posture you want; besides my dense wood-knocking club, I pack road flares, which would, I believe, successfully alarm a bear, wolves or coyotes; an air horn is also a good idea.

Just Do It: The Emotional Side—

- I can guarantee that very frequently, especially if you are camping solo, you will find yourself resisting as the time approaches to depart your safe and comfortable home; you'll come up with all sorts of excuses not to go out; remember, yes, that this is a deadly serious and overwhelming business, this bucking of the eons-long human trend of placing walls between ourselves and the wildwood, this laying of oneself out there, wholly surrendering to the vast unknown, and to the *known* possibility that a primordial giant may come to you; it's honestly terrifying;

- It's also a perfect way of returning to pure childhood wonder and soaring into profound adventure; the petty chattering monkey mind that tries, with clever dodges, to talk you out of this insane pursuit can be hushed with a few deep breaths, when you conjure up the larger, wiser primate side of yourself, the *hominin* you that is, after all, intimately related to Sasquatch; instead of spending just one more night inside, gird up, set forth, and move toward your primordial kin;

- Lying in the pitch dark, far from civilization and probably even from your car, you will undoubtedly experience waves of anxiety, if not panic ("What on Earth am I *doing* way out here by myself?"); but these waves will normally pass in less than a minute; exercise mental control and remind yourself of two things: 1) My level of fascination is much greater than my level of fear, or else I wouldn't be out here doing this in the first place, and 2) I am in possession of excellent audio and video equipment, so that whatever happens, I can document it, which is as good as gold;

- When it's 2:30 in the morning and you are staring into a black wall of nothingness, think of this: If this truly *is* nothingness, then it's not scary; and if you do begin to hear something, now, moving inside the blackness, rejoice, because after all the greatest risk we face when reaching into the rich void is that nothing will bother to reach back.

The 5% Rule of Thumb —

- In Vermont, I have found that 95% of the time I camp out or plant recording equipment, absolutely nothing happens in terms of clear Sasquatch activity, due to either their absence or to their avoidance; of the 112 such "tests" I have conducted from 2007 through 2010, two audio plants have come back positive for wood knocks, and three camping experiences have put me in close contact with the primate;

- You may arrive at a different average ratio in your own research area; I have recently begun visiting a site in New Hampshire and a site in central Florida, where the ratio of activity to inactivity is, thus far, much higher than 50%; a lot depends upon the tactical disposition of the adults (or just the Alpha male) in your local family or clan, the boundaries established and level of discipline instilled in the naturally more venturesome juveniles (I think that so-called "hot spots" represent areas where such discipline is lax); but still, quiet nights will probably far outweigh active nights;

- Whenever you drag yourself home from yet another long night of no contact, or none that you know of, offset the disappointment with confidence that the law of averages is on your side, and that therefore this past night has only moved you closer, with certainty, to an encounter;

- In other words, patience is the key here,

enormous persistence fueled by an enduring desire to transcend the human rut and to prove to your concealed cousins, and to yourself, that you are determined to do whatever it takes to be with them;

- The experience of putting yourself into position to encounter a Sasquatch is like this:
…nothing nothing nothing nothing nothing
nothing nothing nothing nothing nothing
nothing nothing nothing nothing nothing
nothing nothing nothing nothing nothing
nothing nothing nothing nothing nothing
nothing nothing nothing nothing nothing
nothing nothing nothing nothing nothing
nothing nothing nothing nothing nothing
nothing nothing nothing nothing nothing
nothing nothing nothing nothing nothing
nothing nothing nothing nothing nothing
nothing nothing nothing nothing nothing
nothing nothing nothing nothing nothing
nothing nothing nothing nothing nothing
nothing nothing nothing nothing nothing
nothing nothing nothing nothing nothing
nothing nothing nothing contact nothing
nothing nothing nothing nothing nothing
nothing nothing nothing nothing nothing
nothing nothing nothing nothing nothing
nothing nothing nothing nothing nothing
nothing nothing nothing nothing nothing
nothing nothing nothing nothing nothing
nothing nothing nothing nothing nothing
nothing nothing nothing nothing nothing
nothing nothing nothing nothing nothing
nothing nothing nothing nothing nothing
nothing nothing nothing nothing nothing

nothing nothing nothing nothing nothing
nothing nothing nothing nothing nothing
nothing nothing nothing...

Ten Square Miles —

- The dance of evasion and fleeting contact between our two species has been ongoing for eons, but your goal is to intensify and focus it; each year, during your research season, you'll put together a sincere, methodical body of work, to ante up against theirs;
- Gradually, over time, you will mark out your personal research area—mine is ten square miles—and then tend to it, year after year, becoming ever more familiar with its quirks, features, signs, seasonal shifts, its wildlife both primate and not;
- Do not spread yourself too thin geographically; be comfortable with the idea that you cannot, alone, cover the whole of your subjects' territory; I think that every given family or extended-family clan lives, during a full cycle of seasons, in an expansive "house," shaped very differently from our houses and stretching perhaps a couple hundred square miles; there are many rooms, some clustered together (secluded wilderness), some spread out and linked by narrow corridors, strips of forest or watercourses; and the residents travel within this house according to what the rooms have to offer, seasonally, in terms of food and shelter; any one researcher can hope to locate only one good room and then to learn when

the door tends to be opened each year, and the power switched on.

On the other hand, much of the above will be unnecessary if you find yourself in an even rarer position—able to communicate with Sasquatch directly, or lucky enough to team up with someone who possesses this ability; see Epilogue.

Chapter Seven

Mystery Solved!
(on the back of a further mystery)
DNA Results Reveal Half-Human Genesis

His function is to uncover and disrupt the very things that
cultures are based on. Not surprisingly…these more
settled neighbors often tire of trickster's disruptions and set
out to bind or suppress him. [He is] how change might come
to any orderly, self-regulating, and self-protecting world.
Most enduring structures (in nature, society, the human
psyche) are resistant to fundamental change, by which I
mean the change that alters the givens of those structures
themselves. It's almost a matter of logic: No self-contained
world can induce its own fundamental change, because self-
containment means it knows nothing beyond its own givens.
                              —from *Trickster Makes This World*,
                                              by Lewis Hyde

The effect of the Copernican revolution was tremendous, but
it was diluted by the long delay in its acknowledgement. The
results of the Darwinian revolution were no less telling. Yet
the cognitive and emotional shock received from the news [of

Sasquatch reality] by the world of science is likely to be greater than in the previous revolutions. Bigfoot and Yeti are of more interest to common people than abstractions of cosmology and evolution, so billions of listeners and viewers will expect explanations from the spokesmen of the scientific establishment, from the people who for decades have been treating the subject with ridicule. Natural sciences will take an historic lesson from humanitarian sciences...from folklore and mythology. It is these fields of knowledge that have preserved the bulk of evidence for the existence of uncatalogued hominins, the evidence stubbornly ignored and denied by the learned *scoftics*. And it will be a lesson taken by science and scientists from lay people, from the native populations all over the world who have always known the presence of hairy wildmen.

> —Dmitri Bayanov, with the International Center of Hominology in Moscow, in his 2011 essay, "Thoughts on the Revolution in Anthropology"

1543   **1859**   **2013**

1. The Facebook Post Heard 'Round the World

On November 24th, 2012, at 1:16 PM EST, Dr. Melba Ketchum revealed the basic outlines of her team's study results. Controversy erupted immediately because the data themselves remained under wraps; nevertheless, this press release marks the first moment that the human race learned the truth about our enormous next of kin.

FOR IMMEDIATE RELEASE

"BIGFOOT" DNA SEQUENCED IN UPCOMING GENETICS STUDY

Five-Year Genome Study Yields Evidence of *Homo sapiens*/Unknown Hominin Hybrid Species in North America

DALLAS, Nov. 24—A team of scientists can verify that their 5-year-long DNA study, currently under peer review, confirms the existence of a novel hominin hybrid species, commonly called "Bigfoot" or "Sasquatch," living in North America. Researchers' extensive DNA sequencing suggests that the legendary Sasquatch is a human relative that arose approximately 15,000 years ago as a hybrid cross of modern *Homo sapiens* with an unknown primate species.

The study was conducted by a team of experts in genetics, forensics, imaging and pathology, led by Dr. Melba S. Ketchum of Nacogdoches, TX. In response to recent interest in the study, Dr. Ketchum can confirm that her team has sequenced 3 complete Sasquatch nuclear genomes and determined the species is a human hybrid:

"Our study has sequenced 20 whole mitochondrial genomes and utilized next-generation sequencing to obtain 3 whole nuclear genomes from purported Sasquatch samples. The genome sequencing shows that Sasquatch mtDNA is identical to modern *Homo sapiens*, but Sasquatch nuDNA is a novel, unknown hominin related to *Homo sapiens* and other primate species. Our data indicate that the North American

Sasquatch is a hybrid species, the result of males of an unknown hominin species crossing with female *Homo sapiens*.

"Hominins are members of the taxonomic grouping *Hominini*, which includes all members of the genus *Homo*. Genetic testing has already ruled out *Homo neanderthalis* and the *Denisova hominin* as contributors to Sasquatch mtDNA or nuDNA. The male progenitor that contributed the unknown sequence to this hybrid is unique as its DNA is more distantly removed from humans than other recently discovered hominins like the Denisovan individual," explains Ketchum.

"Sasquatch nuclear DNA is incredibly novel and not at all what we had expected. While it has human nuclear DNA within its genome, there are also distinctly non-human, non-archaic hominin, and non-ape sequences. We describe it as a mosaic of human and novel non-human sequence. Further study is needed and is ongoing to better characterize and understand Sasquatch nuclear DNA."

Later, I will explain what is meant by the pivotal terms mtDNA and nuDNA, and explore some of the implications of Ketchum's results. But first, a look behind the scenes and several years into the past.

2. How DNA Samples Were Obtained

Massive curiosity, building for years, has begun to be satisfied now as accounts of the study's background players, and their methods, steadily emerge. Hair, saliva, blood, and tissue samples were gathered in a fascinating variety of ways, of which five are presented below; they account for more than half of the one hundred and nine total organic samples included.

a) New Mexico: J.C. Johnson (Blood Samples)

In 2010, researcher J.C. Johnson investigated a strange incident in which an eight-inch PVC pipe had apparently sustained two punch holes; nearby lay the body of a skunk with its scent glands removed. Johnson and others pieced together what must have occurred and gathered samples from the copious blood found on the pipe. See YouTube: "The Harvest" (search keywords "The Harvest Bigfoot"), in which J.C. Johnson advances a plausible theory as to why the scent glands may have been harvested from the animal:

> With all the young [Sasquatch] that have been sighted in this area this year...[I thought that] if I had a youngster I wanted to hide out and all the animals would leave it alone, the predators, the dogs, the coyotes, whatever, I would take skunk scent and put it all over my youngster, and everything would leave it alone. A skunk lays by the side of a road until he evaporates. Ravens won't touch it, buzzards won't touch it. So, skunk's a good mask, a good smell to hide behind.

For graphic images of what the researchers found at the scene, see YouTube: "Skunk Attack Photos (night before)."

b) Tennessee: Scott Carpenter (Hair Samples)

Scott Carpenter is a habituator in Eastern Tennessee who has had great success, born of persistence and ingenuity, in making contact and gathering hair samples. He speaks about his methods on the November 25th, 2012, episode of "Bigfoot Tonight," hosted by Chuck Prahl and Stacy Hostetler:

> I baited the tree. There were three different methods I used. The first big sample I collected I actually just put [the tape] on the tree, because I had a trail camera and a few weeks before I'd gotten a video where they were hiding behind this tree and peeking out at the camera. So I said, "Aha. I know where you guys are spying my camera." So I went in there with the packing tape and went around that tree backwards, sticky side out. Then I went back in a couple weeks later to check the SD cards, and that's when the tape was torn off the tree and laying on the ground with this huge amount of four-to-six-inch black hair in it, just a huge amount. And so that was my first sample.
>
> And then, I was trying to figure out a way to lure them in, and that's when we came up with the bacon grease. We were looking for something to put on the tree that would get them against it. And I already knew they love bacon. So during the colder part of the weather I would smear bacon grease in the bark of a tree, as high as I could reach, nine foot off the ground. And then I would wrap packing tape at three different levels. Periodically, they'd come by and lean up against the tree and lick the bacon grease and happily give me some hair samples. I didn't get as much with this method. I'd get a dozen or so hairs, but it did work.
>
> Another thing I did like this was, I'd place apples up in the notch of a tree and then I'd wrap tape, and I'd get a few hairs off of their hands or underneath their arms when they'd reach to get the apple out of the tree.
>
> And then the [last] method I used I just stumbled on by seeing

what would happen in nature. I noticed going into one of my areas there had been a holly bush that had broke off, and when it broke off it made like a cone...the splinters...it had actually caught some hair. So I collected that hair and got the idea. I went along this trail, with gloves on, broke some trees off of my own, forming that natural hair-catch. And I actually got about a dozen strands of hair doing that.

So during a two-year period, I collected quite a bit. The low-tech methods work best. I'm sure a lot of scientists out there are going to be swallowing their tongues, seeing that some guy *from the South* has gotten good evidence with bacon grease and packing tape.

[Also,] stringing black sewing thread between trees at seven foot has been a good indicator of whether the Bigfoot are moving through an area or not. That has told me where to put my tape traps [and] my trail cameras.

I had an area that they walked through pretty common and I put the black thread up between two trees, and he broke it three weeks in a row, then all of a sudden he stopped breaking it. But I could see by the ground clutter that he was still moving through, so obviously he'd gotten used to it...Oh, the idiot's putting thread. So I did this 360 around the trail, and sure enough I went back a week later and he'd gone two trees over and tried to go between two other trees. And I'd just love to have been a fly on the wall when he broke *that* thread. That's just a little bit of satisfaction, aggravating them as much as they aggravate me. I think they've got a sense of humor and enjoy screwing with us, so it was nice to pull one over on them.

Low-tech methods like that. In low parts of the trail actually laying a stick on the ground, and seeing if it gets kicked, that sort of thing has worked as well. Or they'll step on it and break it. Little things, that's been my bread and butter.

Carpenter places a "tape trap"; see YouTube channel: joebblack1963

c) *California: Justin Smeja (Tissue Sample)*

Almost two years before the San Antonio event, a twenty-four-year-old hunter named Justin Smeja shot to death an adult and a child Sasquatch; DNA from the former was included in the Ketchum study.

If you wish to, you can watch Smeja discussing the incident on YouTube: "I Killed Bigfoot—A Conversation With Justin Smeja"; more background context is offered by Derek Randles in "Two Sasquatch Shot and Killed (Part 2)"; and below is the transcript of an Internet radio interview conducted by Abe del Rio, Steve Kulls, and J.C. Johnson, which can be heard on YouTube: "Two Sasquatch Shot and Killed (Part 1)." Also, see Bart Cutino's documentary chronicling thermal footage obtained, in 2012, at the kill site.

It was October 8th of 2010, and we were going bear hunting up by Golden Lake. It was just another day. We'd hunted most of the day. We found one small buck and we said it's a young deer, let's let this one grow up. Then we ended up going into another area, and we're coming around the corner. It's probably 5 o'clock. We came around onto an open field but it's a blind corner because you can't see past these trees. So it opens up into a field, we both look, and see this thing at the same exact time. The truck stops. I pointed my rifle at it and I could see it through the scope. I had my scope on 16 power, I could see it pretty clearly. Everybody asks me, What was going through your head, did you think it was a bear? I thought a lot of things. It wasn't that I was a skeptic, it was that I didn't know that anybody believed in Bigfoot at all.

We saw this creature, it was walking on two legs, hairy. The best way I can describe it is it looked like a person in a suit. Probably 3 or 4 seconds had gone by and it started to walk towards us, between 100 and 80 yards, somewhere in there...It had its arms in the air and was waving them, almost like Don't shoot, don't shoot! Kind of a universal thing in any language, anybody raises his hands, sign of surrender. I didn't know what it was. To me it was just a monster, I didn't know what it was. I'm looking at this monster. By this time I have the bullet in the chamber, my finger on the trigger, and it's coming towards us, slowly, it's taking steps, waving. A lot of people are saying I shot it in the back, so if you have a deer and you shoot it behind the shoulder, then you're going to penetrate both lungs. On a person it's a hard area to describe but it's basically right under the shoulder where the lungs are located.

So maybe 5 seconds had passed, and my buddy he says Don't shoot, don't shoot! It's not a bear. Do not shoot. And I'm still kind of locked in on this thing. To me it was a monster, that's all it was. You know the gun's getting ready to go off. We've hunted together a lot over the years and we both knew what was going to happen. Normally when we see something the truck stops, both of us get out and we've got our rifles on it immediately. Well, my buddy was still using his binoculars because he didn't know what to think. I didn't know what to think. I'm looking at this thing and I'm pretty close to pulling the trigger, I've just been squeezing this whole time. And he's getting louder and louder, he's like Hey bro don't shoot, don't shoot! That is not a bear, that's a person in a suit, that's a person in a suit, don't shoot! And I'm thinking Well if that's a person in a suit then we've got a real problem here, 'cause they're walking around during bear season with a fur suit on. Something don't add up about this. I'm halfway thinking in the back of my mind that somebody's going to pull around the corner and it's going to be like a film crew or something. I don't know, my mind's going a hundred miles an hour.

But I see this animal, this furry thing, and we're here to hunt, we're here to kill animals, and it was just a monster. So I pull the trigger and you could see dust shoot off the side of it, like it obviously made a really good hit, definitely got it in the lungs. And it took off running. Just then we see two...I guess you'd call 'em kids, or cubs or something, I don't know. The big one's almost out of sight and these two come right out and my buddy's like Holy shit, really? There's more of them.

So we drive the truck into the field as far as we can, maybe 30 yards, then we take off running. We heard the thing crash, though. It crashed, it sounded like a car wreck. We knew we made a good hit. It's very normal to shoot a deer and have it run 50, 60, 70 yards and expire. So we run up there and my buddy doesn't even grab his gun, I mean we're just running, trying to run over to this thing, and cubs are just out of sight. And we run over there and now we're face to face with these kids. Probably 10 yards away or so, and we can't find the big one. So I decide I'm going to shoot one of the kids, and my buddy's like No, do not shoot, do not shoot.

Okay, okay, alright. We'll find the big one, we'll get it and we'll leave. So we end up looking for 15 minutes or so.

Meanwhile, the kids...they're looking for the parent obviously. They are walking around looking for their parent. We knew we were looking in the right area then...I've made the mistake of shooting a sow, and then the piglets come running out and they always know right where their mom is. They take you to the body. So we knew that it was right there, we just couldn't find it. It's an extremely brushy area. I mean, we could have looked for 2 weeks and not found it.

So there's blood on the ground, we're kind of looking at the blood, we're walking around, we split up probably 10 or 15 times, he'd go one way I'd go the other way. And the kids would do the same thing. They'd walk into the center of the open field and they'd say something to each other, it sounded

like deaf chatter, they'd go Wawwa Wo! They'd say
something to each other then they'd split up. Then about a
minute later they'd come back, almost like, You see
anything? You see anything? No, okay. Did you look by
that tree, did you look by the stump? Yeah I looked by the
stump, did you look by the tree? I'll look by the other tree.

They didn't care that we were there, they were not alarmed at
all. They were just there. And so, maybe 15 minutes goes by
or so, and I keep deciding that I'm going to shoot one of the
little ones. It's like, We'll shoot one of these, throw it in the
back, and we'll figure it out. And my buddy's like, No no
that's terrible, don't do that, there's no reason for that, there's
absolutely no reason to do this. So at the time everything's
running through my head, I'm thinking if we don't get one of
the little ones nobody's ever going to believe us, it's just
going to be a crazy story. We just need to find the big one
and we need to get out of here.

So eventually me and my buddy are split up and I'm down
this hill and it's almost like straight uphill maybe 15 yards
away, maybe 20, and one of them, the little one, is starting to
approach me. It's getting closer…it's getting closer, starting
to make some noise, like the deaf chatter thing…it's getting
closer and I was thinking, I don't know what's going to
happen here but he's going to get too close, it's way too close
for comfort. Screw it, I'm going to shoot.

So I shoot it directly in the neck 'cause I didn't want to mess
up the skull or the face. And it rolled down the hill and
actually…it hit my feet, starts bleeding on my boots, still
alive. So I pick it up and I'm sitting there looking at it and
I'm starting to feel bad, I'm starting to realize, What have I
done, what have I done? And…that went on for a couple
minutes, there was a lot of stuff that happened in there but to
summarize it, make a long story short, it died.

Artist's rendering of the juvenile

And then my buddy walks up and he's like, What have you done? Seriously, really? And I'm like fine, forget this, so I throw it on the ground and I start walking off, walking back to the truck. Then I look back and my buddy's holding it, just holding it, sitting there staring at it. So…I walk back to him like Dude, we gotta get out of here. Somebody just heard a shot, you know that somebody's going to show up, Fish and Game, we're going to get in so much trouble, we're going to go to jail, we need to get out of here, this is crazy, let's go. He says, Okay, okay, let's hide this, we'll come back for it later. We'll come back. So we take it into the bush, get it as deep as we can, throw a bunch of stuff on top of it, and then we leave.

Not saying a word. We actually drove out of there probably 60 miles an hour on that dirt road. It doesn't make sense but we were just afraid we were going to get caught, get in trouble, something. So we drove down to Sierraville, and we stop there. Both of us quit smoking in like the last 6 months, gross habit, but we both walk in, get a pack of cigarettes without saying a word, and we drive all the way home without saying a word. Smoked the whole thing. Then he dropped me off.

A couple days later I get on Taxidermy.net, I've got a few friends on there, and I'm trying to think if there's some way I can talk about what happened, so I make a post like, So if you saw a Bigfoot would you shoot it? That's all I said, and everybody's going back and forth. Taxidermists are outdoor people, they've got a fascination with wildlife, they've hunted all their life. There's a bunch of guys on there who were like, Oh no, I seen one, I seen one, I know they're real. And it turned into this really long topic, so maybe 20 pages goes by and I get on there and I just say, I'll tell you what, you can call it bullshit if you want, I don't care, but I shot something that walked on two legs.

[Word soon reaches Derek Randles, long-time Pacific Northwest Sasquatch researcher and co-founder of The Olympic Project. He got in touch with Smeja.]

I end up telling Derek the whole thing, and he says, Alright, I need you to get back up there and I need you to get the body of the little one, or the big one. We've got to get this done. And I'm like, I don't think so, man, I don't think I'm going to go back there. And he's like, You don't understand, we've worked so hard for this, we need your help, we need to get up there. I'm just going to drive down there, how 'bout I'll drive to your house, I'll drive you up there.

What, you're going to drive 12 hours? And he's like, Yeah, no, this is really important. 27 years of research and this is as big as it gets, this is the Holy Grail.

So eventually I end up saying, Alright, fine, I'll drive up there, and I'll get it, then you can drive down and pick up the body. So I put it off, maybe a week or so, I'm busy with work. And I didn't really get what had happened, and

Derek's calling me up every day, Seriously, you've got to get up there, you've got to get up there, just call into work, this is so important. There could be money involved. But more than that, we've been looking for this thing for so long, and now there's one sitting there.

So I talk to my buddy and we're like, Well, let's go get this thing. So we get a bunch of trash bags, black contractor bags, we get up there, and there's freakin' 3 feet of snow on the ground. So...we couldn't find it. I had my bloodhound with me, she's usually pretty good at tracking, she's a hunting dog. So I take her out there and she's acting like she just shit the bed or something, she's acting so embarrassed, she's acting very timid, she's very bothered by the whole thing. So eventually we decided to gauge where we would dig, 'cause we'd been digging for 5 or 6 hours...we figured out there were 2 or 3 areas she really didn't like, she'd walk in a straight line then all of a sudden she'd turn around and walk the other way. So we based where we dug off of the dog.

We find this flesh sample. It looks like a piece of hide. Some people say there's just no way that something like that would be there that long without the animals getting to it. I say that's ridiculous, 'cause if I shoot a deer, take it to my house, I butcher it, take it back to the woods, drop it off, and a month later I'll go back up there and you'll still see...you'll see bones, you'll see pieces of hair, you'll see hide, you'll see blood, you'll see all that stuff.

So we find it and end up sending a small portion of it, I don't know maybe an 8th of it, to Melba Ketchum. And here we are today. If you were to weigh it, the whole sample, it might be 2 pounds, but that's really pushing it. We ended up taking the rest of the sample, wrapping it in paper, freezing it in a block of ice. It'll be exactly the same 20 years from now. No air can get to it, there's no chance of freezer burn.

We've probably been back up there 20 times, maybe more, we went with a group of researchers, and we looked and we looked and we looked and we couldn't find anything. I've heard about the theory, maybe they bury their young or something. I don't know, I don't know what to think. On one of my trips we found some tracks of a larger one and a younger one with it. I have pictures of those tracks.

The one question everybody asks me, they corner me and ask me, Why didn't you put the little one in your truck. [Very agitated.] I don't know! It bothers me every day. I've got no idea, I'm so tired of that question. If I could go back in time...you're telling me that I had a winning lottery ticket, and I burned it. But...I lose sleep over it, it bothers me, I don't know. I don't know what was going through my head. I was sitting there thinking we gotta get out of here, this is nuts, this is crazy. It was like a bad dream, actually it was *very* much like a bad dream. We felt like once we got out of there, it was over.

There was a while where it was really, really traumatic. And then...you lose sleep enough and you kind of forget about it. But every once in a while I'll see like a little monkey or something in a zoo and I'm like, Fuck man, what did I do? Recently, I saw this boxer and it had this face that was really kind of similar to the young one's face, and I was just sitting there looking at this dog just thinking Oh my God...what happened?

The kid looked like a little black kid. Its face...human eyes, but it had the snout of a boxer, and the lips of an ape. It very closely resembled the snout of a boxer but pushed in a little bit more.

[J.C. Johnson asks if the young ones were walking on all fours or on two legs.]

50/50. They spent as much time on all 4s as they did on 2 legs. They were drastically different color than the adult. The adult was the color of a pale coyote, and the kids were cinnamon-colored, quite a bit darker.

[Abe del Rio asks if they were faster on all fours.]

They were definitely faster on all fours, definitely. They had very long arms and they had huge heads. They basically had an adult-sized head on a kid-sized body, which is really hard to wrap your mind around. And their hands were *huge.* Well, they were the size of mine but you put that on a little frame, it looks oddly proportioned. And they were calloused. I've been saying that they have paws. They're hands, but they're so calloused it looks like paws. It looks like a pad, like two little pads on each finger, and a big pad. Their hands were very cushioned.

[Justin's buddy, the driver of the truck, comes on the line.]

When I first looked at it [through the binoculars], the first thing I ever said, it looked like a person in a bear suit. Someone that had the bear suit on but then where the bear's face would be it was not there, it looked more human. I didn't even really think it looked ape-like at all, it looked a lot more human, but it looked a lot more hairy in the face.

[You actually lifted up the little one. How much would you say it weighed?]

35 to 40 pounds.

[And about how tall?]

I would say 3 feet. The little ones were extremely vocal while we were searching for the big one. The best way to describe it is like when a deaf person is trying to talk. They were loud, they talked a lot, they would come back to each other, they would start making noises, then they would run off in different directions. And they did that probably 5 or 6 times.

[They weren't communicating in English, nothing you could understand, right?]

Correct, yes.

The adult looked very similar to the one in the Patterson Film because it looked like a person in a suit. Not that I'm saying that's what the Patterson Film shows, I'm not saying that. I personally felt like it would have been a female because of the 2 younger ones. I can't tell by looks whether it was a male or a female. [Compared to "Patty"] it was more flat-chested, well, muscular but I felt like it was carrying a lot of weight around with it, like it was thicker more than it was what you would call "cut up" or "ripped." I could tell by the way that the sides shook when it got shot.

I watched the shot enter the body of the big one, and I remember the way the side…it looked like Jell-O. It rocked its side, you could see like waves in the side of the body. And that picture sticks with me more than anything else, was when the bullet entered the big one.

d) Pacific Northwest: Derek Randles and The Olympic Project (Saliva and Hair)

The Olympic Project (OlympicProject.com) is an excellent organization that tends to fly under the radar of publicity. Their main emphases are on public education and the crafty placement of trail cameras, with which technology they have had much better success than most.

This hard-working and professional group submitted more than one hundred samples to the Ketchum study, of which thirty-nine proved usable, making it by far the most fruitful single source. On February 5th, 2012, co-founder Derek Randles appeared on the radio show "Bigfoot Tonight," hosted by Chuck Prahl and Stacy Hostetler, where he discussed an exciting moment of evidence collection. The saliva recovered from the camera lens referenced below tested positive for Sasquatch DNA.

My partner Richard Germeau and I were up checking this camera in a very remote spot, over four thousand feet, and the camera had been moved, manipulated. And it was gooped, like it had been spit on or licked. And the good thing about Rich is that he's trained in gathering DNA in the field, he's a sheriff, and we carry those kits with us in our backpacks. So he DNA swabbed the entire camera very thoroughly, and we videotaped that.

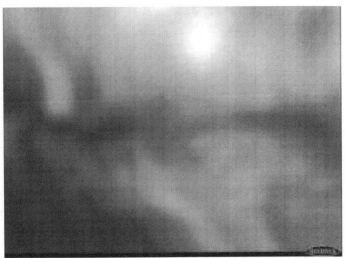

Image of Sasquatch lips snapped by the "gooped" camera (copyright OlympicProject.com)

e) Kentucky: Adrian Erickson (Blood and Tissue)

Earlier (see pages 45-47), I described the birth of the Erickson Project, an effort that contributed many organic samples to the Ketchum study and obtained the best-ever videotape of the species, footage that is due to be released shortly.

You'll recall the famous "pancake eater" situation, in which a juvenile female would consistently visit the home of a woman named Sissy, who'd leave pancakes and syrup on a paper plate on the banks of a catfish pond. This is the story that captivated me in 2005, when I heard it from Matt Moneymaker on my first BFRO expedition.

After the wealthy British Columbian real estate tycoon, Adrian Erickson, purchased the property in question, he installed in the house Dennis Pfohl and Princeton PhD in wildlife biology Leila Hadj-Chikh.

Together, they decided to make use of the long-term habituation pattern and one night glued shards of glass to the paper plate beneath a helping of pancakes and syrup. Sure enough, by the next morning, they had all the blood and little bits of flesh they could have hoped for.

Yes, it's a gruesome method, but the wounds probably healed.

And isn't it better than murder?

3. Mother Loops & Haplogroups: Breaking Down the DNA

There are two types of DNA in each animal cell, nuclear DNA mitochondrial DNA. The former are found in the cell's nucleus. Outside the nucleus, but still within the cell, mitochondria are found, which are tiny structures often called the powerhouse of the cell because they produce the energy that cells need. Each mitochondrion—there are about 1,700 in every human cell—includes an identical loop of DNA (called mitochondrial DNA or mtDNA) that is about 16,000 base pairs long. (A base pair is the smallest unit of genetic information.) In contrast, nuclear DNA (nuDNA) consists of three billion base pairs.

In other words, mtDNA is much easier to isolate (within, say, a Sasquatch hair, blood or tissue sample) and to analyze because there are so many more copies per cell and because each copy is so much simpler than the double helix system within the nucleus.

Rick Groleau, managing editor of NOVA Online, crisply summarizes the most important difference.

Whenever an egg cell is fertilized, nuclear chromosomes from a sperm cell enter the egg and combine with the egg's nuclear DNA, producing a mixture of both parents' genetic code. The mtDNA from the sperm cell, however, is left behind, outside of the egg cell. So the fertilized egg contains a mixture of the father and mother's nuclear DNA and an exact copy of the mother's mtDNA, but none of the father's mtDNA. The result is that mtDNA is passed on only along the maternal line. This means

that all of the mtDNA in the cells of a person's body
are copies of his or her mother's mtDNA, and all of
the mother's mtDNA is a copy of her mother's, and so
on. No matter how far back you go, mtDNA is
always inherited only from the mother.

That is, these loops serve as remarkable, convenient portals into
deep maternal antiquity. This fact enables researchers to trace maternal
lineage far into the past, even to pinpoint specific ancestral population
groups, and here's how.   Since mtDNA never recombines during
reproduction, it is very stable over time, as though persisting in a vacuum,
while mothers' and fathers' nuclear DNA recombine furiously conception
after conception.   mtDNA changes only through chance mutation, and it
turns out that this process occurs at a predictable rate with few and distinct
enough mutations, differing from ancient genealogical group to ancient
genealogical group, for them to be used, now, to identify these groups,
called "haplogroups" or "haplogroups" (from the Greek: *haploûs*,
"onefold, single, simple").

Each of us belongs to a haplogroup, an ancestral clan whose
identifying markers—small mutations called SNPs, or Single Nucleotide
Polymorphisms—permit geneticists to study how modern humans came to
inhabit the Earth. Haplogroups represent the branches of the *Homo sapiens*
tree, and these branches characterize the early migrations of population
groups. As a result, haplogroups are usually associated with a geographic
region. If haplogroups are the branches of the tree then the haplotypes
represent the leaves of the tree; all of the haplotypes that belong to a
particular haplogroup are leaves on the same branch.   Understanding the
evolutionary path of the female lineage has helped population geneticists
trace the matrilineal inheritance of modern humans back to our origins in
Africa and the subsequent spread across the globe.

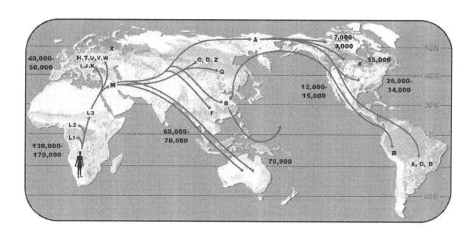

There are actually surprisingly few haplogroups; for instance, the major mitochondrial clan lineages for modern Europeans stand at just twelve, and for the human race worldwide, the number is about two hundred. Had the current breakthrough occurred twenty years ago, it would not be nearly so illuminating as it is today. Refinements in the methodology for categorizing types of mtDNA are what have allowed the Ketchum team to highlight Sasquatch genetic origins with such a startling degree of confidence—at least on the *Homo sapiens* side of the equation.

The rate at which mutations occur in nuclear DNA is extremely low. Mitochondria, on the other hand, are not quite so vigilant with their error-checking and allow through about twenty times as many mutations. This means that many more changes are to be found in mtDNA. In other words, the "molecular clock" by which we can calculate the passage of time through DNA is ticking much faster in the mitochondria than in the nucleus. [Moreover,] although mutations are found all around the mtDNA circle...there is a short stretch where mutations are especially frequent. This section, about five hundred bases in length, is called the *control region*. It has managed to accumulate so many mutations because, unlike the rest of the mtDNA, it does not carry the codes for anything in particular. If it did, then

many of the mutations would affect the performance of the
mitochondrial enzymes.[The mutation rate for
mtDNA is predictable.] On average, if two people
had a common maternal ancestor ten thousand years
ago then there would be one difference in their
control region sequences. If...twenty thousand years
ago...two mutational differences.
—from *The Seven Daughters of Eve*,
by Dr. Bryan Sykes

Another term for "molecular clock" is "mutation clock," and its predictable rate of change allows for the accurate placement of human population groups on the historical timeline.

The Ketchum study has found that Sasquatch mtDNA is a close enough match to *Homo sapiens* mtNDA that we can conclude a) that the species owes its genesis to a female *Homo sapiens* matriarch (or rather, a *regime* of matriarchs in different, far-flung locations), and b) that the SNPs that appear in Sasquatch mtDNA demonstrate how long ago, and roughly where, the various inceptions occurred.

The study has identified four broad haplogroups thus far, all entering the picture about fifteen thousand years ago: Native American, Middle Eastern, African, and Eastern European. Further testing will allow for greater precision, and further organic samples will probably reveal other haplogroups.

On the paternal side, though, the study has been unable to pin down the identity of the hominin involved, because the nuclear DNA does not match any in our genetic database of life on Earth. For now, we can call him simply TOP, The Other Primate.

Some in the media are glad to paint a lurid and titillating scene of forbidden love between the two species—a sort of Paleolithic Peyton Place—but the truth is certainly more brutal. Since 15000 years is nowhere near enough time for Sasquatch to have developed a substantially different body-type, and since today's adult bodies stand in the range of seven to ten feet, what manner of giant must have been required to engender, no doubt without the cooperation of our sub-five-foot mothers, the Sasquatch line? And how few of these girls and women could have survived childbirth?

4. Door Number One: TOP in our Collective Memory?

We are familiar with the archetype of the giant and the folklore that has brought it forward out of prehistory. As with all lore, some of these stories may reference historical truths. They may point to human co-existence with varieties of Sasquatch, or they may reach back to the genesis of this hybrid species.

In *True Giants*, Loren Coleman and Mark A. Hall present a rich array of cultural backstory, featuring such figures as Goliath of Gath, Grendel of Sweden, Og of Bashan, the Titans of the British Isles, among others. I can recommend this book for the light it sheds on potential ancient candidates for TOP.

We might catch a glimpse, as well, in *The Epic of Gilgamesh.* This tale as a complete narrative dates to 2000 BC but likely calls upon a much earlier version surviving in fragments of Sumerian cuneiform (3300 BC). And these fragments, in turn, probably echo an oral storytelling tradition stretching back further still. We can only speculate, of course, on whether this source is rooted in actual events, but it does contain themes that resonate with our topic.

The story features a king, Gilgamesh, who is oppressing his people, such as by exercising his "lord's right" to sleep with newly married brides on their wedding night. The gods respond to the subjects' pleas for help by creating a primitive man, Enkidu, in order to distract Gilgamesh. Enkidu is covered with hair and lives in the wild with the animals. He is spotted by a trapper, whose livelihood is being ruined because Enkidu is uprooting his traps. The trapper tells Gilgamesh of the man, and Enkidu is eventually domesticated and becomes friends with the king. Gilgamesh proposes a journey to the Cedar Forest to slay the monstrous demi-god Humbaba.

In Akkadian mythology, Humbaba was a monstrous giant of immemorial age, who was guardian of the Cedar Forest. "When he looks at someone, it is the look of death." "Humbaba's roar is a flood, his mouth is death! He can hear a hundred leagues away any rustling in his forest! Who would go down into his forest?!"

One of many portrayals of Humbaba

When the heroes enter the Cedar Forest, Humbaba insults and threatens them. He accuses Enkidu of betrayal, and vows to disembowel Gilgamesh and feed his flesh to the birds. A long battle ends with Gilgamesh dispatching him with a blow to the neck. The two heroes cut down many cedars, including a gigantic tree that Enkidu plans to fashion into a gate for the temple. They build a raft and return home along the Euphrates with the giant tree and the head of Humbaba.

The story continues, but we can take stock here.

What strikes us immediately is the presence of three distinct types of primate—modern *Homo sapiens*; the hair-covered wild man, who is able to cross between worlds, entering the human realm and forming alliances with us; and then the even *wilder* wild figure, who stands entirely outside the circle of domestication. Since the latter blocks our way to the primeval forest, he must be destroyed, thus clearing the way for human dominion over nature, even allowing us to co-opt it to serve as the very *entrance* into what lifts us above our mere animal natures—the temple to the gods.

Another relevant wrinkle is that Humbaba "accuses Enkidu of betrayal," which carries a suggestion beyond the obvious; not only did the wild man begin life in the forest and then turn his back on his origins, on nature itself, but Humbaba also seems to consider himself and Enkidu more specifically connected, because one can only truly "betray" an ally or family.

Since *The Epic of Gilgamesh* is, let's remember, a product of *Homo sapiens* authorship, the inclusion of this shade of character bond may reflect a primordial awareness, on our part, of Sasquatch pedigree, of its deep relatedness to another, even less human creature.

5. Or Is It...Door Number Two?

Perhaps TOP was not, after all, a larger, more monstrous primate than Sasquatch, but rather one of comparable size, or even *smaller*.

As we know, offspring can sometimes outgrow their parents, though this is not generally the case. In certain inter-species hybridizations, however, it *is* generally true. Let's take, for example, the liger, which is a cross between a male lion and a female tiger.

The male liger stands six feet tall at the shoulder and eleven feet tall on its hind legs, whereas the male lion averages four feet at the shoulder and seven feet on hind legs, and the female tiger, three feet at the shoulder and eight feet on hind legs.

> The liger is the largest known cat in the world. Imprinted genes may be a factor contributing to huge liger size. These are genes that are expressed only when maternally inherited and cause the young to grow larger than is typical for either parent breed, because in the paternal breeds, such genes are normally "counteracted" by genes inherited from the female of the appropriate breed. (Wikipedia)

Weights of Three Largest Wild Cats Measured in Pounds

LIGERWORLD.COM

A liger beside average-sized people

6. What Ever Became of TOP?

Well, if the identity of the Sasquatch forefather turns out to be found behind either Door Number One or Door Number Two, then we might expect certain concrete remains to be lying around or buried intact, ready for our trowels. And indeed, many candidate fossils have been located through the years, though according to accounts, not handled with adequate scientific care.

Here again, Coleman and Hall's *True Giants* proves a useful archive for historical examples of what may indicate Sasquatch or TOP. See especially Appendices C: "Giant Bones"; D: "Giant Skulls" by Ivan Sanderson; F: "The Teeth of the Dragon" by Eric Pettifor (about *Gigantopithecus blacki*); and Appendix G: "*Meganthropus*: Giant Man from Old Java."

I can't accept, however, the book's central claim that this form of primate lurks still today, in remote places, and occupies a very different classification from Sasquatch. The authors present no credible evidence for this distinction, and even place the average True Giant's height at "twelve to fourteen feet," a size falling well within the range of Sasquatch proportions as assessed in eyewitness encounters; people do tend to emotionally inflate their estimates when facing a creature nearly twice as tall, and five times as bulky, as themselves.

Let us step back from the logistical issue of the disposition of their fossilized bones and consider two plausible pathways, probably overlapping, to the extinction of TOP in the first place: 1) They were outcompeted for resources by the increasingly group-cohesive, cooperative and technically advanced *Homo sapiens*; 2) they were systematically tracked down and exterminated by same, just as Gilgamesh smote Humbaba, and for a broadly similar reason.

In that story, the monster guarded the Primeval Forest, and his destruction allowed for the forward march of civilization, the control of nature, its transformation from a source of jeopardy, unpredictability, and death, into a reliable source of raw materials.

On the issue of crossbreeding between our species and TOP, let's not fool ourselves into projecting some titillating scene of taboo transgression, dangerous liaisons, a Paleolithic Peyton Place; far more likely, these couplings were seldom consensual, the monsters instead emerging from the wildwood to snatch away our mates and daughters. We can read TOP, too, as descriptive of literal sexual posture—a much more powerful male on top of a diminutive human female, our foremother, raping her.

It would become imperative for *Homo sapiens* to subdue and eliminate this constant and destabilizing threat, even as they domesticated nature itself. After perhaps a centuries-long regime of forced couplings, her people would eventually succeed in taking up arms against the brutalizing horde, whose members were not as socially, strategically adept as we.

Indeed, our developing social order would enable just such a concerted campaign. Recall that this time in human history saw the dawn of the Agricultural Revolution, the wide-scale transition of many human cultures from a lifestyle of hunting and gathering to one of agriculture and settlement, which supported an increasingly large population. Archaeological data indicate that various forms of plant and animal domestication evolved in separate locations worldwide, starting around 12,000 years ago. This period would overlap with the trailing end of the epoch of Sasquatch births.

Once TOP was stricken from the picture, this left in their wake only their half-*Homo sapiens* children. The original few generations must have been much more like us than Sasquatch is today, because over the succeeding thousand generations, they would have reproduced largely amongst themselves—this incidence approaching 100% as humankind grew its villages into cities, walled itself off from nature, and codified its social structures—which served increasingly to purify their race, their mighty bodies, their nuclear DNA gene pool, even as those mitochondrial loops never ceased to bear the eternal signature of their tiny matriarch.

7. Seeking an Apt Research Paradigm
a) Pivoting from Primatology to Anthropology

We are all keenly aware of the need for a fresh approach to the study of Sasquatch, because the "field," such as it is, has been essentially spinning its wheels for the past fifty years, except on two fronts: 1) the increasing recognition of habituation sites as a source of reliable contact, and 2) the sequencing of their DNA. To move beyond what is offered by these avenues, however, to begin to learn how Sasquatch live when they are not visiting us, we'll need to arrive at a methodology that draws upon the heritage of Goodall and Fossey—in their practice of passive, respectful, endlessly patient observation—and yet embraces the reality that our subject species is dramatically more intelligent and sophisticated than the other great apes. That is, they deserve their own domain within the realm of scientific inquiry, a discipline akin to that of cultural anthropology.

Some feel strongly that when Sasquatch is not visiting us, when they are off by themselves and minding their own business, they ought not to be "studied" at all, that we should take our cue only from *their* overtures toward us, if and when these occur. I think this is a legitimate stance, and one that will certainly enter into the healthy debate going forward. And yet, now that the curtain has been parted, their existence revealed, it's simply not credible to expect the human animal—with all the boundless curiosity that has driven our evolution—to refrain from pursuing further knowledge; the imperative will be to pursue it peacefully, an aspiration on which, admittedly, this same evolutionary history casts doubt.

More than a century ago, pioneers in the emerging field of anthropology helped nudge Western civilization out of its benighted, self-enclosed and self-congratulatory worldview by shedding light on the phenomenon of diverse cultures worldwide. The breakthrough, here, lay in successfully challenging the comfortable notion that people living in radically different ways from those of Europeans or Americans were "primitives" languishing on some lower rung of the ladder of human development.

The parallel to our situation in 2012, and through the near future, is that now the entire human race itself—well, the 99% of us who have remained in the dark concerning Sasquatch—has been caught out in the same falsely entitled posture as the "advanced" societies of old, and finds itself waking from a vast parochial slumber.

Starting with rigorous fieldwork among the Nuxálk of British Columbia, Franz Boas, considered the father of modern anthropology, advanced the concept of "cultural relativism." In an 1883 letter, Boas wrote, "I often ask myself what advantages our 'good society' possesses over that of the 'savages' and find, the more I see of their customs, that we have no right to look down upon them, to blame them for their forms and superstitions which may seem ridiculous to us."

It was Boas who originated the notion of "culture" as learned behaviors. His emphasis on research first, followed by generalizations, stood in marked contrast to the British school of anthropology which emphasized the creation of grand theories. Although serious work was being done in anthropology at the time, the field was heavily peopled with untrained adventurers and armchair philosophers. It was common practice to use small scraps of information, or preconceived pet theories, to further prognosticate on the "nature of Man." (NNDB.com)

This could just as well describe the rag-tag state of Sasquatch research today, and the crying need for a coherent set of procedures for the collection and assessment of data; but an interesting question will become, To what extent can we really model our new discipline after the example of anthropology?

> Boas further helped develop the basic methodology that underlies anthropological research. He felt that one could only begin to understand a culture by taking on a complete survey of its mythology and tribal lore, religion, social taboos, marriage customs, physical appearance, diet, handicrafts, means of obtaining food, and so on. The new standards as applied to cultural anthropology required that ethnographers go on location, learn the language, and

undertake an intense survey that catalogued all the
elements mentioned above as well as whatever other
unique features that were apparent. (NNDB.com)

Margaret Mead in Papua New Guinea, 1931

It's difficult to imagine how, in the present case, we'd even *begin* to
aspire to such a level of studious engagement, given that the very first step,
"go on location," is of course the whole dilemma in a nutshell. Human
groups, even in the most far-flung locations on Earth, have, for better or
worse, proven willing to stay put, in their jungles, mesas, villages and
valleys, beneath the anthropological lens, and they've hung together in
stable societies; but here we have, in Sasquatch, an exceedingly mobile
and nomadic style of existence—a perpetually receding target—that
furthermore aggressively fragments itself, avoiding congregation (except
perhaps on rare occasions), making itself scarce instead in disparate cells,
each occupying its own territory.

As for "learn the language," we are thankful for Scott Nelson's
crucial spadework, his cataloguing of morphemes from one dialect in the
Sierra Nevada Mountains, uttered in the early 1970s, as well as a handful
of further morphemes recorded recently, elsewhere in North America, and

his assembly of a preliminary "phonetic alphabet." But this analysis and transcription still leave us light-years away from an actual translation of what these towering speakers are saying. And even if we could comprehend them, the Berry/Morehead tapes only capture what's shouted in a highly atypical setting, in the presence of encroaching men at a hunting camp, rather than shared through the presumably much subtler, wider-ranging articulations of private communal and family life.

As quoted in Chapter Six, Nelson holds out hope for a major interactive breakthrough. "To truly discover them as a people we need contact, to *speak* with them. One property of language, for something to qualify as a language, is that it be learnable. I think we will be able to learn how to communicate with them someday. I don't think we will ever learn their language fully, because I think secrecy and self-preservation will always be important to them. Again, I can use the example of the Romano Gypsies: I think they will always keep part of their language to themselves. But if nothing else I think Sasquatch will be able to communicate with us through our own language. So it will be an effort on both our parts. We may end up communicating in what we would call a *pidgin*—half human and half Sasquatch."

We can all devoutly share Nelson's vision, of course, though we lack any means to assess its likelihood in the near term. Perhaps there may eventually arise some willing go-between—a sort of Sasquatch Sacagawea (the Lemhi Shoshone woman who served as guide and translator for the Lewis and Clark expedition)—a sympathetic emissary who first grows to trust one of us at a habituation site, and whose *own* anthropological leanings and curiosity compel her or him to bend and snap tribal taboos. After all, if the phenomenology of habituation sites has taught us anything, it is that they, not we, are the observers here, the true researchers, that they know worlds more about our lived routines, our daily culture, than we do of theirs—because their survival depends upon this knowledge. Thus, the catalyst of transcendence, of bridge-building, is likely to come from their side of the chasm, if it comes at all.

And yet, barring some mass (and foolishly risky) sea change in Sasquatch ethos, wouldn't such wayward flouting of ancient tradition ensure ouster from the clan, after which we'd be obliged merely to take on faith whatever information the ostracized individual could impart? That's hardly a solid basis for a social science.

Rarely, certain persistent investigators from our side *will* be able to "go on location." We remember that Mike, in Autumn Williams's *Enoch*, gained access after four years of consistent forays into that thick swamp in Florida, interacting not only with Enoch himself but also with members of his family, and once, even with the larger group. But Mike could only accomplish his feat solo, whereas, again, the cornerstone of any scientific discipline is corroboration, observational repeatability; we can't rely long-term on trust, on the accuracy of such isolated reportage.

This brings us to the category of video surveillance. Many have tried this over the years, and the success rate is vanishingly small. We've already covered the fact that Sasquatch seem to abhor cameras, and for an excellent reason: Their welfare has always required that they remain unseen. So from a purely ethical standpoint, any secret filming would seem to be ruled out, never mind the pesky drawback that they're nearly always able to sense and eschew our best efforts along these lines; as soon as they realize a spot is not secure, they simply pick up and relocate.

Frustration will give rise to people who do not go in peace. Say someone peppers leaves and branches beside prime trails with sticky transponders the size of bee-bees until one eventually gets lost within the thick, unruly coat of a Sasquatch. Through GPS, the quarry's travel, and that of the clan, could be steadily monitored, even allowing for a signal chopped by tree cover.

Depending on the legal state of play at the time, the pursuer may then choose to emulate Rick Dyer, armed with bullets or tranquilizer darts. Or he may wait to discover some longer-term refuge, probably underground. What then? Storm the place? This would accomplish precisely nothing, other than a pointless stand-off or else a bloodbath.

Some will attempt to employ this same transponder trick benignly, for purely tracking purposes, as we do with bears, porpoises, migratory birds, etc. But the lowest-impact technology, and one that apparently bothers Sasquatch far less, is audio surveillance. As we know, researchers have managed to capture a great deal of high-quality sound in the field—wood knocks, rock clacks, tree pushes, branch breaks, and most importantly, a remarkable variety of vocalizations up to and including speech. One could easily envision, unfolding next, a far more concerted and systematic program of audio collection, with concealed recorders arrayed liberally across the land, capable of live-streaming data back to headquarters where it may be remotely analyzed. Could this not provide us with as lavish a soundscape as National Geographic visuals, an acoustical version of Goodall's peripatetic fieldwork (following chimps from place to place), and letting us track our own subjects' movements, so long as they remain within our study zone?

Presumably, too, using the finest microphones, we could often guess what they were *doing*—eating, playing, sleeping, fighting, loving, building, hunting, above all talking; and after we gather a critical mass of the latter, we ought to be able to work out their language, gradually, dialect by dialect. In this manner, we might freely learn without resorting to pursuit or pressure.

Our equipment would need to be capable of recording infrasound. Although in its raw form infrasound is beneath the range of human hearing, it can be brought forth as data to be analyzed, allowing us to access an entire secret world of communication. Zoologists are beginning to employ this means in the study of other large mammals. For instance, according to Cornell University's Elephant Listening Project:

> One way to discover if you have recorded infrasonic
> elephant calls is to speed up the recording, raising all
> the frequencies to a level that you can hear. Typically, if
> you speed up a recording containing infrasonic elephant
> calls by a factor of three, you will be able to hear them.
> Sounds can also be represented visually using spectrograms.

Along these lines, I've obtained some promising early results myself by installing a long-term audio system on a mountain top overlooking the area where I recorded the 2009 "Sasquatch Stakeout" wood knocks; see YouTube: "The Sasquatch Listening Project 2012: First Steps," which also contains advice on setting up your own such system.

This kind of intimate ear upon the subjects' realm may be the softest, most feasible option, because in contrast to classical anthropology, must we really strain to embed ourselves among, or even wish to visually monitor, these folks? There's something avaricious about our prying vision. And let's not forget that their physical morphology had already come into quite good focus even before San Antonio, thanks to all the previous video clips we do possess, bolstered by thousands of detailed eye-witness accounts. See, for example, Henner Fehrenbach's paper, "Sasquatch: Size, Scaling, and Statistics," which is based largely on John Green's decades' worth of rigorous witness interviews. David Claerr, too, has been at the forefront of Sasquatch physical anthropology with such studies as "Bigfoot Back: The Upper Torso of a Sasquatch—Posterior Anatomical Study" and "Bigfoot Bones: Sasquatch Skeleton Analyzed and Compared to Human"; these complement the valuable anatomical insights contributed by Dr. Jeffrey Meldrum (on the foot/locomotion) and by M.K. Davis's video analyses of the Patterson/Gimlin figure, posted to YouTube by Greenwave2010fb.

We will always yearn to feast our eyes on Sasquatch directly, yet our sharpened priorities can lead us, for the sake of knowledge, to renounce such appetite.

Luckily, the question *whether* to study Sasquatch will, I think, lag far behind the numerous and severe practical impediments entailed in *how* to study them. When and if the time finally arrives that we're forced to confront the ultimate moral issues involved, a cautionary touchstone would be The American Anthropological Association Code of Ethics.

> Anthropological researchers have primary ethical obligations to the people, species, and materials they are studying. These obligations can supersede the goal of seeking new knowledge, and can lead to decisions not to undertake or to discontinue a research project. These ethical obligations include:
>
> • To avoid harm or wrong, understanding that the

development of knowledge can lead to change which may be positive or negative for the people or animals worked with or studied;

- To respect the well-being of humans and nonhuman primates;
- To consult actively with the affected individuals or group(s), with the goal of establishing a working relationship that can be beneficial to all parties involved;
- Anthropological researchers must do everything in their power to ensure that their research does not harm the safety, dignity, or privacy of the people with whom they work. Researchers must present to their research participants the possible impacts of the choices, and make clear that despite their best efforts, anonymity may be compromised;
- Anthropological researchers should obtain in advance the informed consent of persons being studied, providing information, owning or controlling access to material being studied, or otherwise identified as having interests on which the research might have an impact. It is understood that the degree and breadth of informed consent required will depend on the nature of the project and may be affected by requirements of other codes, laws, and ethics of the country or community in which the research is pursued;
- While anthropologists may gain personally from their work, they must not exploit individuals, groups, animals, or cultural or biological materials. They should recognize their debt to the societies in which they work and their obligation to reciprocate in appropriate ways.

(Aaanet.org)

b) Same As It Ever Was...with a Twist

Despite our revolutionary leaps forward in this field of inquiry, Sasquatch will continue to operate Old School; perhaps, then, we should learn to value the resources contained in our own vivid, pre-technological observations of the species, arising organically in the course of our lives— today as in bygone eons—whether near home or off in the wilderness.

The several thousand sightings reports catalogued by the BFRO, other contemporary outlets, and John Green before them, represent a small fraction of those people who have been fortunate enough to see Sasquatch—sometimes viewing nuances of behavior for luxurious minutes on end—but have refrained from coming forward for fear of ridicule. In the wake of Ketchum and Erickson, these witnesses will tend to feel vindicated and many, tens of thousands, will finally share their accounts, adding significantly to this treasure trove of anecdotal data. Moreover, the current explosion of awareness and fascination among the general public will result in an ever-expanding regime of encounters—primarily peaceful, instructive ones—as fresh ranks of avid amateurs seek to participate in this primordial outreach. The smart ones will venture forth free of cameras, to project the right spirit and increase their odds.

The methodological trick will become: how best to manage the incoming information flow, to synthesize the disparate sources of past observational data, channel new data daily accumulating, and to analyze both in such a way that salient patterns emerge. Various "data mining" projects will compete under this banner, several distinguishing themselves, each with its own strong points, all building on the foundation of low-tech and no-tech personal experience. The effort that separates itself from the rest, however, will be that which successfully recruits an ongoing labor pool of worthy contributors, and nurtures a budding alliance between professional and amateur researchers.

An analogy already exists in astronomy: Volunteers are helping to scan the heavens.

The International Centre for Radio Astronomy Research (ICRAR) is set to launch the Square Kilometer Array, a "citizen science" application based on the open source Nereus V Cloud computing technology developed at Oxford University. The application, dubbed "theskynet" by Australian researchers, would grant anyone not affiliated with the global telescope project access to the datasets formed out of the Array's work. (Computerworld Australia)

The SKA will consist of 3,000 radio dishes, spread as far as 2,000 miles in every direction from a central core, offering a full 1,000,000 square meters (that's one square kilometer) of collection surface. (PopSci.com)

Let's compare these 3,000 dishes, cast skyward, to our millions of newly wide-open eyes today and tomorrow, searching the forests, and to our ears as well, attuned to subtle, telltale clues in our backyards.

8. How Many in North America?

Oddly enough, we will never know the answer, even approximately; you'll hear various researchers advancing widely divergent ballpark estimates. Here's my own reasoning.

Canada contains ten provinces and three far-northern territories. Let's exclude the territories (due to their harsh climate) and Prince Edward Island (due to its small size and isolation)—not that there are no Sasquatch in these places, just probably few enough to set aside when deriving a conservative overall estimate. This leaves nine provinces.

There are no credible sightings in Hawaii. North and South Dakota combine for only 2.5 million acres of forest, so let's consider these two as one. Add the resulting forty-eight states to the Canadian number and we get fifty-seven.

(I can't include Mexico, because we don't possess accurate records of encounters below the border.)

I'm going to conservatively estimate one thousand Sasquatch per state/province, understanding that many contain fewer, others far more.

- Between them, Canada and the United States contain 15% of the Earth's forest cover. North American forest cover expanded nearly 10 million acres over the last decade;

- The United States is 2.263 billion acres, of which 745 million acres, or 33 percent, is forested, which represents 5 percent of the world's forested area;

- Today, the United States has about the same area of forestland as it did in 1920, even though there has been a 143 percent increase in population;

- Canada's forests occupy 1.5 times the land area of the entire European Community and represent 10 per cent of the world's forested area;

- Acres of forest in Canada: 1 billion
  (forestinformation.com)

- Average number of forested acres for *each* of the 57 states/provinces included in my count: 27 million.

Here are one thousand dots:

....
....
....
....
....
....
....
....
....
....
....
....
....
....
....

Under my projection, the average state/province would provide each individual with twenty-seven thousand acres of forested territory all to itself; but this neglects the fact that Sasquatch tend to cluster in family and extended-family groups.

My estimate, then, is that North America supports—*at bare minimum*—a population of fifty-seven thousand Sasquatch, the vast majority of whom will never interact with, or even be glimpsed by, a member of our own species.

9. *Worldwide Variations on a Theme*

It's almost certain that different breeds or subspecies exist within North America under the umbrella term Sasquatch. Quite diverse appearances are reported, and even filmed. For instance, "Patty" in the Patterson/Gimlin Film has a clear sagittal crest while Matilda, the Kentucky subject shown in the Erickson Project clip, does not. In *Enoch*, Autumn Williams' long-term witness, Mike, relates that certain of the Florida Sasquatch he comes across look nearly human whereas others possess a face and head-shape much closer to a gorilla's. In Michigan, there is a long history of encounters with a type of primate figure known as "the dogman," and indeed, many across the continent have seen Sasquatch with protruding, doglike snouts; these are reportedly more aggressive than their flatter-faced counterparts.

Other regions of the world, too, are home to varieties of hairy, upright-walking hominins. We cannot speculate on whether their DNA will reveal the same ancestry profile as that of the North American Sasquatch. Here's a sampling.

a) Almas or Almasty

Inhabiting the Caucasus and Pamir Mountains of central Asia, and the Altai Mountains of southern Mongolia, Almas stand between five and six and a half feet tall, their bodies covered with reddish-brown hair, with humanlike facial features but a pronounced browridge, flat nose, and a weak chin.

Sightings have been recorded as far back as 1430, when Hans Schiltberger set down in his journal observations of these creatures spotted in Mongolia while he was a prisoner of the Genghis Khan. British anthropologist Myra Shackley, in her book *Still Living?*, describes Ivan Ivlov's 1963 observation of a family group of Almas. A pediatrician, Ivlov interviewed some of his Mongolian patients and discovered that many of them had also seen this creature; it seems that neither the Mongol children nor the young Almas were afraid of each other.

Russian researcher Alexei Sitnikov was travelling to Kake Tonee in 1993 when he and his team of researchers encountered an Almas. They were crossing a river on a raft when they noticed a man covered with reddish fur lurking on the opposite side of the river. He made a few grunting noises and then scampered into the nearby woods. The weather was sunny and clear and the creature was plainly visible to Sitnikov and several of this research team. Its head was somewhat triangular in shape, widening toward its base. The creature had small eyes and wide nostrils. The neck was not visible—the head looked as if it were placed directly on wide shoulders—and it possessed a powerful chest. Sitnikov has collected many descriptions of the "snow man" and gathered statements from the local populace, including hunters who have encountered the figure. Secret settlements have been found deep in the thick woods.

b) Orang Pendek

Though these creatures are historically documented throughout Sumatra and Southeast Asia, recent sightings have mostly occurred within the Kerinci regency of central Sumatra, in the Bukit Barisan Mountain Range that features some of the most remote primary rainforest in the world. Because of its inaccessibility, the park has been largely spared from the rampant logging that occurs throughout the rest of Sumatra.

Witnesses describe this primate as covered with short fur (black, gray, brown, or reddish-brown) and standing between two and a half and five feet tall, with extremely long, powerful arms. The tracks display a "divergent big toe," separated from the other digits as a thumb is from the other fingers; and these tracks often bear four, rather than five toes.

Debbie Martyr, long-time Orang Pendek researcher, says that what most impresses the Kerinci villagers is the sheer physical power of the creature. They speak in awe of its broad shoulders, huge chest and upper abdomen, and the powerful arms. It is apparently able to uproot small trees and even break rattan vines. The legs, in comparison, are short and slim, the feet neat and small, usually turned out at an angle of up to forty-five degrees. The head slopes back to a distinct crest—similar to the gorilla's—and there appears to be a bony ridge above the eyes. But the mouth is small and neat, the eyes set wide apart and the nose distinctly humanlike. When frightened, the animal exposes its teeth, revealing oddly broad incisors and prominent, long canines.

c) Yeren

Native to the remote mountainous forests of western Hubei Province, China, these hominins are reported to be covered, again, in reddish-brown hair, though white specimens have also been sighted. They are said to have a sloping forehead that rises up above the eyes like a human's, eyes set deep, and the whole face, with the exception of its nose and ears, is covered in short hairs. The Yeren's arms hang below its knees. The height is estimated to range from six to eight feet, somewhat smaller than the North American Sasquatch. But like Sasquatch, the Yeren is peaceful and will generally walk away quietly when encountering people. The Yeren has been a part of the folklore of southern and central China for centuries. Ancient Chinese literary works and folk legends include references to big hairy man-like creatures that live in the vast forests of the Quinling Bashan Shennongjia, a mountainous region of central China. Roughly two thousand years ago, during the Warring States period, Qu Yuan, the statesman poet of the State of Chu, referred in his verses to mountain ogres. His home was just south of Shennongjia, in what is today the Zigui country of the Hubei Province. During the Tang Dynasty, the historian Li Yanshou, in his Southern History, described a band of hairy men in the region of modern Jiangling country, also in the Hubei Province, which is home to the Shennongjia Mountains, an area of approximately 1,250 square miles that is composed of steep, rugged mountains reaching up to ten thousand feet.

Regional officials have recorded nearly four hundred credible sightings in and around this region since the 1920s. In 1940, biologist Wang Tselin claimed to have examined the corpse of a Yeren that had been killed in the Gansu region. He stated that the specimen was a female, over 6 feet tall, with striking features that appeared to be a cross between ape and human. Also, geologist Fan Jingquan reported seeing a pair of Yeren, what he thought was a mother and son, in the forests of the Shanxi province in 1950.

d)Yeti

This famous type hails from the Himalayan region of Nepal, India and Tibet. Stories of the Yeti first entered Western popular culture in the 19th century, though the frequency of reports increased during the early 20th century, when Westerners began making determined attempts to scale the many mountains in the area and occasionally reported seeing odd creatures or strange tracks.

In 1925, N. A. Tombazi, a photographer and member of the Royal Geographic Society, saw a creature at about fifteen thousand feet near Zemu Glacier. Tombazi later wrote that he observed the creature from about two to three hundred yards, for about a minute. "Unquestionably, the figure in outline was exactly like a human being, walking upright and stopping occasionally to pull at some dwarf rhododendron bushes. It showed up dark against the snow, and as far as I could make out, wore no clothes." About two hours later, Tombazi and his companions descended the mountain and saw the creature's prints, described as "similar in shape to those of a man, but only six to seven inches long by four inches wide."

Western interest in the Yeti peaked dramatically in the 1950s. While attempting to scale Mount Everest in 1951, Eric Shipton took photographs of a number of large prints in the snow, at about twenty thousand feet above sea level.

In his memoir *The Long Walk,* Sławomir Rawicz recounts his 1940 journey with fellow escapees from a Siberian labor camp.

> In all our wanderings through the Himalayan region we had encountered no other creatures than man, dogs, and sheep. It was with quickening interest, therefore, that in the early stages of our descent of this last mountain Kolemenos drew our attention to two moving black specks against the snow about a quarter of a mile below us. We thought of animals and immediately of food, but as we set off down to investigate we had no great hopes that they would await our arrival. The contours of the mountain temporarily hid them from view as we approached nearer, but when we halted on the edge of a bluff we found they were still there, twelve feet or so below us and about a hundred yards away.

> Two points struck me immediately. They were enormous and they walked on their hind legs. The picture is clear in my mind, fixed there indelibly by a solid two hours of observation. We just could not believe what we saw at first, so we stayed to watch.

> I set myself to estimating their height on the basis of my military training for artillery observation. They could not have been much less than eight feet tall. One was a few inches taller than the other, in the relation of the average man to the average woman. They were shuffling quietly round on

a flattish shelf which formed part of the obvious route for us to continue our descent. We thought that if we waited long enough they would clear the way for us. It was clear they had seen us, and it was equally apparent they had no fear of us. The American said that eventually he was sure we should see them drop on all fours like bears. But they never did.

Their faces I could not see in detail, but the heads were squarish and the ears must lie close to the skull because there was no projection from the silhouette against the snow. The shoulders sloped sharply down to a powerful chest. The arms were long and the wrists reached the level of the knees. Seen in profile, the back of the head was a straight line from the crown into the shoulders. We decided unanimously that we were examining a type of creature of which we had no previous experience in the wild. There was something both of the bear and the ape about their general shape but they could not be mistaken for either. The colour was a rusty kind of brown. They appeared to be covered by two distinct kinds of hair, the reddish hair which gave them their characteristic colour forming a tight, close fur against the body, mingling with which were long, loose, straight hairs, hanging downwards, which had a slight grayish tinge as the light caught them.

e) Yowie

In the 1870s, accounts of "Indigenous Apes" appeared in the *Australian Town and Country Journal*. The earliest account in November 1876 asked readers, "Who has not heard, from the earliest settlement of the colony, the aboriginal people speaking of some unearthly animal or inhuman creature...namely the Yahoo-Devil, or hairy man of the wood?" In an article appearing six years later, a Mr. H. J. McCooey claimed to have seen such a creature on the south coast of New South Wales: "I should think that if it were standing perfectly upright it would be nearly five feet high. It was tailless and covered with very long black hair, which was of a dirty red about the throat and breast. Its eyes, which were small and restless, were partly hidden by matted hair that covered its head. I threw a stone at the animal, whereupon it immediately rushed off."

The leading contemporary Yowie researcher is Dean Harrison; see his videos on YouTube channel YowieHunters. Here is an account from a 2006 interview by Harrison. The encounter took place in December of 1986, near Mount Kembla, New South Wales:

One morning, while engaged on upgrading the Unanderra to Dumbarton railway at the base of Mt Kembla, plant operator Ron S. arrived on site early, parked his car in a small clearing and began to read the paper.

"It was just coming up light when I had this feeling, 'somebody's behind me.' I'm a big bloke, but it put the wind up me…an eerie feeling."

He got out of the car, took a few steps and found himself only four feet away from "a dark shadow—and it was big, probably seven feet tall, broad and strong-looking. The head was like ours, but broader and maybe a bit narrower at the top. I weigh 120 kilos [260 pounds]. This was double my weight, if not triple. It might have been a browny colour, scruffy, hairy—I'd say 100 mill [4 inches] long.

"I froze—I didn't know what to do – run, scream or what. It took off down the hill—hard, rocky terrain, a lot of thick lantana trees…underscrub. It went crashing through. Long strides. The arms were down near the knees, [they] were swinging. It wasn't a person." It left "a real horrible smell…like when your dog goes out and rolls in something. Filthy, dirty, musty. I got back in the car and just shook. Even now [20 years later, as he recalled the event] I'm shaking…goose pimples.

"I was bewildered. All day blokes were saying, 'What's wrong with you?' and I'd say, 'Nothing, nothing'—I wouldn't tell anybody.

"Then, about two weeks later, about a kilometre up the escarpment, me and another bloke seen it–clear as a bell this time. We were having lunch at 12 o'clock, and my mate…looked up and says, 'Jesus Christ—what's that?' Straight across the train line there's a bank that rises up—and this thing was standing there, 50 metres away, just inside the tree line, in clear view.

"I reckon it was the same one—same size and

dimensions. It was like an orang-utan–because it had orangey hair. The head hair was thick, wild and dirty; on the chest it seemed sparser, but around the lower abdomen it was so thick that it was impossible to say if the creature was male or female. One hand was on a tree and it was, like, looking at us, saying 'What are *you* doing here?' A face like a monkey's... shiny, dark, probably like a gorilla...didn't have a nose like ours...more broad. His eyes were deep, dark...the contact was there between me and him...an aggressive look that was overpowering and scary. I was shaking like an autumn leaf again [but] it just turned and walked away up the escarpment ... torso bent forward slightly."

10. Okay, Just How Big *Anyway?*

I'm not sure what this says about me, but I'll confess that at least half of what captivates me about this creature is its immense size; if they were our size or smaller, they would still be fascinating and important, but not heart-stopping.

North American Sasquatch males reach between seven and a half and ten feet in height—some even taller—while females average about twenty percent smaller. Both can be astonishingly bulky, muscular, broad-shouldered, though some are described as quite lanky.

In other words, Sasquatch are at least as much larger, in every dimension, than Shaquille O'Neil and Tiny Sturgess as O'Neal and Sturgess are larger than Earl Boykins and Scott Fleishman; see next page.

But whoever TOP was in the beginning, his descendents are currently making mischief in my backyard.

Shaquille O'Neal (7'1") and Earl Boykins (5'7")

The Harlem Globetrotters' Tiny Sturgess (7'8") and WCAX sports reporter Scott Fleishman (5'9")

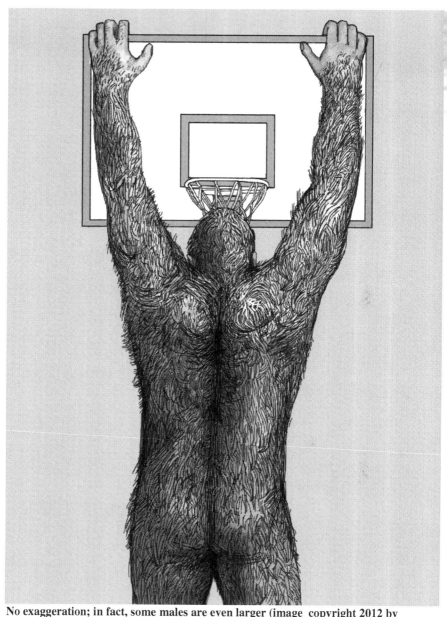

No exaggeration; in fact, some males are even larger (image copyright 2012 by Christiopher Noël & Jeff Caramagna)

The Yeahoh, An Old Kentucky Folktale

Once they was a man out huntin' and he got lost and after a while he begin to get hungry. He come to a big hole in the ground and he thought he would venture down into it. He wen down in there and he found that the old Yeahoh lived in there and had deer meat hangin' up and other foods piled around the walls. The man was afraid at first, but Yeahoh didn't bother him and he went toward that meat to get him some. The Yeahoh walked over and looked at the knife and said, "Yeahoh, Yeahoh," a time or two. He cut it off a piece of the meat and it started eatin' it.

Well, the man stepped over to the middle of the pit and took out his flint and built him up a fire. And the Yeahoh watched him and looked at the fire and at the flint and said, "Yeahoh, Yeahoh" again. The man put his meat on a stick and br'iled him a nice piece and started eatin' it. The Yeahoh watched him and acted like it wanted a piece. The man cut it off a piece of the br'iled meat and reached it over, and the Yeahoh commenced to eatin' it up and smackin' its lips and saying, "Yeahoh, Yeahoh."

Well, the man lived there with it a long time and they got along all right. After so long they was a young'un born to 'em, and it was half-man and half-Yeahoh. And the Yeahoh took such a liking to the man it wouldn't let him leave. He got to wanting to get away and go back home. One day he slipped off and the Yeahoh follered him and made him go back. Went on that way for a good while, but he picked him a good time and slipped away. This time he got to the shore where they was a ship ready to set sail. He got on this ship and he looked and saw the Yeahoh comin' with the young'un. It screamed and hollered for him to come back and when it saw he wasn't goin' to come, why, it just tore the baby in two and helt it out one-half to him and said, "Yeahoh, Yeahoh."

Chapter Eight

From Ancient Forests
To my Apple Tree
(The Vermont Project 2011-2012)

Bigfoots all across North America live where the habitat is viable. Animals basically need food, water, and cover. And where you find lots of all three of those things, you generally have a history of Bigfoot activity.

> —Cliff Barackman of "Finding Bigfoot," interviewed on "G4's Attack of the Show," November 26th, 2012

They have had 15,000 years to expand their population and spread throughout our continent. Probably even by several thousand years ago, they'd come to occupy every suitable tract of territory. And as an apex predator, they would have had no natural reason to permanently vacate any area unless actively rebuffed by human development.

> —Sarah Galloway

Why Me?

I am lucky enough to live in a spot that fulfills the baseline requirements for Sasquatch habituation: plenty of woods. I am surrounded by several thousand acres of the stuff, interrupted by fewer than thirty houses. Also, I'm at the end of a long driveway, with nothing between my backyard and miles of pure habitat.

Add to this three further factors in my favor:

First, I have spent many nights alone in a ravine, just two miles from here, where their presence is evidenced by stick signs, two eyewitness reports, and my own harrowing "Thumper" night; after the latter, I found three "gifts" by my car on three successive mornings (see Chapter Two).

Second, aside from these forays into "their" territory, I have made consistent overtures to them, here at home, over the past five years— vocals, knocks, food, and gifts.

Third, I have had a small daughter running about the place very enthusiastically the whole time.

Now mind you, I believe that I comfortably surpass the minimum qualifications here, and that you can likely foster an habituation just by living near a sizeable forest (not even right up against it) and applying yourself to patient outreach, emphasis on *patient*. It takes time, tons of it, because although I think they definitely do scout around, during idle hours, looking for intriguing human situations and personalities to engage with, it may take years for your efforts to be recognized as such and meet with reciprocal energy. And once you finally experience your first iron-clad response, don't expect the waiting game to get any easier: They do not like to overplay their hand. Between the interactions of 2008 and the next clear-cut gesture, nothing happens for two years, during which I continue my Vermont Project solo camping method.

2011: Object Communication

Inspired by Lisa Shiel's book *Backyard Bigfoot,* in which she discusses trading stick configurations with her hairy neighbors, I undertake a similar experiment at my place, using rocks, during the late summer and fall. The campaign is kicked off by the appearance, in late July, of a pine tree beside my woods that has obviously not been sawn down or ripped up roots and all. It's been broken at the base, but there's no corresponding stump anywhere in sight.

These pictures were taken weeks later; when the tree was first "delivered," it was fresh and extremely thick, loaded with green, sap-oozing pinecones

I decide to interpret this as an offering and set up a reply on the spot.

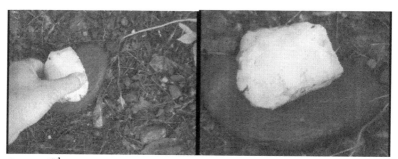

August 2nd, I place this three-pound piece of quartz on top of another rock

August 15th, I find them separated   **August 15th, I set them back up and add a quartz pebble on top**

August 16th, I find the pebble moved off and, August 16th, I reset the pile
beside it, a new pebble has been added

August 25th, I find them removed again   August 25th, I set up a new configuration

October 16th, I find top rock reoriented; note 52-day gap

I leave two pretty gourds, which are quickly taken, and then the dialogue ceases.

But the October 16th event reminds me of other subtle (yet unmistakable) tweaks, like Sylvester's quarter left on a stump in the woods, oriented north/south, and then later found carefully rotated to east/west, or like the toy dragon at the Oklahoma site.

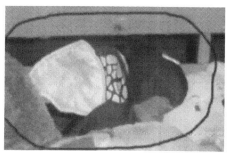 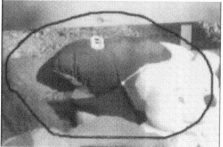

Dragon left face-down at night...   **...flipped over by morning**

Being attuned to such a high level of refinement in these games requires, of course, great precision of awareness on the human side. We recall Robert W. Morgan's method, as described in his *Bigfoot Observer's Field Manual.*

> Instead of being cleverly hidden to snare your guest, your harmless lures will be even more cleverly placed *in the open*, yet the slightest touch will be easily detected. For example, I routinely place on a stump or a flat rock my steel signal mirror, an open plastic case containing aromatic soap, toothbrush, toothpaste, dental floss, and my razor, each arranged with its tip touching a curved line that I faintly etch onto the rock or the stone with the point of my knife.

If you suspect you may have ongoing Sasquatch activity near you, I encourage you to try something similar yourself. A word of advice, however—depending on the personalities of your visitors, you may experience long gaps (often lasting months or even years) between responses. Try not to fall into the trap of becoming mopy and resentful; Sasquatch are busy beings, driven by the demands of survival and the avoidance of prying human eyes. Also, they operate in general at a much more deliberate pace. I think their curiosity about friendly human beings clashes with ancient taboos against consorting with our species, even against consorting obliquely by means of mediating objects.

It may be, too, that some Sasquatch are conducting numerous similar games with certain of your neighbors far and wide—each person probably assuming that she or he *alone* is thus blessed with an invisible playmate—like a chess grand master who is able to match wits with dozens of opponents simultaneously; in this manner, your periodic partner could remain engaged and mentally stimulated while making the rounds, a constantly moving target, distributing and diminishing the risk.

Many habituators attempt to read specific messages in the configurations they find on their property, and some reliable translation might eventually be possible. At this early point in my own experiment, though, I prefer to accept each new manifestation as a good-humored gift that means simply, "I acknowledge you."

Meanwhile, at a Friend's Place

On the afternoon of September 1st, 2011, at a family cabin in southeastern New Hampshire, Sasquatch researcher Joshua Megyesy and his two-and-a-half-year-old daughter play with small clumps of moss. The next morning, Josh finds that one of these clumps has been speared onto a branch ten feet high.

At this same cabin, family members have heard, for many years, night-time branch breaks and bipedal footsteps in the forest, and then recently: distinct, single and double slaps on the outside wall the moment after the last light is turned off and everyone has settled down for sleep. Some of these recorded slaps are included in the YouTube video "Moss Gift" (search under "Moss Gift Sasquatch").

In this case, I'd say the message is not "I acknowledge you," but closer to "Ha!"

Josh's wife and young daughter beneath
the speared moss

2012: Escalation

One night in late March, my daughter and I are reading *Charlotte's Web* in bed when we hear three distinct knocks on the back wall of the house. We look at each other and joke that it must be a ghost, but I just continue reading, because even knowing what I know, it's hard for me to believe that what all habituators have routinely experienced could be happening, also, *right here.*

On April 13th, she rushes inside to tell me there's a squirrel up in our apple tree. I don't give her the proper reaction till she fills me in that it's a *toy* squirrel. I reach it out and find that it's a surprisingly pristine one at that, not ratty or weathered. And we've never seen it before. Of course, my mind immediately jumps to those for whom the appearance, disappearance, and relocation of stuffed animals is commonplace.

We ante up a stuffed monkey in the tree, where it remains untouched all spring, summer, and fall. Perhaps this choice was insulting. Perhaps they think we think they are just monkeys.

A friend rents a cabin from me about two hundred feet behind the house, and during March and April she, too, begins experiencing odd things. First, a clump of mud appears on her upstairs window, as though tossed; then, she notices that the upstairs window around the corner, at the same height, has had a length of screen somehow removed from it.

Approxomately 1.5 by .75 inches

Not long afterward, she is (to say the least) startled by a very loud bang on the mud-side of the cabin, up high by her bed, followed by a slow downward scrape. Her cat freaks out appropriately, but the two dogs, downstairs, don't even wake up, though normally they are on a hair-trigger. The next day, she is eager to tell me about the incident, and to ask how the dogs could possibly have slept through it; she's almost questioning her sanity—well, and her cat's. I show her the passage about those home entries reported in Navidad River, Texas, 1835-1850 (page 97):

> In addition to owning firearms, nearly all the settlers kept two or more large and fiercely protective dogs. The dogs were the alarm systems of the day and were kept to protect the families from interlopers be they man, big cat, bear, or something else. The wild woman, seemingly, was able to step right over these dogs and enter the premises.

My friend does not enjoy learning this bit of history, so I don't share with her the other potentially related phenomenon, as described by Rita in Chapter Three (page 108):

> I walked up there, with my video function on my camera running, and didn't see anything, that I *remember*, because once I got over there and I turned off my video camera I got another infrasound experience. It's like when you're

about to put your hand on a TV screen, you get that
tingling all over the surface of your hand, it was like that
all over my whole body, and worse on my arms and legs.
And I said something to her about it, and then I stepped
backwards. In my mind, it only took two seconds. But
she informed me later, "Oh no, you were frozen and
staring straight ahead for about twenty seconds." And...I
didn't take her seriously, but I happened to have an audio
recorder in my hand, so I played it back and you could tell
by the beep when I turned off the video function on my
camera, and when I spoke to her. I actually spoke to her
twice, and then you hear when I finally do step
backwards. It was a total of thirty-six seconds.

Crescendo

Nothing much happens during the summer, except that I record a
single knock on my outside wall.

On September 15th, something occurs that I want to dismiss, because
it seems too far-fetched. A tomoato appears in my front yard. We have
not grown tomatoes here for years, and just like the one I found on my
back path in 2008, this one is entirely lacking in claw or teeth marks. I'm
hurrying to go on an overnight trip, so I just let it be. The next day, when I
return, it's gone; my friend who rents the cabin did not touch it. If I didn't
know better, I'd say this places the emphasis of meaning squarely on the
date September 15th, but no—the only possible significance is that it's the
anniversary of the time, three years ago, when the tree came down six feet
from me on the mountain above the wood knock witness's home, and
would have broken me had it not landed parallel to my body.

In any case, I hold that synchronicity in suspension, and then, early
on the morning of September 23rd, after a night full of hard rain, I glance
out my window toward the two flat gray rocks on the back porch. They

have sat there undisturbed for more than two years, and I've long since given up on this gift, assuming they're just too close, too risky to mess with. Yet I still reflexively check them each day; they have become simple, familiar fixtures in my home landscape.

You'll understand how startling it is to find them missing this morning, their resting place suddenly blank. The rain must have provided safe cover. Neither my daughter nor my friend was home.

And how much more shocking, then, a few minutes later, to find the larger, bottom rock now lain atop a two-piece stack of quartz, more than a hundred feet away, at a bend in the path.

Before...   **... after**

Six days later, at 3:49 AM, my recorder picks up a distinct double knock on my back wall; doubles seem to me about fifty times more significant than singles because they convey clear intent, whereas singles can be explained away as an errant bird. You can see how I narrowed down the location of this signal, and watch a round-up of all the activity at my place, on YouTube: "Sasquatch on the Home Front: Vermont Habituation Site 2007-2012."

On the same wall, I hang two laminated pictures, one by the artist Jeffrey Caramagna (whose illustration graces the front cover), and beneath it, the famous frame 352 of the Patterson/Gimlin Film.

My aim is to convey respect, admiration, and just the simple message: "I know who you are, and you are welcome."

Three weeks later, I find the bottom picture removed and lying on the ground. I'm doubtful that the elements can be to blame, as both pictures were firmly tacked into the wood, and the much larger one—with far more surface to catch the wind—has remained in place. Never once did it cross my mind, before now, that an image of Patty would be problematic, but now that it has been apparently "rejected" like this, I see it makes perfect sense and leaves me ashamed of my naivete. This image represents, after all, a low point in Sasquatch history, for forty-five years the most successful "capture" of their kind by our technology, whereas the top image is only a drawing, an affectionate human impression.

But by far the strangest event in the series takes place on October 5th, and represents the first *daylight* mischief perpetrated by my visitor(s). I drive my daughter to school in the morning, then travel back home, a round trip of more than one hour, during which I notice nothing awry, parking on the only side of the house without windows. I then spend the next five hours, from nine until two, working at my computer inside the house. Again, nobody else is home.

When I get in the car again and begin down the driveway, I instantly notice it—my radio antenna has been bent way back and tightly wedged into the slot between the side mirror and the door; when I stop and get out, I find it's really hard to dislodge. It's hard to make out in the picture below (much easier in the video), but what's been done matches exactly how saplings are arched and pinned in the woods.

Cold weather closes in and nothing new has occurred since the antenna. Perhaps they were saying goodbye for the winter, marking their adopted territory before departure on the very contraption that I use to come and go.

What a full circle it's been—from jetting around North America for BFRO expeditions, to discovering Sasquatch activity right here in northern Vermont, to now finally experiencing repeat visits. The Vermont Project will certainly be recast if this attention keeps up, however sporadically. Who would continue wearing himself out in the mountains for little return—tresspassing, risking backlash—if he can stay home and play chess with a grand master?

Essentially, I find myself back at No-Bite's place, the northern version, yet without benefit of her gifted intercession.

Reflections by Thom Powell
Author of The Locals and Shady Neighbors
From the Documentary Coda to The Film
"Letters from the Big Man," by Christopher Munch

Once, I spent all night wood knocking, always whacking three times just like a good little BFRO Investigator, and finally gave up at the crack of dawn and drove home. And as soon as I got home, after traveling a hundred miles between there and here, I didn't get out and shut the car door before "Whack Whack Whack!" came from the woods behind my house. The repercussions of that were obvious: Somebody was messing with me. I thought I was being the experimenter and the table just turned.

I found that the more I studied the subject, even in remote places, the more I got subtle indications that the subject was studying me. That really put a chill in me, because that's not something you can undo, how they—at least hypothetically—know where you live. So that was a sobering thought. But I also could see that there was no menace to it.

My initial reaction to it all was actually skepticism and doubt, because that's the science guy I still was. So it really took a lot before it all started to sink in.

So now when people say, "I've got them going on back there, what should I do?" the first thing I tell them is, "Well, you should decide what you want out of your 'research.' Do you want understanding or do you want proof? They're sort of mutually exclusive. If you chase after proof, you may or may not get it, but you're also going to find that it distances you from understanding and inspiration."

But what does oddly tend to happen is you get these synchronicities, these coincidences. Opportunities come your way that seem to be somehow *steered*. It gets a little spooky. And it's nothing that you can ever prove, but once you learn to just go with it and maybe use it, to the extent that they're willing to let you use it, it becomes potentially beneficial.

Epilogue
Through the Looking-Glass

Perhaps the most significant discovery [within quantum mechanics] is *"entanglement,"* a phenomenon that Einstein called "spooky action at a distance." Erwin Schrödinger, one of the founders of quantum theory, used the word to refer to connections between separated particles that persist regardless of distance. These connections are instantaneous, operating "outside" the usual flow of time. They imply that at very deep levels, the separations that we see between ordinary, isolated objects are illusions created by our limited perceptions. Reality is woven from strange, "holistic" threads that aren't located precisely in space or time. Tug on a dangling loose end from this fabric of reality, and the whole cloth twitches.

—Dean Radin, *Entangled Minds:*
Extrasensory Experiences in a
Quantum Reality

"I can't believe that!" said Alice. "One can't believe impossible things."

"I daresay you haven't had much practice," said the Queen. "When I was your age, I always did it for half an hour a day. Why, sometimes I've believed six impossible things before breakfast."

—Lewis Carroll, *Through the Looking-Glass*

Dirt Bridge

I always try to keep an open mind, but this was a tough one; what could be more far-fetched than telepathy?   Here's what: telepathic communication with *Sasquatch*? Talk about piling stretch upon stretch.

And yet, for the sake of argument, if such a thing is even *remotely* possible, why not in this particular species? After all, Sasquatch brains are significantly larger than our own, and they don't use them to write symphonies or books or to build cities, computers or universities, so perhaps, just perhaps, they may have edged us out in developing certain faculties distinctly advantageous for survival, beyond night vision, infrasound, photographic territorial memory, and strategic genius. And if so, why should such specialized gifts be expected to fit neatly within *Homo sapiens'* standards of plausibility?

From my first visit to No-Bite's place in November, 2008, she made no secret of her extraordinary claim, though presenting it humbly; indeed, when the "mind-talking" had begun, not long before, it jarred her worldview as much as anyone's.

"A friend suggested I address my visitor by name, and that her name had come to him: Nantaya. So one day I decided to give it a whirl. I thought: 'Nantaya?' And immediately I heard, '*What!?*' It was a clear female voice in my head, and she sounded annoyed."

Apparently, this was the very same enormous creature whom No-Bite had startled mid-hunt that past June (see Chapter Five), and the two had since debriefed about it, the Sasquatch confessing to having been every bit as shaken by the incident as her much punier counterpart.

I'll admit I was captivated by what my host shared with me, and pitched myself into the sheer speculative *fun* of it, like a character in some bizarre fairytale; I mean, nothing ventured, nothing gained, right? Yet of course I didn't have the foggiest notion how such a thing could be actually, *literally* true. Maybe there was a more straightforward explanation, like trickery or insanity.

Before my first visit ended, it occurred to me to ask whether Nantaya might have any advice for me on where to investigate in my own area, back in Vermont. No-Bite looked into space and then returned with, "Directly west of you: big water."

"Yes, twelve miles west, that's where a young man saw the seven-foot male running through the woods." I had never mentioned the direction, or the presence of the water.

"And she says you should not look on the side with the dirt bridge, but the other side."

Nor had I shared with No-Bite that this body of water is a reservoir, with a dam constructed of earth.

And in fact, the other side (out of frame) is where the sighting occurred, and where, the following May (2009), I would obtain audio of six hours of clear wood knocks.

There on No-Bite's front lawn, I held my head, as the idea not only of mind-talk but also of some type of remote viewing suddenly became a real, if still tenuous, possibility.

Neurons communicate with each other through the release of neurotransmitter molecules. When an electrical signal reaches the end of a neuron, it causes channels in the neuron to open through which calcium ions can enter. If a sufficient number of ions are accumulated, the neuron releases neuro-transmitters, which in turn increase the tendency of surrounding neurons to "fire" their own electrical signals. Multiply that process by a few billion neurons and trillions of synapses, and that's the basic infrastructure of the brain. The quantum element enters at the ion channels, because at some points these channels are less than a billionth of a meter in diameter, and at that size quantum effects become noticeable.

—Dean Radin, *Entangled Minds*

Deer Machine

That same first visit, I asked No-Bite to convey to her friend that my thermal camera was nothing to feel threatened by, that it was only used for spotting *deer* in the dark. This lie bore a nugget of truth because, one evening, I did scan the tree line and registered two deer-shaped heat signatures.

No-Bite told Nantaya where they were, and later that night heard back: "We got both deer and ate very well." She thanked me profusely and said that her group "loves your deer machine."

The next night was the bonfire and my lucky break with the "Woodpile Sasquatch" footage.

After I returned to Vermont and realized just what I'd filmed behind that woodpile, No-Bite told Nantaya, who initially flexed toward denial. "Dumb cat! Dumb cat!" she kept repeating, as if what's moving beside that tree is not clearly a forearm and hand.

A few days later, the video subject fell into a morose mood and changed her refrain. "I am in big problems. I am in BIG problems." That is, not only was the moving bright object, yes, a forearm and hand—it was *hers*. And she was quickly shunned for being caught out: "I didn't get low enough. The others have all turned their backs to me."

Nantaya conveyed to me, through our intermediary, a sense of betrayal, because wasn't the deer machine supposed to see *deer*? My awkward answer was that this was a mistake, that the machine must have malfunctioned, and that I was sorry.

Fortunately, it seems that Nantaya can "hear" only what No-Bite chooses to "tell" her; that is, she can't *probe* the other's mind at will. In this regard, the process of mind-talking is exactly the same as that of ordinary spoken dialogue.

And she doesn't speak English as such; this communication takes the form of thoughts beneath the level of language. No-Bite's mind translates it into English words.

In the middle of the night of November 9th, 2008, my recorder captured a dramatic moment. The microphone was placed beside a bowl of black plums, which I'd set on a rock at the tree line. Later, I sent the audio file to No-Bite and asked her to ask Nantaya if she could shed any light. Nantaya answered, "A young one was getting too close to the plums and an adult female had to stop him." (Listen at YouTube: "Black Plum Reprimand.")

> Entanglement would lead to a Darwinian
> advantage. It could coordinate biochemical
> reactions in different parts of a cell, or in
> different parts of an organ. It could allow correlated
> firings of distant neurons. And…it could coordinate the
> behavior of members of a species, because it is independent of
> distance and requires no physical link.
>
> —Johann Summhammer

A Whole Lot to Swallow

Now it is early June of 2011, and I make my third visit to the site. Nothing much happens for the first five days; since it's one hundred degrees outside, No-Bite and I spend hours every day sitting perfectly still in the shade of her hickory tree, sipping sweet tea.

Her place is well stocked with kittens, cats and dogs, whose various antics and personalities are on full display around us. Her daughter (present at the 2008 bonfire) now has a toddler, whom we play with in the wading pool.

I've brought from Vermont a drawing made by my daughter, who's just turned five, depicting a Sasquatch (large) standing next to Daddy (tiny). I've had it laminated, against the elements, and offer it as a gift on a chair at the corner of the backyard. For the first two nights, the picture stays put.

No-Bite and I do a lot of "chatting" with Nantaya, just casual conversation about ordinary life. I'm now about 50/50 on the possibility of telepathy.

"How was the hunt last night?" I ask in the morning.

"Bad. We didn't get a deer or a hog. We ate fish. I don't like fish because they're slimy."

One night they switch to eating frogs.

"How do you handle this terrible heat during the day?"

"We get in water or sit under trees."

I picture No-Bite's grandson splashing in the pool; and here are *we*, also sitting beneath a tree.

"Sometimes, we lie under the straight little sticks."

No-Bite thinks about this. "Oh, pine needles! You pile them over you to keep cool?"

"Yes."

One afternoon, while we're eating ham, potato salad, and corn on the cob, Nantaya comments, "We eat the same as you. Same-same. Except ours isn't cooked." Don't ask me how, but it seems she's able to actually look through No-Bite's eyes, down at the lunch plate.

"So you don't use fire?"

"We know fire but we don't use it for food. We do make fires, never where the hairless ones can see. We use it sometimes for light."

After lunch, I introduce a delicate topic. "Nantaya, I noticed on the map that there's a huge forest starting right here behind the house." It's

1550 uninterrupted acres with no structures or roads visible on Google Earth. "Would it be okay for me to go down in there and look around?" "No, please don't. That's our territory. You have the yard. Don't antagonize us. You have the *yard*."

Digesting this, I ask No-Bite to ask Nantaya whether she has a special place where she goes to be alone.

"Yes, Sam's barn. Sometimes I go there." No-Bite's neighbor Sam lives in Dallas most of the time; she keeps watch on his property next door.

I think aloud, "Hmmm, maybe I'll just sleep in that barn tonight…"

"DO NOT ANTAGONIZE US. *You have the yard*."

So I obey, spending my nights at the farthest corner of the backyard, sleeping in my rental car beside the ravine. As far as I can tell, I'm not being visited while I sleep.

One afternoon, as we sit out again in the stifling heat, Nantaya mentions that she's not very far away just now, in the dense woods. It occurs to me to request a wood knock. No-Bite: "She says, 'Wait.'"

I allow myself to get excited, but thirty seconds later comes the follow-up: "She says, 'There are no good trees here.'"

(Uh…huh.)

Reportedly—regardless of my wavering level of credulity—there has been much spirited discussion within the Sasquatch group about my daughter's picture. Should Nantaya accept it or not? Final authority rests with the Big Man—the Alpha male—who sets and enforces the rules.

This is not an easy question for them. Most possessions are held in common by the clan, though each individual does have a small stash that he or she keeps at a private spot; these possessions, however, are what they have collected themselves, not what comes from humans.

When items are *borrowed* from humans—such as stuffed animals, garden tools, lawn furniture, etc.—they are typically kept for a while and then returned, or returned *approximately,* habituators finding a missing item weeks or months later hanging in a tree, up on the roof or porch. This is the playful side of the relationship.

But when an item is sincerely *gifted* by a human, it's a whole different story. Accepting it can throw off the balance between our two kinds unless a suitable gift can be bestowed in exchange—that is, if the situation involves a long-standing trust relationship like the one No-Bite has established with her hairy friends here. For example, if four apples are offered, usually only two will be taken.

In the case of something very special, like my daughter's drawing, the dynamic becomes even trickier.

I stage a simple re-enactment of the woodpile footage, minus the woodpile, which has since been removed. No-Bite wields the thermal camera as I crouch beside the same tree, extending my left arm like Nantaya.

The temperature today is probably fifty degrees warmer than on the original night, so my eyes do not stand out warmly like hers did. In the comparison images, though, it's clear that my head is shaped very differently from hers—an upright oval compared to her broader, flatter dimensions. My entire head is a bit narrower than the 6.5-inch tree, and about the same width as between Nantaya's eyes.

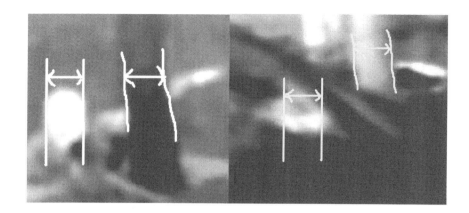

As for our left arms, they appear to stick out about an equal distance past the tree, though her hand is considerably larger, but while my arm is held out straight, what can't be determined is the degree to which her elbow is bent, out of view, so any comparative arm length can't be estimated.

The Higgs Field is to physics what DNA is to biology. It has been called the most fundamental stuff of the universe, or "what binds everything together," yet it is so elusive that it took nearly fifty years to finally prove its existence, as announced by a panel of scientists in July of 2012. This Field may be the very medium that makes the mysterious phenomenon of "quantum entanglement" possible.

— Sarah Galloway

"No Buttons"

All drama waits until the final night.

Inside, No-Bite and I watch an NBA Finals game, Miami vs. Dallas. During time-outs, I trot to my car, parked near the chicken coop and goat house, to make preparations—changing the batteries in my audio recorder; making sure the memory card has enough room; mounting the thermal camera snugly in the back passenger-side window—but I do this in brief bursts of activity rather than one long session, because I don't want to arouse suspicion. I know this strategy is more for the benefit of my Superspy self-regard than it is apt to fool any onlookers.

On one such foray, I climb in the driver's seat and switch on the dome light in one motion. After a minute of double-checking the audio recorder, I kill the dome light. What the *heck*? In the backseat, my flashlight is burning bright. I haven't used it since last night, and I always turn it off before going to sleep. Even if I'd somehow forgotten to, though, the batteries would be well dead by now, more than twenty-four hours later.

In the house again, I ask No-Bite, "So...do you know if they've been to my car?"

She looks off into space. "The young one was in the backseat."

I get a little chill. "Did he...*touch* anything?"

"No buttons!" she blurts, then laughs. She reports that one of the local juveniles once had a bad experience touching buttons in a car, and so this has been forbidden ever since.

"Right," I say, laughing along, "it wasn't exactly a *button*." The on/off switch on the flashlight is the kind that slides. I tell No-Bite what happened.

After quizzing the young one, Nantaya says that when the light came on, he got scared and ran.

"How old is he?" I ask.

"Seven years."

After the Mavericks win a decisive Game 4, my host wishes me luck out there, and I bed down in the extremely reclined driver's seat. All windows are wide open except the back right, which houses the thermal camera. One glaring drawback of this "deer machine" is that it makes a distinct double-click every two minutes, which I hate—Sasquatch hearing is remarkably acute.

From 11:30 till about 1:00 AM, I flip-flop, unable to settle into sleep; my own hearing magnifies the trouble, as my camera's metallic clicks blare out like hammer-blows. All my supposed stealth is a joke.

I sleep at last, and the audio recorder, running through the night on my car roof, picks up numerous percussions and, more interestingly, two nearby snarls and a potential "speech event" (at 2:11 AM). Listen at YouTube: "Possible Sasquatch Speech and Snarls."

When, from time to time, I wake up briefly, I always turn the key in the ignition just enough to illuminate the dashboard clock's LED display. At sunrise, I open my eyes and turn the key once again. No LED. To make sure my battery isn't dead, I start the car. Fiddling around, I discover that the ring on the wand that sticks out to the left of the steering column, the ring that turns the headlights on and off, has been rotated to the on position. This means that when you turn the key, the dashboard lights are much dimmer. I restore this ring to the off position, then retry the key, and again the clock shines brightly, even in the sunlight.

This wand is located directly behind the steering wheel, so that my restless legs couldn't have knocked it, much less rotated the ring.

Over morning coffee, I ask No-Bite whether the young one might have paid me a visit last night…and did he touch anything inside the car?

"No buttons!"

I tell her about the ring. To perform this bit of mischief, he had to reach right over my midsection.

"He says you were *very asleep*." She looks into space. "Also? He bounced your car from the back." Only later do I find the evidence of this.

Directed where to look, No-Bite crosses her backyard and finds something placed on an overturned white barrel, not far from my car. She picks it up and hands it to me. "This is from the young one. He wanted to put it in the car, but the Big Man said, 'That's enough with the car!'"

It's a piece of petrified wood.

"She says he found it in a fast-running river."

I hope this means that Nantaya can now accept my daughter's drawing; and indeed, two days after I leave, No-Bite reports that it has disappeared.

> It may well be the case that evolution has taken advantage of telepathy, but we haven't noticed it yet. For example, physicist Johann Summhammer, in a 2005 paper entitled "Quantum Cooperation of Insects," showed that if insects shared entangled states they could accomplish tasks more efficiently than if they had to rely on classical forms of communication. Two quantum-entangled ants pushing a pebble that was too heavy for one ant could push it up to twice as far as two classical ants.
>
> —Dean Radin, *Entangled Minds*

Caught in the Cookie Jar

On the way to the airport, after thanking my friend, as always, for her hospitality, I stop for gas, and that's when I notice them—a set of fingerprints on the hatchback.

Luckily, the car is black, so these strange remnants really stand out, representing digits clearly smaller than my own.

These prints seem deposited by fingers uniformly covered in dirt, or earth mixed with oil. (I recall Jerry's story of touching a Sasquatch's back, when we was a child, and finding the hair extremely oily.) An alternate explanation is that my own fingers could have left "latent prints," which then picked up blown dust or pollen. Yet, besides the size difference, another objection arises: During my week's rental of this car, I've opened and shut the hatchback many times, certainly leaving lots of latent prints, but this morning's discovery shows just one set from a right hand, and another, two feet to the left, apparently from the other hand:

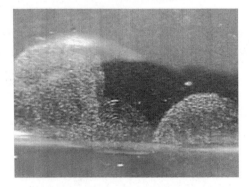

This left-hand set of prints includes one finger pad with a much coarser-grained "whorl" than that of any human print I have been able to locate through subsequent research.

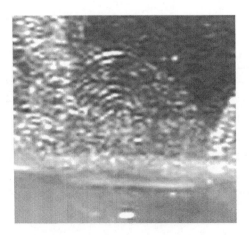

The clearest finger on the right hand (below) shows side striations that also don't appear in human print patterns.   Notice, too, the odd pointedness of the digit.

 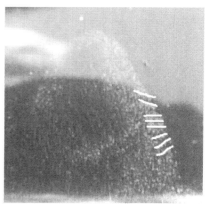

Striations marked

(See YouTube: "Sasquatch Fingerprints: East Texas Habituation Site.")

But even as I stand here pumping gas and marveling at this donation of plain evidence, I've already crossed through the looking-glass—because what occurred just before I left No-Bite's house still rings in my ears.

> Telepathy has probably more to do with physics than with psychology.
>
> — Albert Einstein

One Hour Earlier

We sit on the front lawn, finishing our last coffee together.

"Can you tell Nantaya that it would make me so happy if she could make some kind of goodbye sound?"

No-Bite: "She says to wait."

(Okay, here we go again...)

But within ten seconds...SMACK!   It comes from about a hundred feet away through the dense forest, over my left shoulder.   So close.   I cannot breathe correctly. No-Bite and I gape at each other. During these past six days, we've probably spent twenty-five hours sitting at this spot and not heard a single knock or 'Squatchy vocal, even faintly, from these surrounding woods.

The knock is forthright, frank, and brain-shattering. How on Earth to fathom such a thing?

(I don't have my audio recorder running at the time, but five months later, I do manage to capture a knock from these same woods, in the middle of the night, which sounds exactly like it; hear it on YouTube: "What the Goodbye Knock Sounded Like.")

I slap my hand on my chest and call out several times, "Oh my God!" and "*Thank you*, Nantaya. I will hold that in my heart forever."

No-Bite says, "She's laughing. And she says, 'The Big Man is just sitting there shaking his head.'"

Not till minutes later are we able to return to some semblance of normal conversation.

"I can't believe it, this is so *confirming*," I say, still breathless.

"You know," says No-Bite, "it's a good confirmation for me, too."

"But you *know* you've been talking with her, right?"

"Well, really, this is still so strange for me. You always wonder if you might have crossed over and lost your mind."

In the face of what just happened, I don't know how to cling onto my natural skepticism anymore. What, this woman stationed a human *being* in the woods this morning on the off-chance that I'd ask for a "goodbye sound"...*and then she telepathically signaled him*? Or check that, I've got it...she's wearing a *wire*!

No, this single solid rap of wood on wood has swatted away my last shred of doubt, and the implications are vast and unavoidable: "Mind-talking" is quite real; Sasquatch can use it to exchange thoughts with some humans; No-Bite is a gifted medium; Nantaya is not a figment of my friend's imagination but an actual entity living in the woods with her own kind, and likely, as she herself concedes, the very figure giving off heat in my 2008 thermal footage.

Back in Vermont, I show off my gift, often rubbing it, its surfaces worn smooth by water, by the "fast-running river." I can't believe the appropriateness of the choice, but then again, my belief system has been well eroded as well. Wood is elemental in Sasquatch life—their structures, their playthings, their percussive messages—and so is stone; they clack rocks together, and sometimes stack them, building simple sculptures. What could better express their world, and their cavernous time scale, than a piece of wood *turned to stone*, a process that, aided by water, can take a century?

I'm so grateful for what has befallen me on this trip. And truly, none of it would have been possible had I not crawled way out on this limb, leveraging my life financially and professionally, casting in my lot with Sasquatch study no matter the consequences.

I wait five long days before reviewing the thermal footage taken that last night from the back window of my rental car. I'm afraid to look, afraid that young No-Buttons won't appear, afraid that he will. Of course, he does not. How crafty would this trickster be—how would Sasquatch have remained "undiscovered" over eons—if he put himself easily in front of a loudly clicking mystery machine, one that gave his female elder "big problems"? Instead, he elected to make mischief on the other side of the car, and at the back, where he bounced me. Yet, he did get caught with dirty hands in the cookie jar.

I sell my thermal camera on Ebay. Two weeks ago, this would have destroyed my most prized self-image—daring nocturnal documentarian— but I now understand that we don't belong in their territory, in their night, driven by ulterior motives and toting fancy deceptions. It runs against a primordial division of our world, which is "big enough for the both of us" only if we observe the boundaries.

I'll bet this was the exact message of last year's Vermont Project: "We'll agree to play sometimes, knocking, but just by day."

Indeed, through this lens the tree crash of 2009 now looks more like reprimand than welcome, the fact that it landed parallel to my body rather than *across* it...a mercy. While my night camping method has praised itself as guided by "passive receptivity," beneath this label have I been any less an interloper than the cast of "Finding Bigfoot"?

Indeed, with regard to this whole notion of "fieldwork," my earlier Tips are a useful tool that will, if fully implemented with sincerity and benign patience, almost certainly result in exciting "action," no harm done—and who knows, while out there in your local site, you might find yourself able to "mind-talk," and then your sizeable new friends can guide you from there—but since I wrote them, my priorities have shifted.

I have to laugh at my previous posture, how I let myself go, indulged in feeling lovelorn in the Vermont forest, as if one can pine for an entire *species.* From the instant of Nantaya's reply, her momentary release of secrecy, the whole matter has turned on its axis, so that I've stopped straining to be embraced by *them* and cherish instead being acknowledged by *her.*

When I return in the fall, however, the whole situation on the ground has transformed radically.

> If telepathy is a real fact, it is very possible that it is operating at every moment and everywhere, but with too little intensity to be noticed, or else it is operating in the presence of obstacles that neutralize the effect at the same moment that it manifests itself. We produce electricity at every moment, the atmosphere is continually electrified, we move among magnetic currents, yet millions of human beings lived for thousands of years without having suspected the existence of electricity. It may be the same with telepathy.
> —Henri Bergson

Power Play

The summer of 2011 will go down in East Texas history. The region experiences seventy-three straight days of temperatures above a hundred and no rain for months. Nantaya's clan has trouble finding game and battles these oppressive conditions. Wildfires rage out of control, reaching to within twenty-two miles of No-Bite's house. One day in early September, Nantaya announces, "We are leaving." She's traveling east, to the territory where she spent her childhood, while the Big Man, No-Buttons, and the rest of the group head due north, to a "big river."

No-Bite hears nothing for six weeks, and then one evening, she mentions Nantaya to her daughter and a sudden familiar voice in her head replies, "Here." The Sasquatch has returned now that the wildfires are extinguished and the weather has cooled, but her group is staying north for now. Nantaya tells No-Bite that she found her former home ground occupied by hairy ones she didn't recognize and who did *not* welcome her. But furthermore, she doesn't feel at home back here, either, because the thickly wooded area surrounding No-Bite's house has been taken over by seven rogue males, adolescents who were previously exiled to a nearby forest.

Nantaya explains that until they mature, young males within the extended clan are kept strictly at a remove from the others, especially from young females; they do not behave well and are even capable of violence. (Learning this, I instantly recall the horse attacked in Iowa.) Ever since the exodus, these opportunists have shouldered into the better hunting and hiding topography available in No-Bite's ravine. Thus, the social order has broken down, and Nantaya finds herself vastly outnumbered and ill-treated by the new Alphas; they do not permit her to enter her favorite spots near the house, and establish a firm boundary line just this side of Sam's barn, which, if crossed, earns her painful thrown rocks and even hands-on reprisals.

She adds, "They've taken over my cave where I kept all my things. That's what makes me the most mad. They took your young one's picture." The one I gave her last June. "I told them, '*Mine,*' and they laughed. And they *peed* on it." She calls them The Bad Boys, and under their irresponsible authority, she's angry, sad and lonesome.

When I arrive in November of 2011, I bring Nantaya two gifts—a photograph from home and a Walmart cake. The latter is a combination platter of red velvet and cheesecake. The first evening, No-Bite and I walk it up toward Sam's barn, to which thankfully our abandoned friend still has access. As instructed, I leave the cake (under its clear plastic hood) on a flat fence-post.

I also carry the picture, a laminated print showing my front lawn in Vermont, with full birch and maple trees at the lush height of summertime. Nantaya asks No-Bite to ask me to please hold it up for her to see; apparently, she's concealed back in the trees a hundred yards away across a field.

As if I needed more proof, for fun I've held this gift image-side-down from the moment I removed it from my shoulder bag, and now I raise it toward the far forest, No-Bite standing behind me, unable to see. Immediately, she affirms, "So *green!* Is that where you live?"

Indeed, the represented scene stands in stark contrast to this drought-stricken Texas landscape.

Sam's barn is a tumble-down affair with gaps in the walls and containing old lumber, rusted machinery, mildewed sheetrock, but a still-solid, empty loft. It's up there, Nantaya explains, that she occasionally sleeps, when the weather is "very bad."

"Maybe *I* can sleep in here one night this time?"

She doesn't answer me.

Later, I'm preparing to "car camp" again in my rental, out by the chicken coop, when No-Bite warns, "Nantaya says some of the Bad Boys are in the woods behind the chicken coop, and they are *not* happy you are here."

I'm thinking, *Good.* With no thermal camera anymore rolling while I sleep, I'll need raw, waking experience.

And sure enough, while my hostess and I stand talking in the backyard, we're startled by a sharp knock—WACK!—issuing from directly behind the coop. There's a bright moon overhead, but that area is deep in shadow.

Nantaya: "That means, 'Go back inside, this is *my* place now.'"

No-Bite: "I'm getting such a strong feeling from her. She keeps on saying, 'I hate them. They're *stu*-pid. *Stu*-pid!' It's like she's spitting the word."

Though I'm hoping, of course, for a rare lack of impulse control, some truly scary, thoughtless behavior emerging from those shadows, even hormonal rogue males understand, it turns out, that they must be disciplined when it comes to our race, brazen intruders included; after all, the survival imperative, the code of moderation, runs deep within every ancient Sasquatch cell.

What I *am* allowed to experience, though, is quite striking enough. I cover my audio recorder's red lights with heavy black tape and place the unit, as usual, on the roof of my car. I worry that the delightfully pissed-off wood knock won't repeat itself. But then, at 1:14 AM, I'm jolted awake by the exact same stern order to vacate the yard, and from the same spot, that we heard three hours earlier. Instead of fleeing, I reply with a defiant "Woo!" Fifteen minutes later comes an even louder reprimand, which I also parry off: "Woo-woo!" Both are captured by my recorder.

Night #2, I repeat the procedure except for three aspects: I manage to position my car not in the yard forty feet from the chicken coop but *behind* the structure, among trees; I put the recorder on the coop's metal roof, rather than on top of the car; and then I proceed to sleep through all the action, because it's so much subtler than last night's.

Reviewing the audio file back home, I learn once again that percussion and extreme patience are at the core of the Sasquatch being-in-the-world, that while they do sometimes indulge in blunt, intimidating tactics, when it becomes clear that the outsider has no intention of leaving, they often switch to a protracted program, even lasting throughout the night, with long, diagnostic silences in between, in order to provoke him into reacting, to get a rise out of him, to determine what he's made of and whether he constitutes a threat. When listening to the audio, note the great variety of surfaces used and sounds produced, as if the striker is trying to find the one that finally provokes a response.

(See YouTube: "Typical Night Sounds: East Texas Habituation

Site.")

Once I return to Vermont and discover the array of raps, taps, rolls and ricochets, No-Bite agrees to climb her ladder and check the nearly flat chicken coop roof, which turns out to hold rocks and clods of dirt, plus one small piece of wood; I suspect the latter is what landed on the roof at 1:53 AM, bouncing several times.

It astonishes me that while I snored, curled inside the sub-compact, all of this was going on beside me; of course, I can't tell how close the Bad Boy was, but the items that wound up on top seem not fired from a distance (if so, wouldn't they have skipped off the roof?) but tossed from closer range. Nor are we talking about a particularly high arc; the way that piece of wood behaved, for instance, suggests a gentler landing.

In other words, he was close, but thoroughly under control. Being gigantic, they can't afford imprecision, as though their margin for error is inversely proportional to their size.

And yet, fascinatingly, they are not infallible—they'll leave fingerprints, telltale debris lying on a roof and, as we found out the hard way, they even need to watch what they eat.

When I return to check the gate-post at Sam's barn, I find that the cake is gone—plate, plastic hood and all. Back at the house, No-Bite reports that she feels Nantaya holding her head and moaning, "Owww… owww…oww…I am poisoned."

"What?!" I say. "We'd never poison you."

"Oh," No-Bite realizes, "it must be the *sugar*. A sugar headache."

"What part of the cake did you eat, or all of it at once?" I ask.

"No. First, I ate the red one, and that was good, it didn't hurt me. Later, I ate the other one. It was like mud in my mouth, but without stones." The cheesecake. "Owww… owww…owwwwww."

No-Bite muses, "They never have pure sugar in nature," then adds from Nantaya: "'We share all the food. We don't eat anything all by ourselves, even if it's a little bit.'" She's got nobody to share with now, certainly not the renegade bullies.

The next three mornings, we ask after her health. First, she tells us she caught and ate an armadillo last night. I wonder aloud how she ate it, exactly, and No-Bite gets the image of her prying open its "shell" like an oyster. The second night: a young pig. "It squealed, so I ran away with it, to get away from its mother." It strikes me funny to picture this giantess scared of a lowly hog, until No-Bite reminds me that with nobody to take care of her these days, she must avoid injury like the plague. How strange to think of an adult Sasquatch as isolated and vulnerable.

I ask if Nantaya thought the pig looked cute before she killed it.

Rather sarcastically, she answers, "It wasn't a *baby* pig."

The third morning, she tells us that during the night, she finished off the second half of the pig. She's rationing herself.

> All science is empirical science; all theory is subordinate
> to perception; a single fact can overturn an entire system.
> —Frederik van Eeden

> This life of yours is not merely a piece of the entire
> existence, but is, in a certain sense, the whole; only this
> whole is not so constituted that it can be surveyed in one
> single glance.
> —Erwin Schrödinger

Barngate

On my last day, I finally receive permission from Nantaya to spend the night in Sam's barn.

I cajole both No-Bite and her other daughter, Allison (she of 1998 "rock fight" fame), who has been staying here, to join me. As we're gathering blankets and bundling for a forty-degree night, No-Bite gets a message: "Nantaya says, 'Not you.'"

At first I think this means not *me*, but she clarifies, "Allison's okay, because she might bring the Bad Boys close so you can see them, but I'm not wanted in the barn."

"Aw, c'mon," I say, "she's just trying to protect you. You'll be fine, tell her not to worry."

So we all three traipse off to Sam's, where I set myself up on the hard wood of the loft and (each packing a side-arm) the other two choose the softer, leaf-and-dust-covered ground floor.

Nantaya has fallen into a funk at the disobedience, but our focus is elsewhere, especially after No-Bite sees a huge male.

She and Allison have just made a return trip to their house for a few forgotten items. At Sam's front gate, she noticed him in the bright moonlight.

"There's a big male over by the shed, right there by the road," she tells me upon their return.

"Really?! You walked right past him?"

"I didn't realize till it was too late. His eyes were even with the roof. I could see part of the outline of a shoulder, from the head to the shoulder."

"You see his eyes glow?"

"Yes."

"Weren't you so freaked out?"

"Yes. However, I made a promise to a *friend* [me] that I would come back here."

"What color were his eyes?"

"Yellow."

(The next day, we find that the eye-level was roughly nine and a half feet. See YouTube: "Big Male Near Sam's Barn.")

I don't venture out there at this news of our visitor, because I'm all dug in up here in Nantaya's loft; there's an opening below the eaves that lets me survey the area in front of the barn and I fully expect curiosity to draw in these mammoth teens later on. For good measure, the two ladies gamely pee in the grass.

But as far as we can tell, in our sleepy vigilance, they come no closer than that shed, three hundred feet away. And while it registers our snoring, the audio file contains no sounds of approach.

In the morning, not only does Nantaya *not* agree to send me off to the airport the next morning with another goodbye knock, she will say just one thing to No-Bite, over and over and over—"You're *stu*-pid. That's my space...*my space*"—and then she falls into a heavy seething silence.

Throughout my visit,   I've   been   hoping   to   take   what seems the logical next step, asking whether Nantaya can perhaps let me finally *see* her, if only far away across the field. Here's one typical exchange:

> **Chris:** Just tell me a place to go where you could come out. I
> will go there and wait.
> **Nantaya:** That is so bad, so bad. I'm more than thirty years
> old and have never intentionally shown myself to a
> hairless one.
> **Chris:** But I've been visiting here for three years and no
> problems have come.
> **Nantaya:** It only takes one mistake and everything gets torn
> up. I like it the way it is.
> **No-Bite (deciding to lay it on thick):** Okay, but keep in mind
> that if Chris can see you, he will be more likely to
> return here again and again, and even bring his little
> girl along someday. If he finds another place where
> they interact with him more openly, he'll probably
> start going there instead.
> **No-Bite (to me):** She's thinking. I'm getting a strong sense of
> agitation…like separation anxiety.

But now, in the wake of this scandalous "Barngate," Nantaya's even less willing to bend her ways; apparently, there has been major damage to the trust alliance. We're not sure why No-Bite's insubordination was so serious, but the bottom line is that she was told not to sleep in the barn and she did not listen.

Two days after I get back home, I receive an email:

> She certainly is pissed off. Earlier today I attempted to
> reach out to her. I experienced something new—she
> bounced my thoughts back to me. If you stick your head
> in an empty 55-gallon barrel and talk, that's what it felt
> like. I apologized for going with you on your camp-out in
> the barn, apologized for going to the bathroom TWICE in
> "her" area, and told her I knew I was overstepping my
> boundaries but didn't realize how far I had gone. Tomorrow I'll
> take her a peace offering—some sugar-free

cooked apples with cinnamon on them. Hopefully that
will appease her.

On the one hand, of course, this is a disaster; but on the other, how
very instructive. Of course, we can't know much about their interior lives,
but the nature of Sasquatch survival points to an externalized existence.
Yes, we humans are famously territorial, but mostly not in the old-school,
dear-life sense anymore. We do help ourselves to "private property," and
yet, once we have staked it out, we spend 90% of our time indoors, safe
within walls, doing our "personal work," feeding The Self, surrounded by
resources designed to enrich our inner worlds.

Meanwhile, our hairy counterparts are loose upon the land,
surrounded by wave upon wave of risk, pressured each moment to craft
and recraft a subsistence strategy, exposed to injury, sickness, hunger, the
elements, and fierce competition from their own kind. Am I missing
something? Oh yes…Mankind, in the face of whose constant patrolling
"one mistake" can mean death to you and yours, even to your entire race.

This is why boundaries, routine, group discipline and honor are all-
consuming; the smallest turf infraction can rupture the cosmos.

I have to stop and mentally re-educate myself on all of this (and yes,
the specter of forestsful of Justin Smejas and Rick Dyers certainly helps)
each time the facile complaint bubbles up in me again: For Pete's sake,
why don't they just come *talk* to us?

And in Nantaya's case, the alienation is magnified: She was already
rejected out east in her childhood homeland, forsaken then by her current
clan back here and thwarted by the Bad Boys, and now comes a
"poisoning" at the hands of a supposed hairless friend from up north, and
then…and *then*, her main human ally flatly ignores a direct order, invading
her one refuge.

Is it any wonder she's inconsolable, that they don't let themselves
"need us"? In essence, every such relationship teeters on the brink of
forfeit.   Behind enemy lines, they can't afford nostalgia; we'll always be
the treacherous *others* who—however trustworthily we may act, and
however nobly we *mean* it—can never swear any ultimate oath.

They can't even need their own, if it means group jeopardy. Out of the blue, while I was still on site and before the communication blackout, Nantaya asked No-Bite about a friend's profoundly disabled daughter.

"Why doesn't she take it down to the river? That's what we do when one is born sick or not strong enough."

"You actually *drown* it?" I asked.

"Yes, we hold it under. But tell your friend she should do it *soon*. The longer you wait, the harder it is to do, but it has to be done."

> This evening I made the cooked apples & cinnamon. I waited until it was dark out and headed for the same spot where you put out the cake. I got to the intersection and received a deep growl. Sooo, I took the apples to the area of the compost pile near where you parked your car. I don't know if Nantaya did the growling or if it was one of the rogue males—either way, I made a peace offering.
>
> [Next night's email:] I talked Allison into accompanying me to check the status of my peace offering. There were two cleanly licked slices of apple left in the bowl—which means about 9/10ths of the apple-cinnamon mixture was "accepted." Now the question is: Who accepted it?

Crystal Ball

Here's what I foresee: This great reckoning process will unfold in two phases.

Phase One—the human race will need time to accept the very fact that our planet plays host to a broader spectrum of upright, talking hominins than we ever suspected, and that some of them, the fresh club inductees, are, in terms of sheer physical prowess, akin to superheroes.

Phase Two—we will gradually (*very* gradually) learn to absorb the truth that these folks are far out ahead of us not just physically but psychically as well, perhaps even spiritually. Of course, this will be a terrifically bitter pill for most human beings to swallow.

May those who sincerely wish to learn, to push out ahead of the curve in this reckoning process, either develop their own psychic gifts or find the good fortune to meet up with a willing liaison, someone adept at this presumably ancient form of communication between our two species; it's a prestigious inside track, a royal road.

Sasquatch has always seemed, in relation to us, a striking combination of Self and Other, but now this quality turns out to be quite literal—the first, 100% precise in terms of maternal genesis, the second, perfect as well, the sire side 100% unknown, and thus far unknowable.

What if we *never* identify this sire, no matter how hard we hammer upon the DNA? Science would surely reject such a possibility, quaking at an open end, but perhaps we are not meant to nail down this element of the mystery; perhaps our closest pass is to learn that we ourselves are intimately woven into these shadow figures.

I believe that all our thinking will have to evolve, become far more fresh and limber. While we remain locked in the dusty old ape/human dichotomy, yes, this primate fits much better into the latter basket, surely feels much more like people. Yet, in light of the DNA revelations, we know already that even though the *first* Sasquatch were half human, this has not been true for a thousand generations; today's Sasquatch (*Homo something*) are not human (*Homo sapiens*), any more than jaguars are leopards because they share the genus *Panthera*.

"But we both have spoken *language!*"

"But we both have *spots!*"

If we're to refer to them this way, we should put "people" in quotation marks. Until we open new avenues of thought, this word is our closest available approximation.

But it's an analogy.

Indeed, the similarities do leap out at us more vividly and persuasively than the differences, which take longer to sink in. This is why most viewers' instinctive reaction, upon first seeing the Patterson/Gimlin footage, Erickson's Matilda, or the San Antonio figure, is: Oh, that's a *person* in a *suit*.

Unless we're ready to adopt a new, broader definition of "human," one that straddles species, we must be clear-eyed and realistic about this issue, even amidst the hypnotic dazzle these days.

Though many will wish to rub out the boundary altogether, Sasquatch occupies its very own zoological category that does not include us. The great temptation to avoid this plain fact arises, of course, from the uncanny resemblance involved; but then again, isn't this same resemblance just why we've always been so captivated by our fellow primates generally— the sensation being simply a whole lot more powerful in the present case?

Erasing the boundary between us is as inappropriate as falsely thickening it. And think of this: If Sasquatch *were* just a huge and hairy human being, nothing else, nothing more, how disappointing this would actually be, what an anticlimax, how much less we'd have still dancing out ahead of us to discover, or at least to grasp at; we'd need to lament, with C.S. Lewis in *A Grief Observed*, "The rough, sharp, cleansing tang of her otherness is gone."

So let's celebrate instead the very infancy of our insight into this kin and how she makes her world, as we continue humbly learning the ten thousand wiles, powers, knacks and nuances that animate her name.

Chris: How should we handle our curiosity about your race, as it grows?

Nantaya: There is aggressive curiosity and gentle curiosity. Get to know us like you get to know a new neighbor. You don't go in a neighbor's yard, cut down the neighbor's trees. You don't take the neighbor's children. Peaceful curiosity is not a problem, just don't try to take us over. Your children have a gentle curiosity, that's why we come to them; they're not a threat. We've been interacting with children in the hopes that eventually we CAN come out.

Chris: Why would you want to come out?

Nantaya: So we don't have to be in fear. This has been going on since the days of the wagons. Your people were afraid the natives would steal their children, but part of the time it was US interacting with them. Children would step into the woods and sometimes they'd come back, sometimes not. The children would go off with us and PLAY with us. We've been hoping that if we teach your young ones, they will still know us when they grow up.

Chris: Do ALL of you share this goal of being able to come out?

Nantaya: Some yes, some no. It's like having a dangerous secret: Sometimes it's good to come out, sometimes it's bad. The more the hairless ones know about us, the more dangerous. Even when the secret is out, there will still be places the hairless ones can't go.

Chris: But wouldn't more understanding make the secret less dangerous, too?

Nantaya: More knowledge means more danger, because not all people use the knowledge the same way. If I told you we all like peanut butter, some of you would use peanut butter for bait, some for friendship. But that's not the secret.

Chris: The motivation of No-Bite and myself and many others is to shed light and increase the peace.

Nantaya: Yes. We won't ever be able to come out everywhere, because it's not safe. Why the Big Man is so worried about my interaction with No-Bite is that we never know who's going to come here. At what you call "habituation sites," you are always being tested—what you do with gifts, who you tell, what chain reaction occurs. Habituation clusters are happening all over the place, but it is a more recent thing. The native peoples knew we were here and respected territories. But as the settlers came in they didn't respect boundaries, they just took over. When there was respect, there was less need to test hairless ones all the time. Now we have this new problem to deal with. The settlers and now their descendents keep invading—they see a place they like, they build on it and destroy it. You clear the land because you are fragile. Weak. You can only fight with weapons, not rocks or sticks, bare hands.

Chris: More and more of us today are finding out about your race, but much of what's being said is untrue. If you could speak to the human race, what would you tell us?

Nantaya: The best thing I can say is "DON'T." Don't harm
the little ones. If you see one little one, there are
definitely more. Don't assume anything. Don't think
because you know one of us that we are all the
same. Don't think because you know many of us that
you know the personality of all of us. Don't seek us
out because we will hide. Don't avoid us because if
we want to find you, we will. Don't think we are
stupid because we will embarrass you. Don't think
we are intelligent because we will make you appear
foolish. Don't feed us because you think we are
starving, because we are experts at hunting—you
feed us, it's because you want to share. Don't hunt us
because you cannot catch us. DON'T.

Index

Behavior

Stick/Tree Manipulation

29011872R00240

Made in the USA
Lexington, KY
12 January 2014